The Cigar that fell in Love with a Pipe

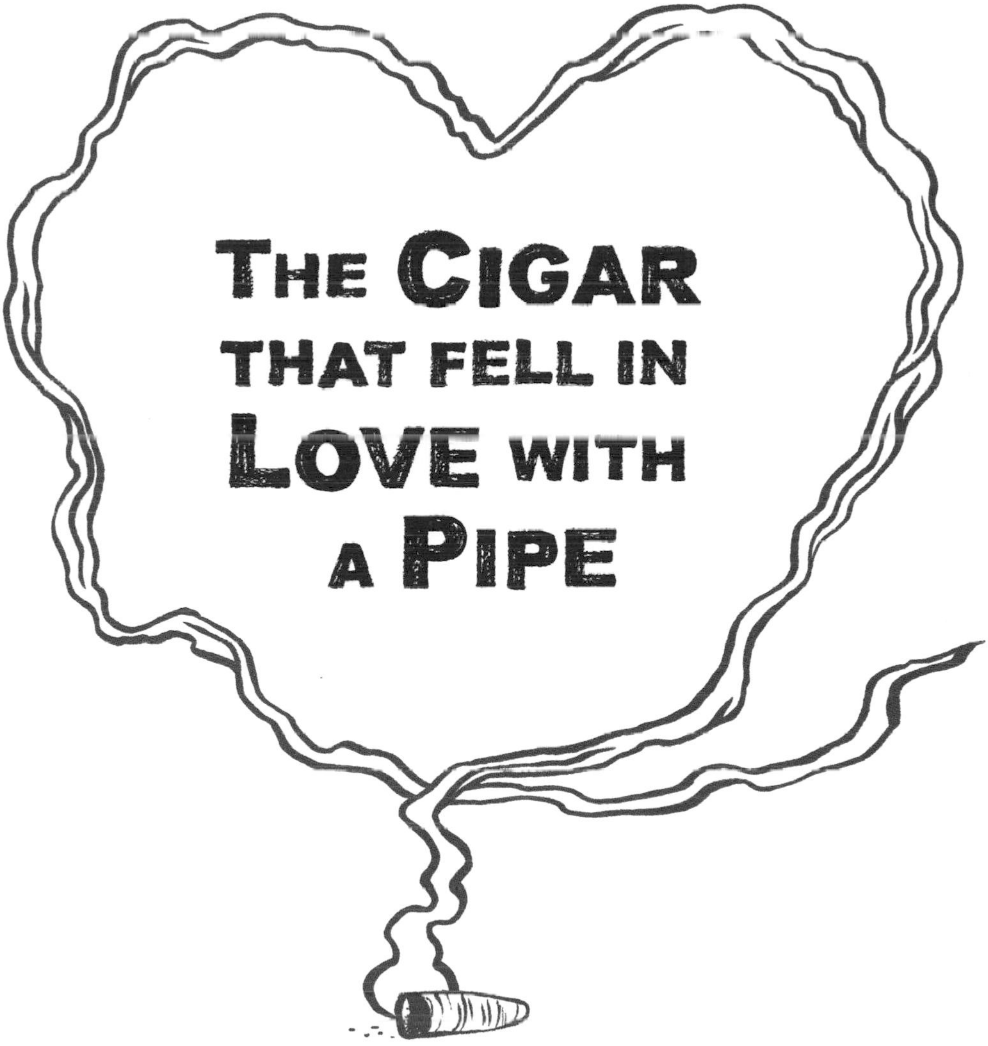

THE CIGAR THAT FELL IN LOVE WITH A PIPE

WRITTEN BY
DAVID CAMUS

ILLUSTRATED BY
NICK ABADZIS

SELF MADE HERO

First published in 2014
by SelfMadeHero
139–141 Pancras Road
London NW1 1UN
www.selfmadehero.com

Written by: David Camus
Illustrated by: Nick Abadzis

Original text translated from French to English by Jeff Probst

Publishing Assistant: Guillaume Rater
Editorial and Production Manager: Lizzie Kaye
Sales and Marketing Manager: Sam Humphrey
Publishing Director: Emma Hayley
With thanks to: Dan Lockwood and Jane Laporte

A CIP record for this book is available from the British Library

ISBN: 978-1-906838-48-5

10 9 8 7 6 5 4 3 2 1

Printed and bound in China

For Cécile, who inspired it.

- DC

For Angela, at home in both the Smoke and the Big Apple.

- NA

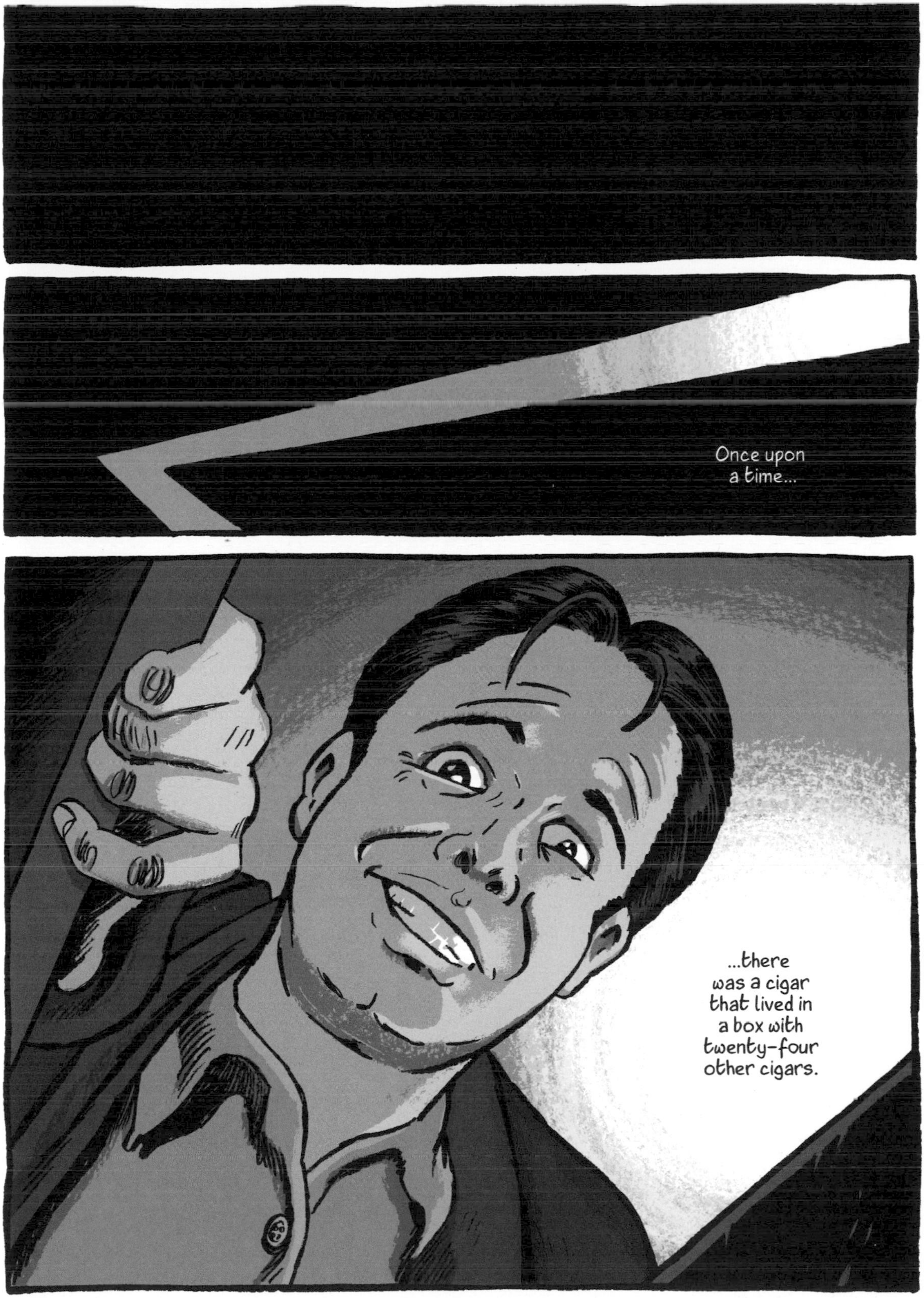
Once upon a time...
...there was a cigar that lived in a box with twenty-four other cigars.

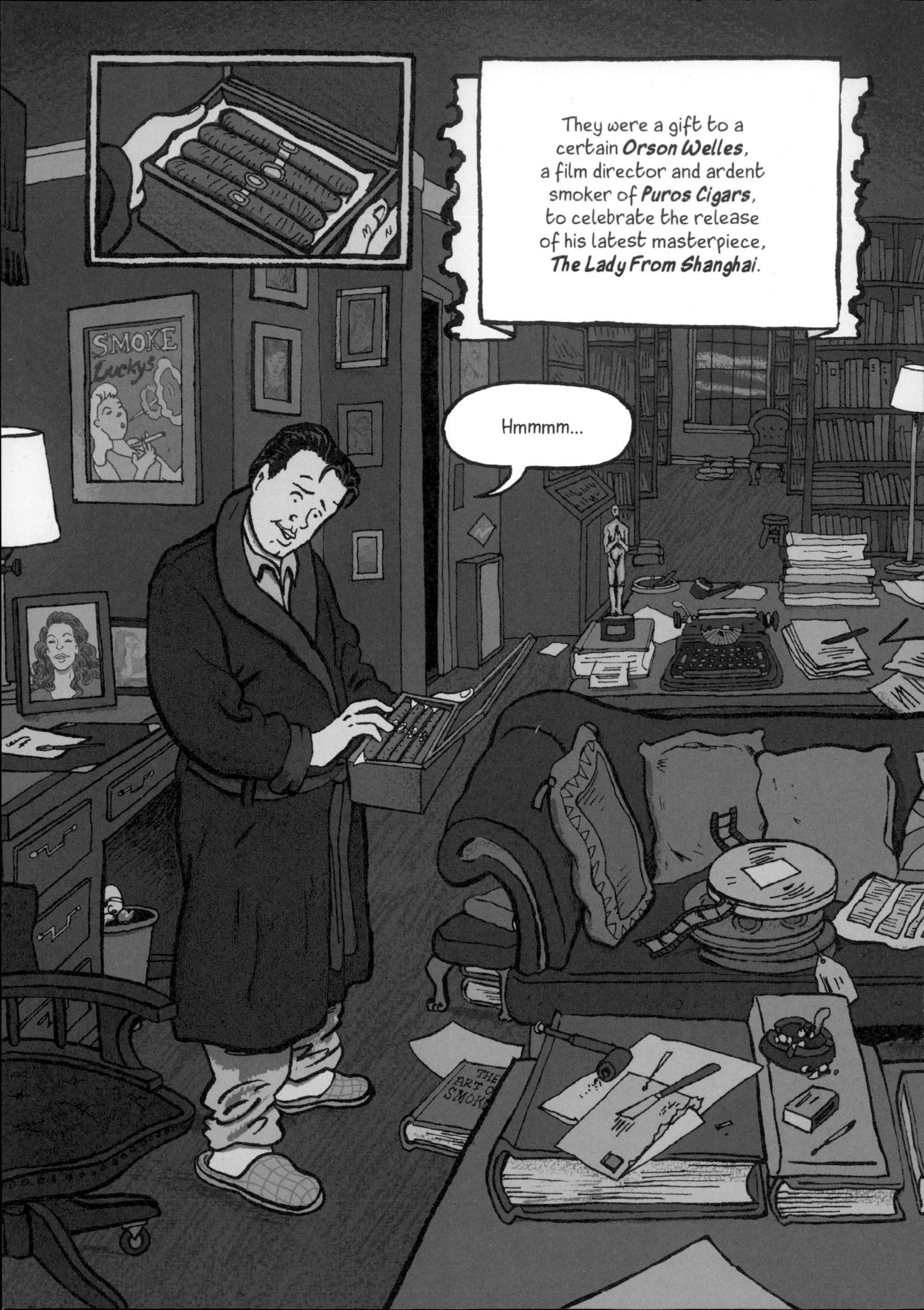
They were a gift to a certain **Orson Welles**, a film director and ardent smoker of **Puros Cigars**, to celebrate the release of his latest masterpiece, **The Lady From Shanghai**.
SMOKE Lucky's
Hmmmm...
THE ART OF SMOKE

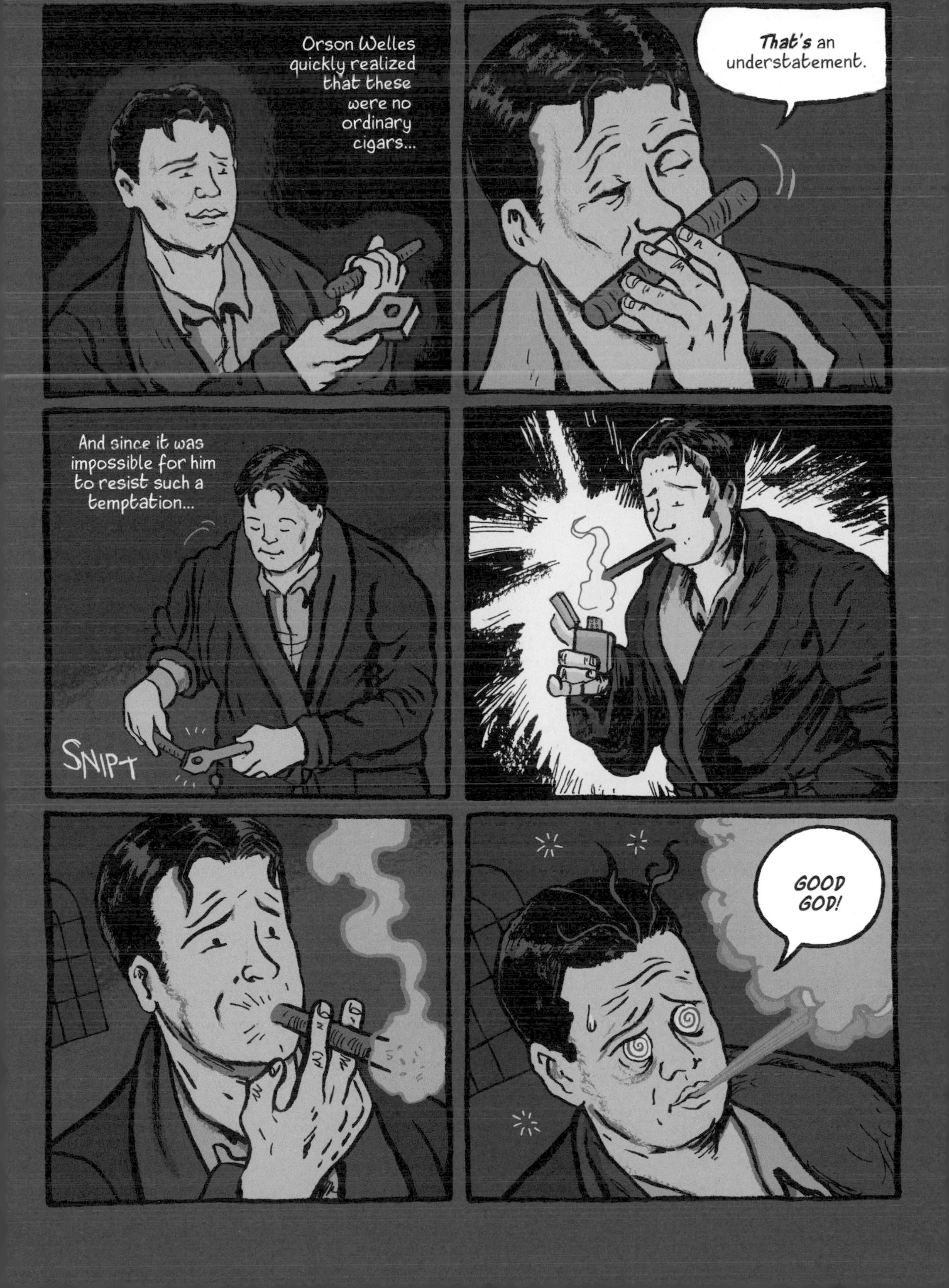

Orson Welles quickly realized that these were no ordinary cigars...
That's an understatement.
And since it was impossible for him to resist such a temptation...
SNIPT
GOOD GOD!

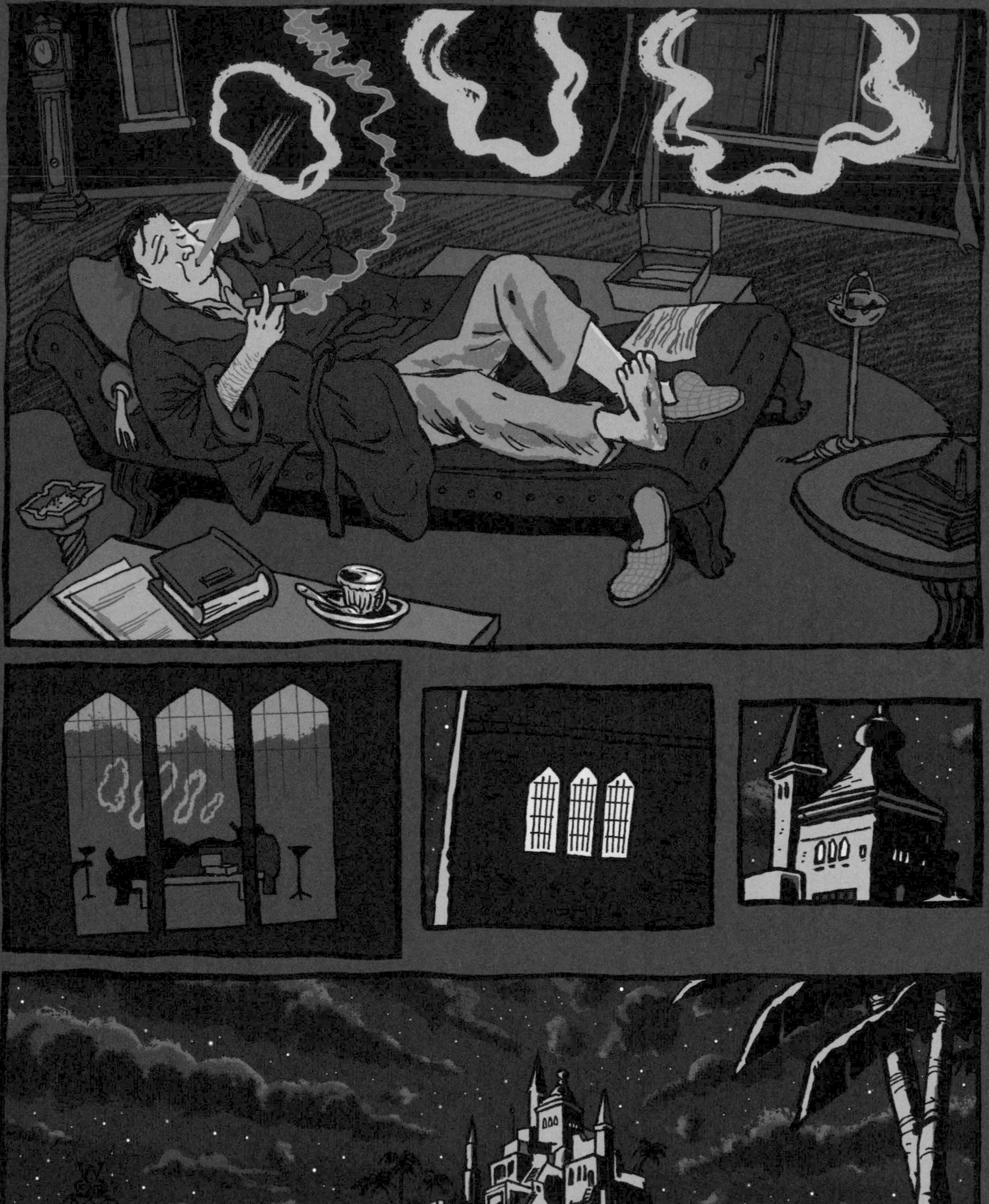

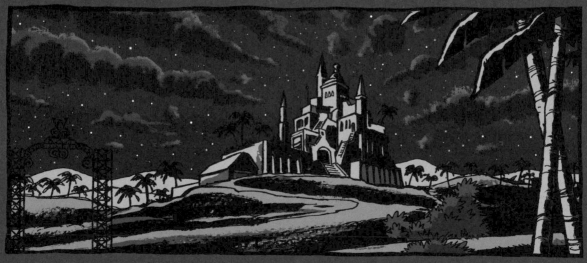

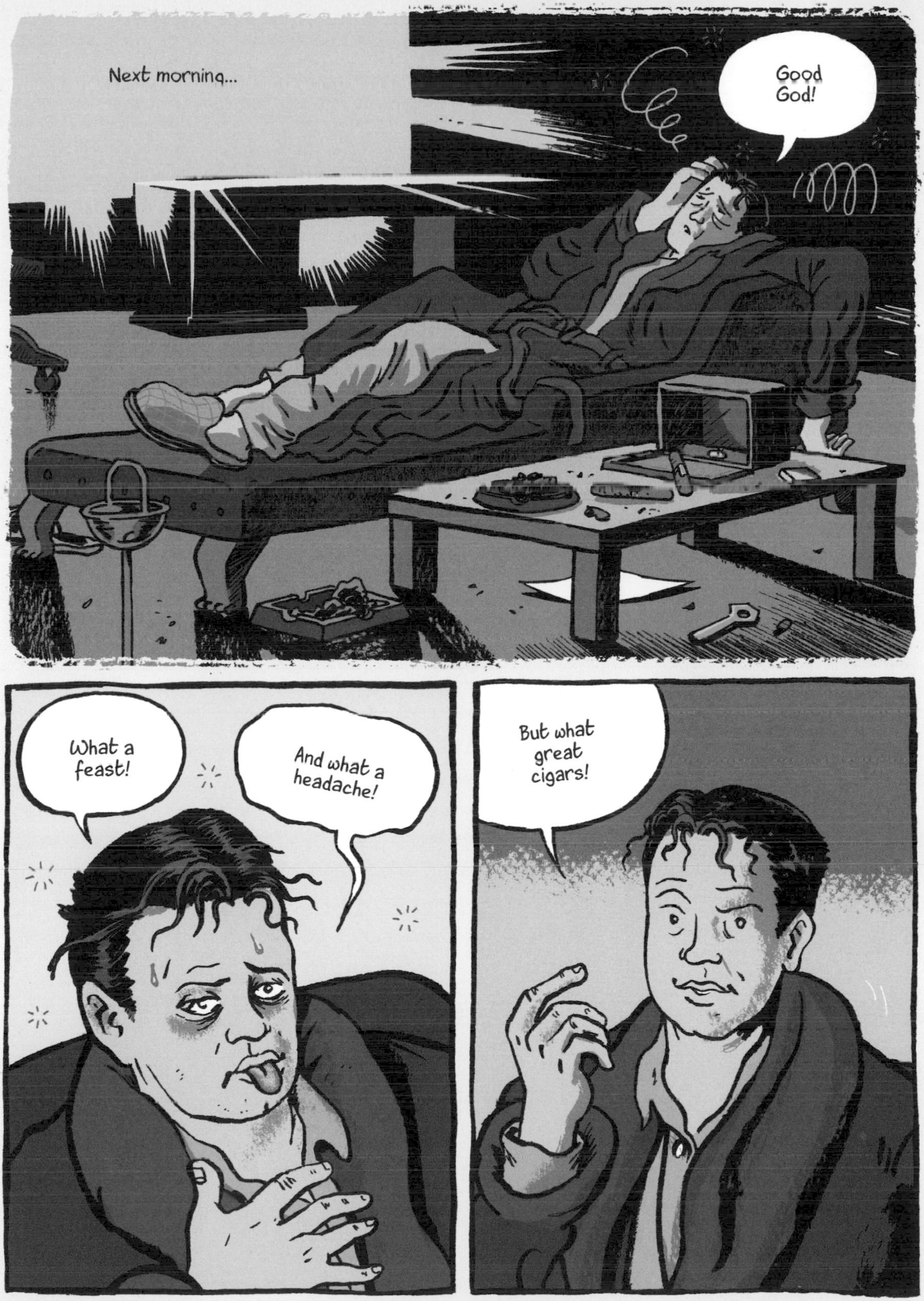
Next morning...
Good God!
What a feast!
And what a headache!
But what great cigars!

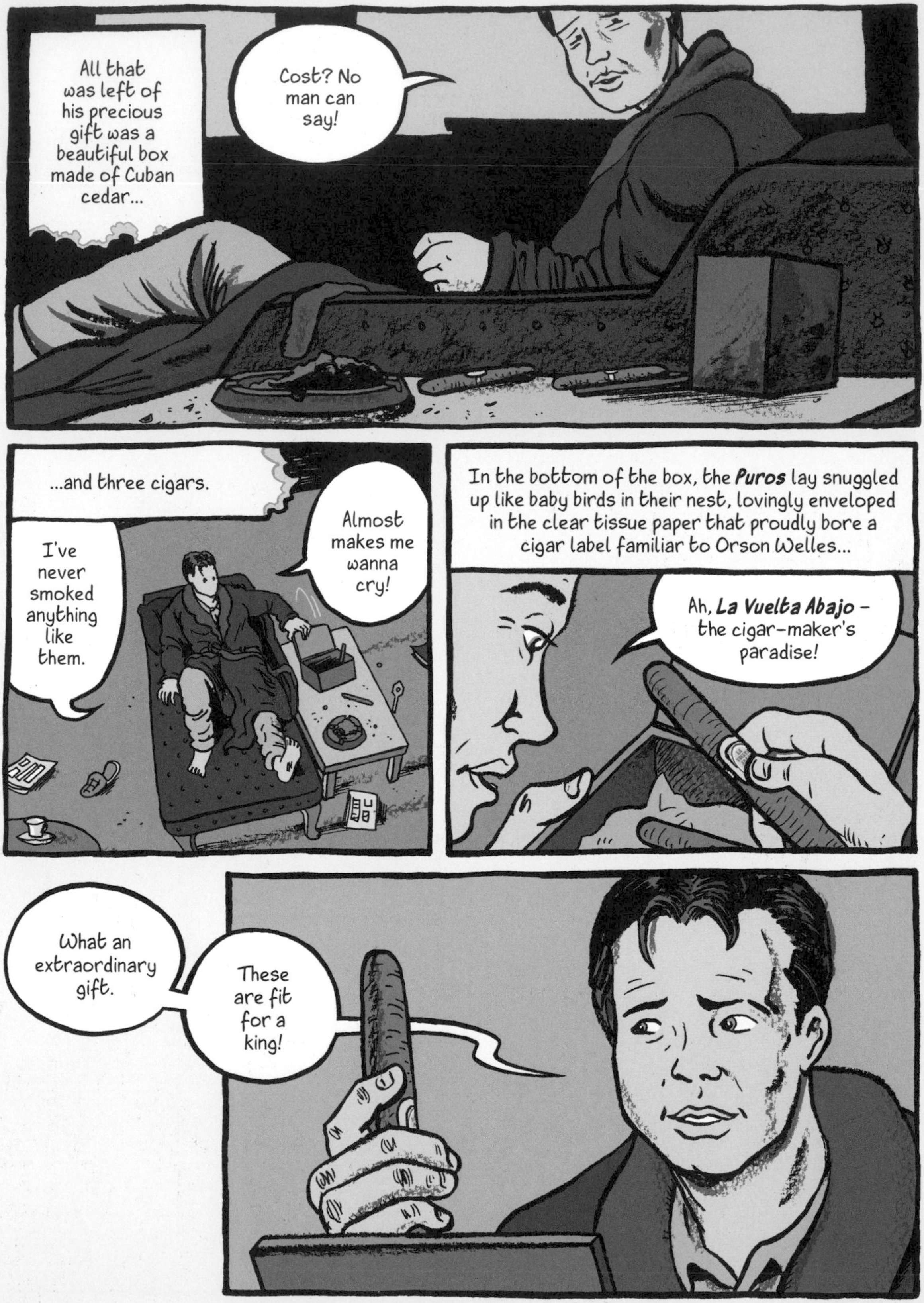
All that was left of his precious gift was a beautiful box made of Cuban cedar...
Cost? No man can say!
...and three cigars.
I've never smoked anything like them.
Almost makes me wanna cry!
In the bottom of the box, the **Puros** lay snuggled up like baby birds in their nest, lovingly enveloped in the clear tissue paper that proudly bore a cigar label familiar to Orson Welles...
Ah, **La Vuelta Abajo** – the cigar-maker's paradise!
What an extraordinary gift.
These are fit for a king!

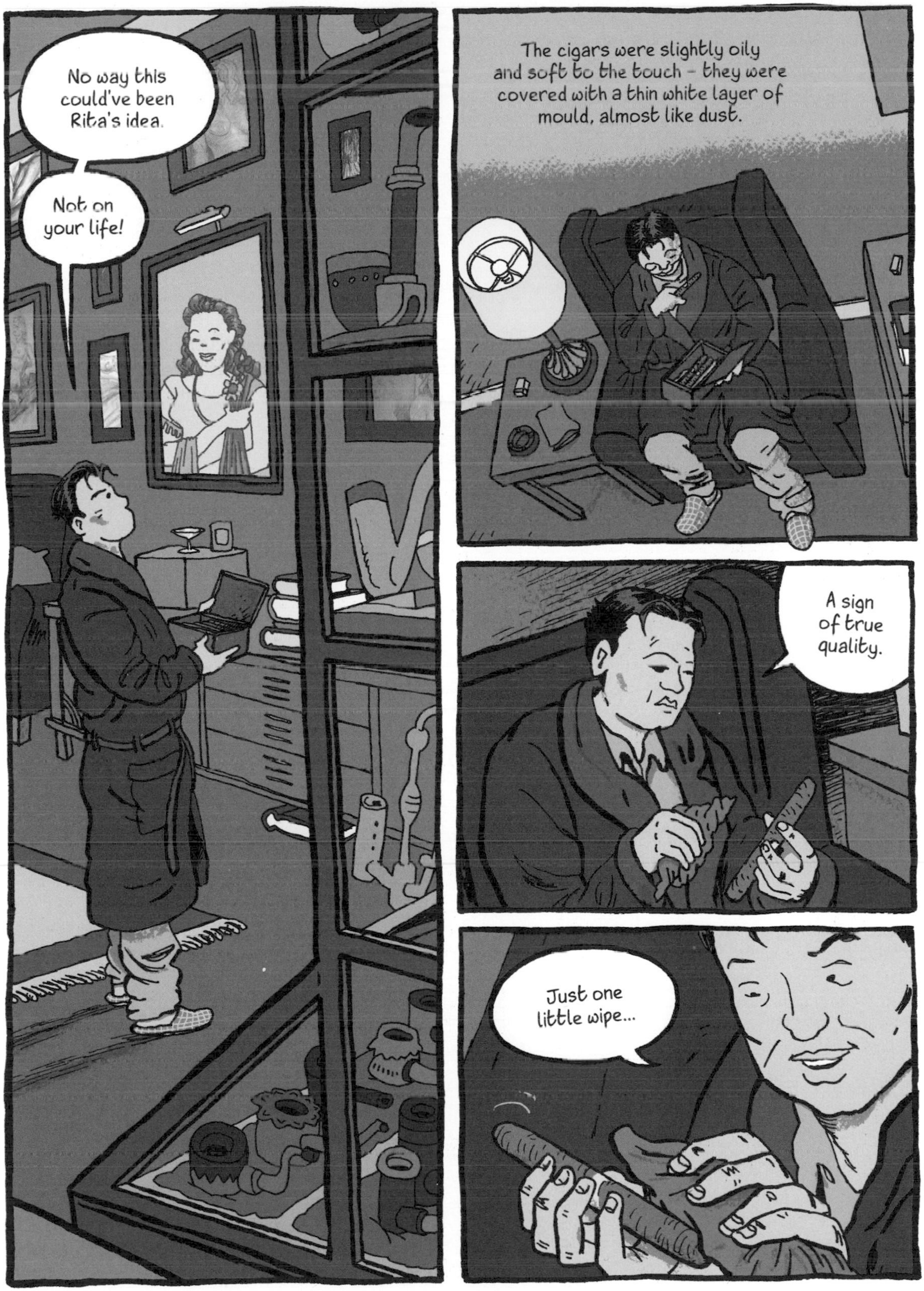
No way this could've been Rita's idea.
Not on your life!
The cigars were slightly oily and soft to the touch – they were covered with a thin white layer of mould, almost like dust.
A sign of true quality.
Just one little wipe...

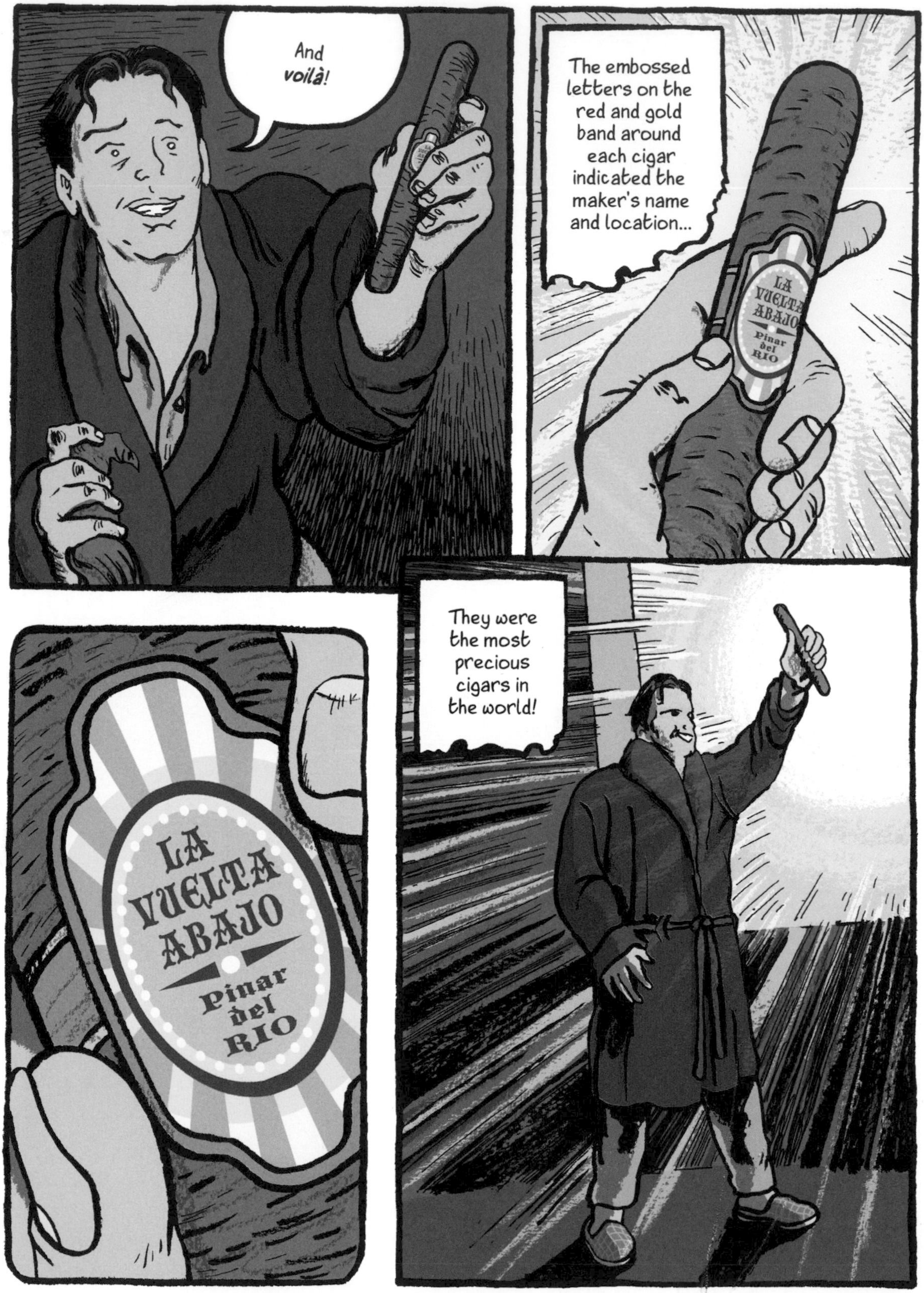
And voilà!
The embossed letters on the red and gold band around each cigar indicated the maker's name and location...
LA VUELTA ABAJO Pinar del RIO
LA VUELTA ABAJO Pinar del RIO
They were the most precious cigars in the world!

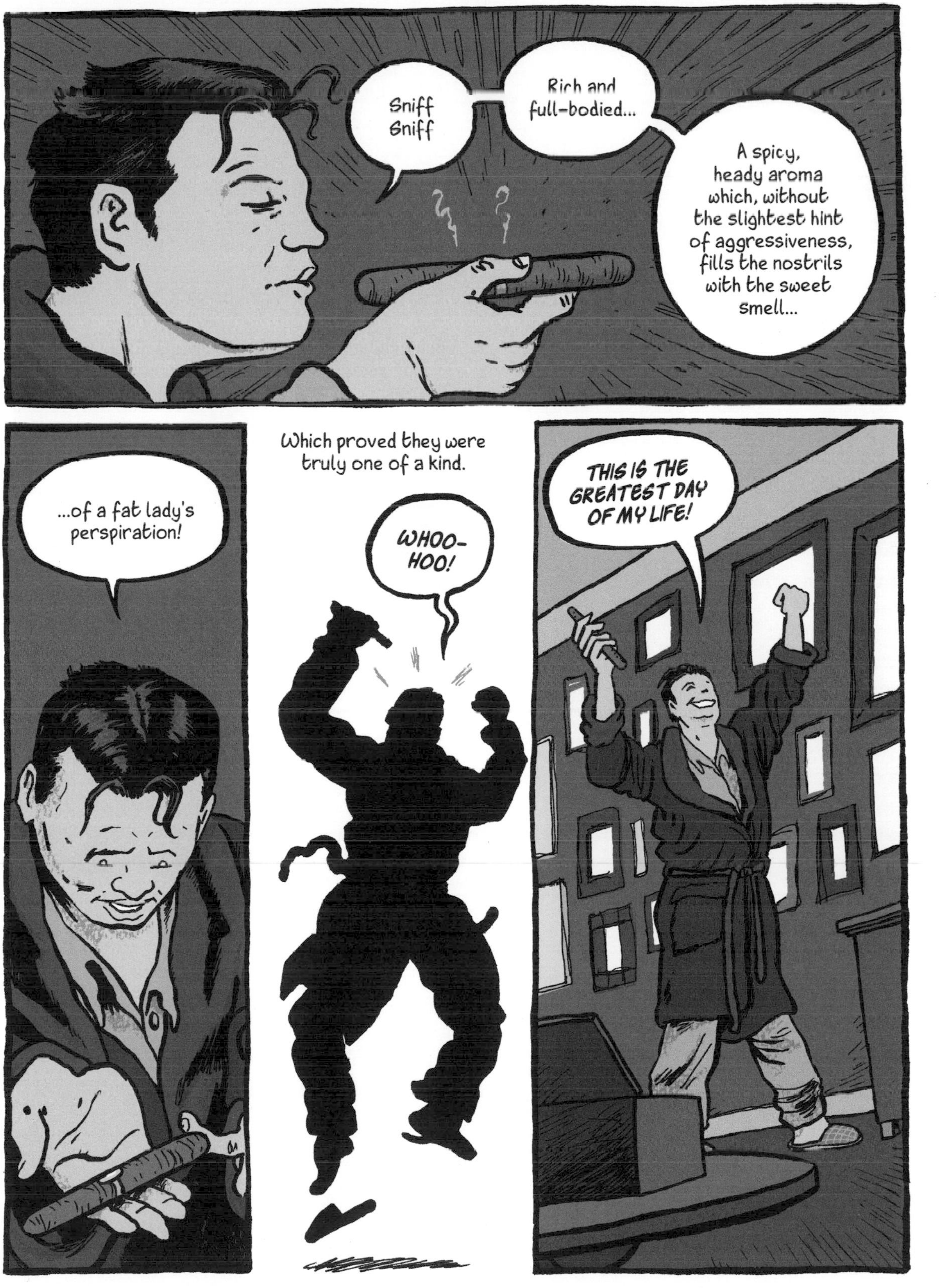
Sniff
Sniff
Rich and full-bodied...
A spicy, heady aroma which, without the slightest hint of aggressiveness, fills the nostrils with the sweet smell...
...of a fat lady's perspiration!
Which proved they were truly one of a kind.
WHOO-HOO!
THIS IS THE GREATEST DAY OF MY LIFE!

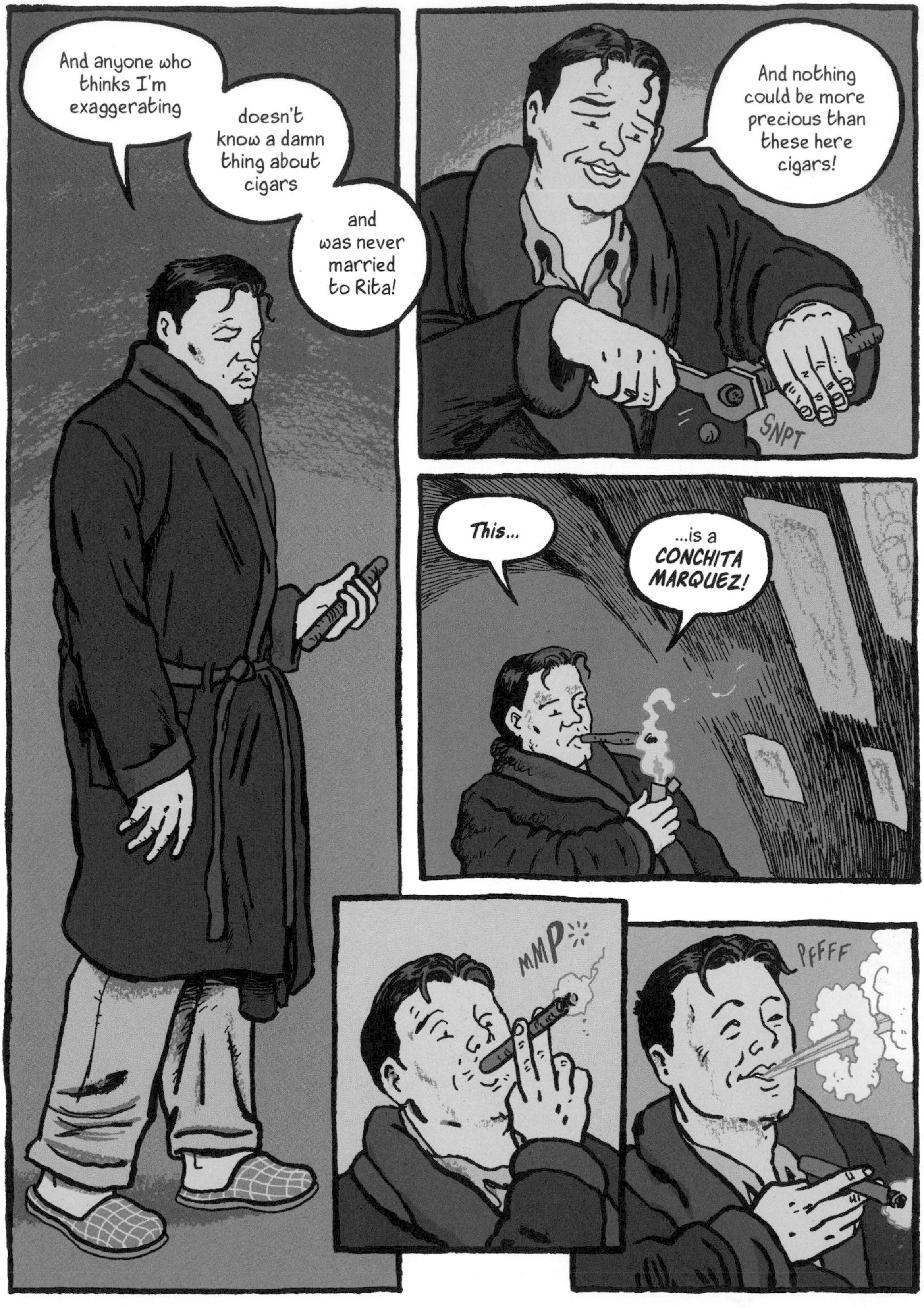
And anyone who thinks I'm exaggerating
doesn't know a damn thing about cigars
and was never married to Rita!
And nothing could be more precious than these here cigars!
SNPT
This...
...is a CONCHITA MARQUEZ!
MMP
PFFFF

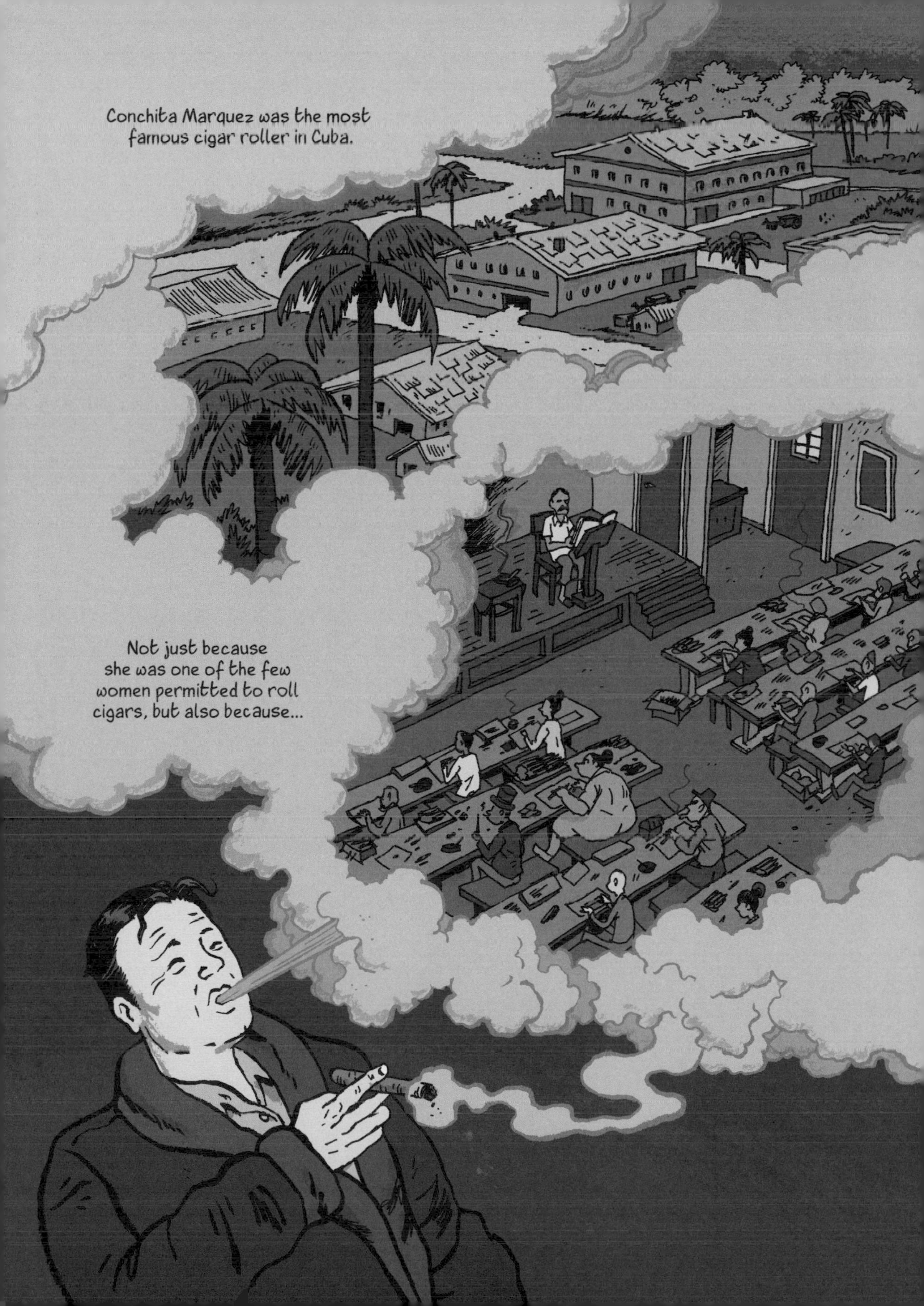
Conchita Marquez was the most famous cigar roller in Cuba.
Not just because she was one of the few women permitted to roll cigars, but also because...

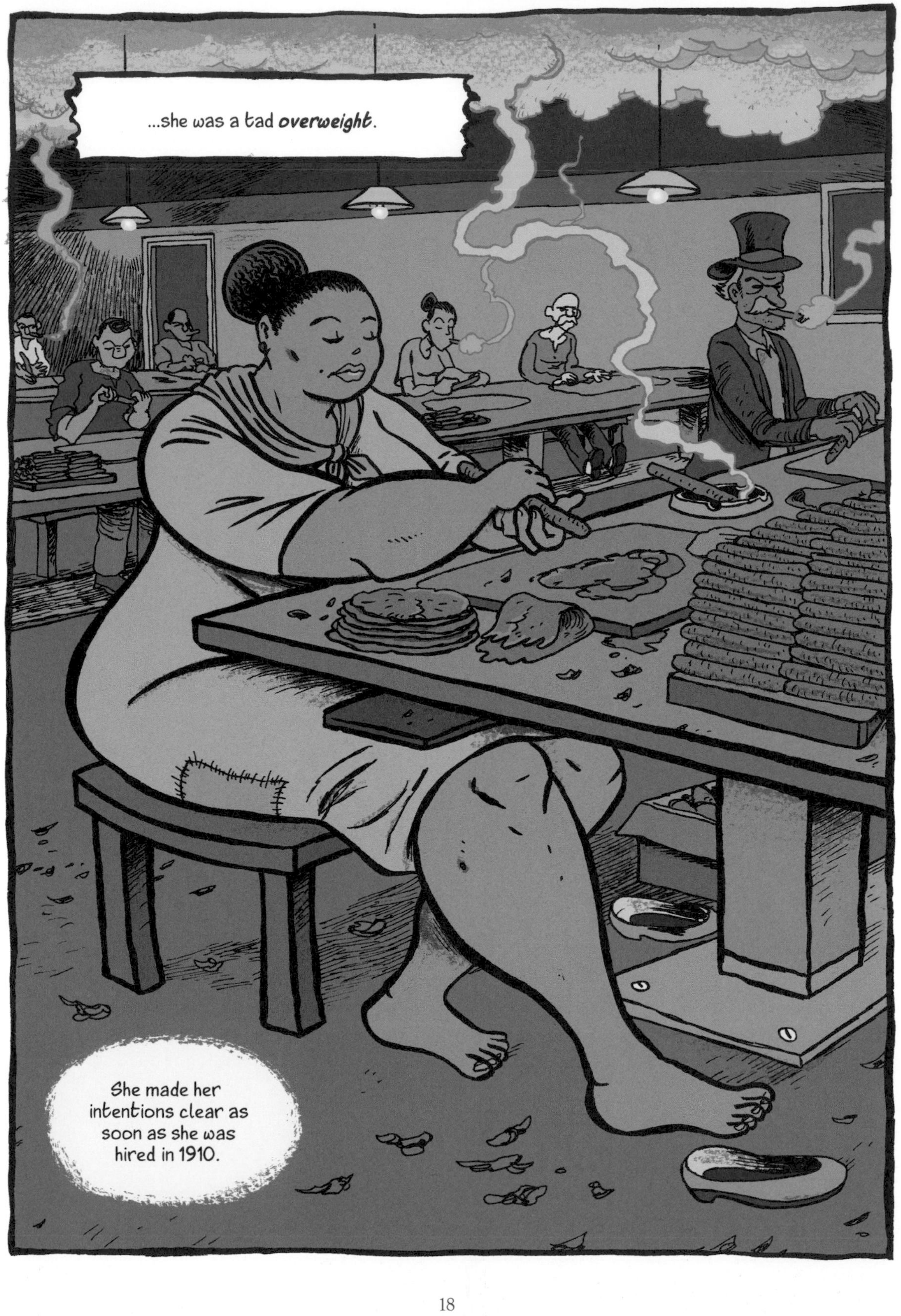
...she was a tad **overweight**.
She made her intentions clear as soon as she was hired in 1910.

It was all part of her plan.

Since *torcedores* were paid by the cigar...

...it was better to have big hands...

...meaty thighs...

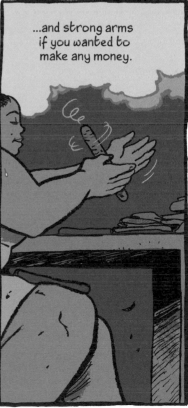

...and strong arms if you wanted to make any money.

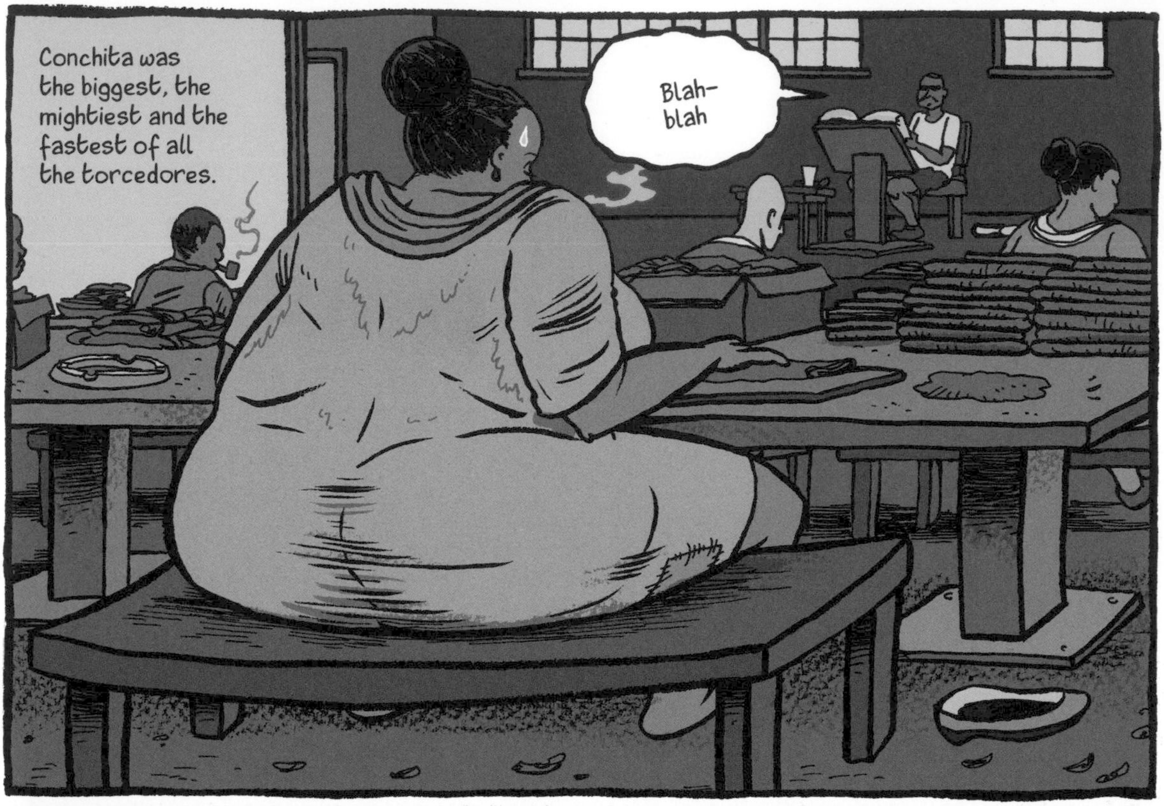
Conchita was the biggest, the mightiest and the fastest of all the torcedores.
Blah-blah

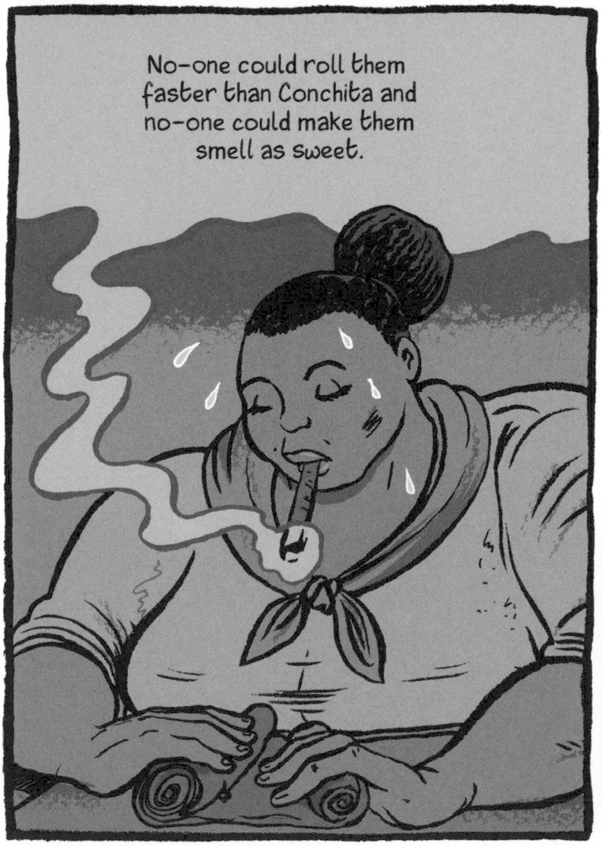
No-one could roll them faster than Conchita and no-one could make them smell as sweet.

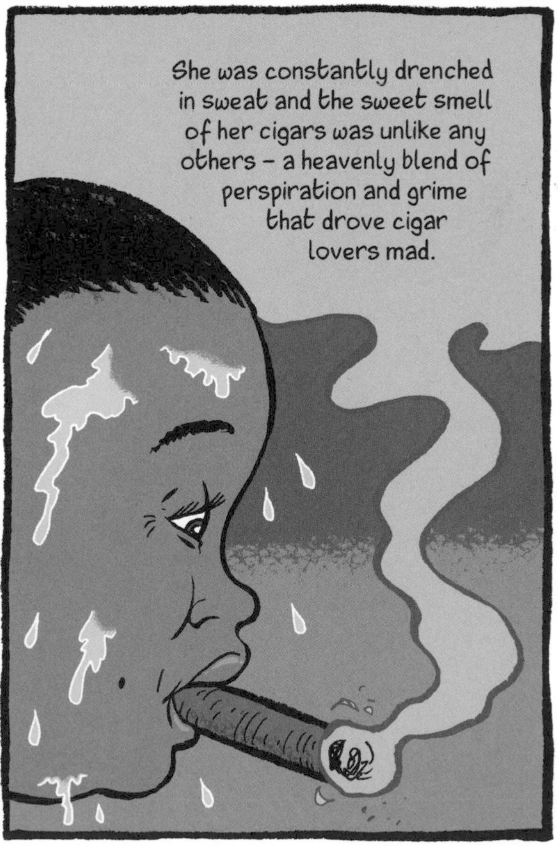
She was constantly drenched in sweat and the sweet smell of her cigars was unlike any others – a heavenly blend of perspiration and grime that drove cigar lovers mad.

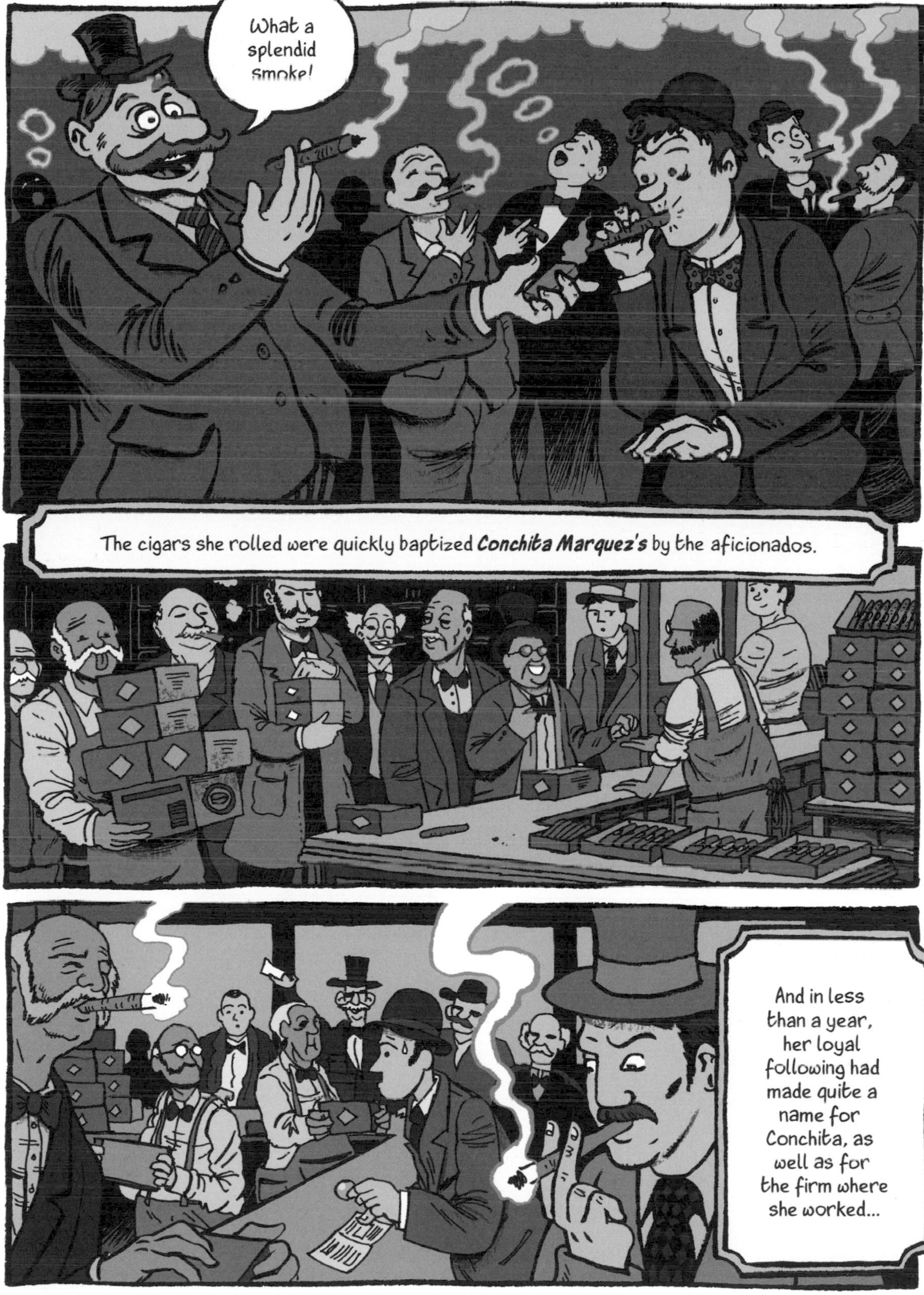
What a splendid smoke!
The cigars she rolled were quickly baptized **Conchita Marquez's** by the aficionados.
And in less than a year, her loyal following had made quite a name for Conchita, as well as for the firm where she worked...

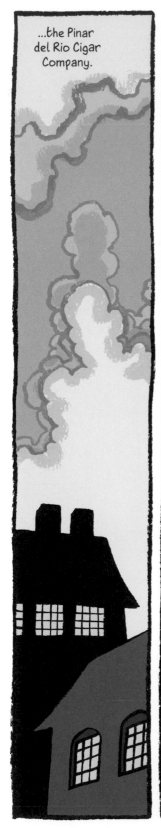

...the Pinar del Rio Cigar Company.

Being a God-fearing woman, Conchita worked every day except Sunday.

PINAR DEL RIO CIGAR COMPANY

EXCLUSIVE MANUFACTURER OF CONCHITA MARQUEZ CIGARS

Thanks to Conchita, the Pinar del Rio Cigar Company made bushels and bushels of money.

Heh, heh, heh!

Other women were hired to work for Conchita and quickly grew jealous of her fame.

C'mon now, keep it moving!

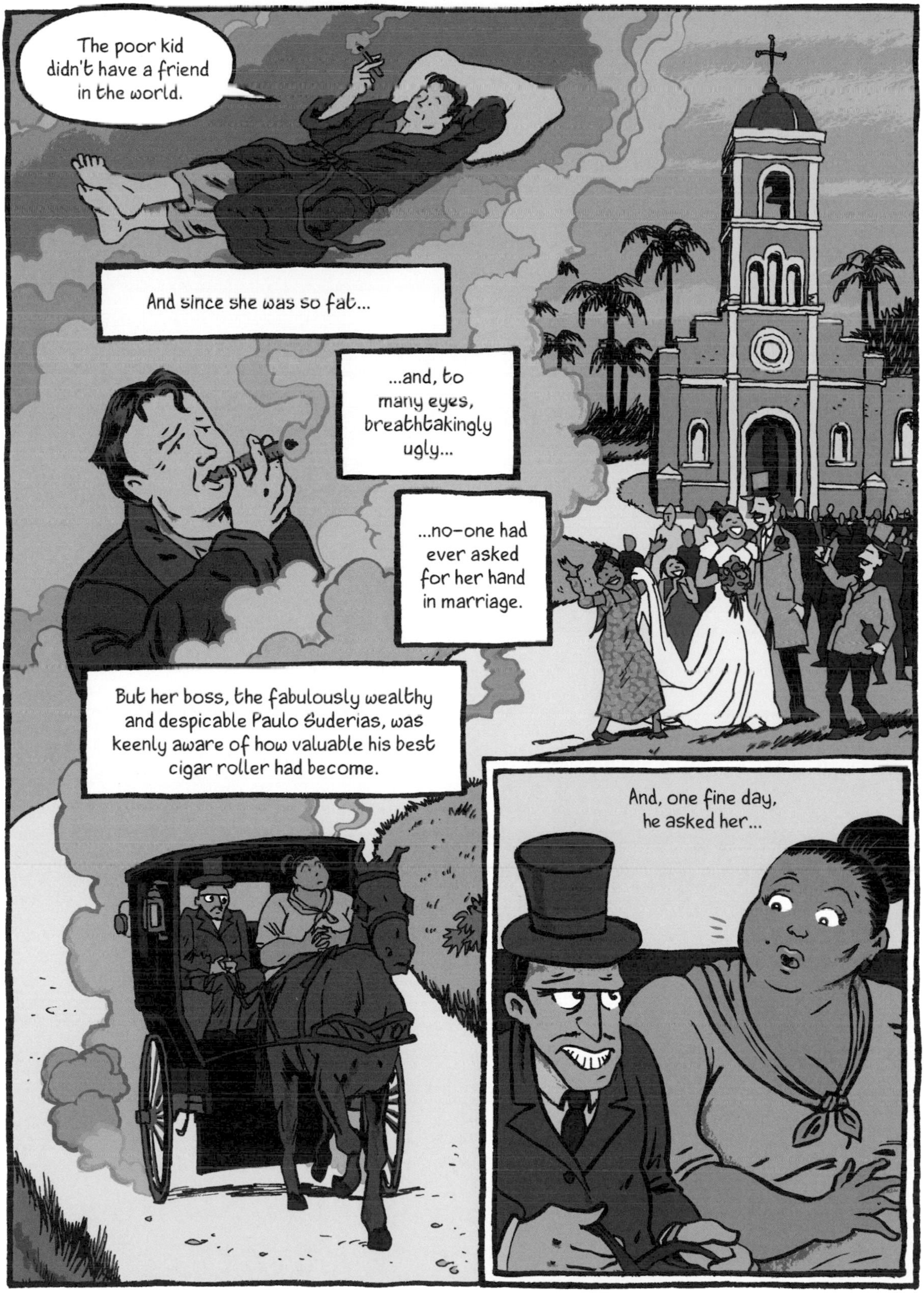
The poor kid didn't have a friend in the world.
And since she was so fat...
...and, to many eyes, breathtakingly ugly...
...no-one had ever asked for her hand in marriage.
But her boss, the fabulously wealthy and despicable Paulo Suderias, was keenly aware of how valuable his best cigar roller had become.
And, one fine day, he asked her...

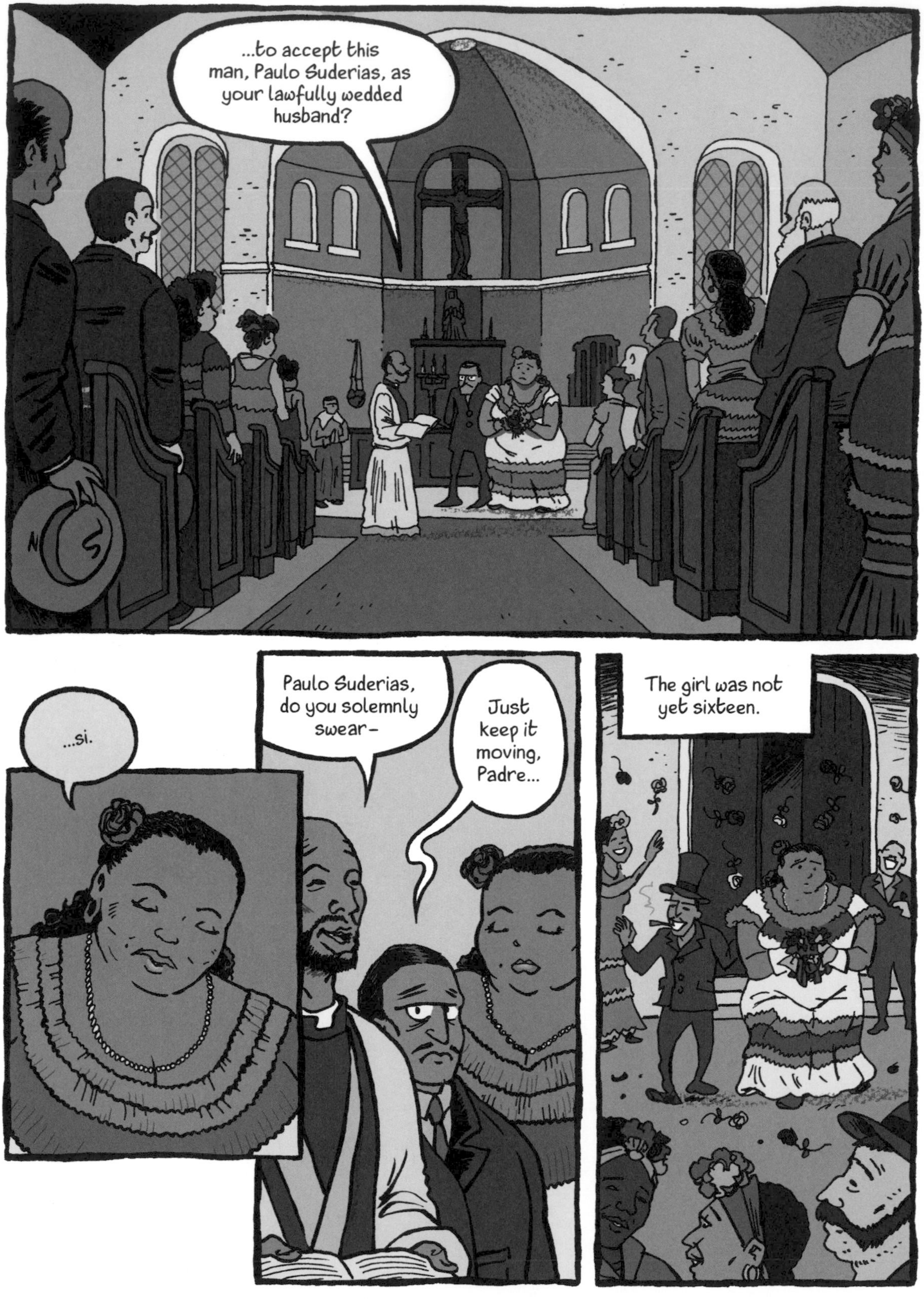
...to accept this man, Paulo Suderias, as your lawfully wedded husband?
...si.
Paulo Suderias, do you solemnly swear–
Just keep it moving, Padre...
The girl was not yet sixteen.

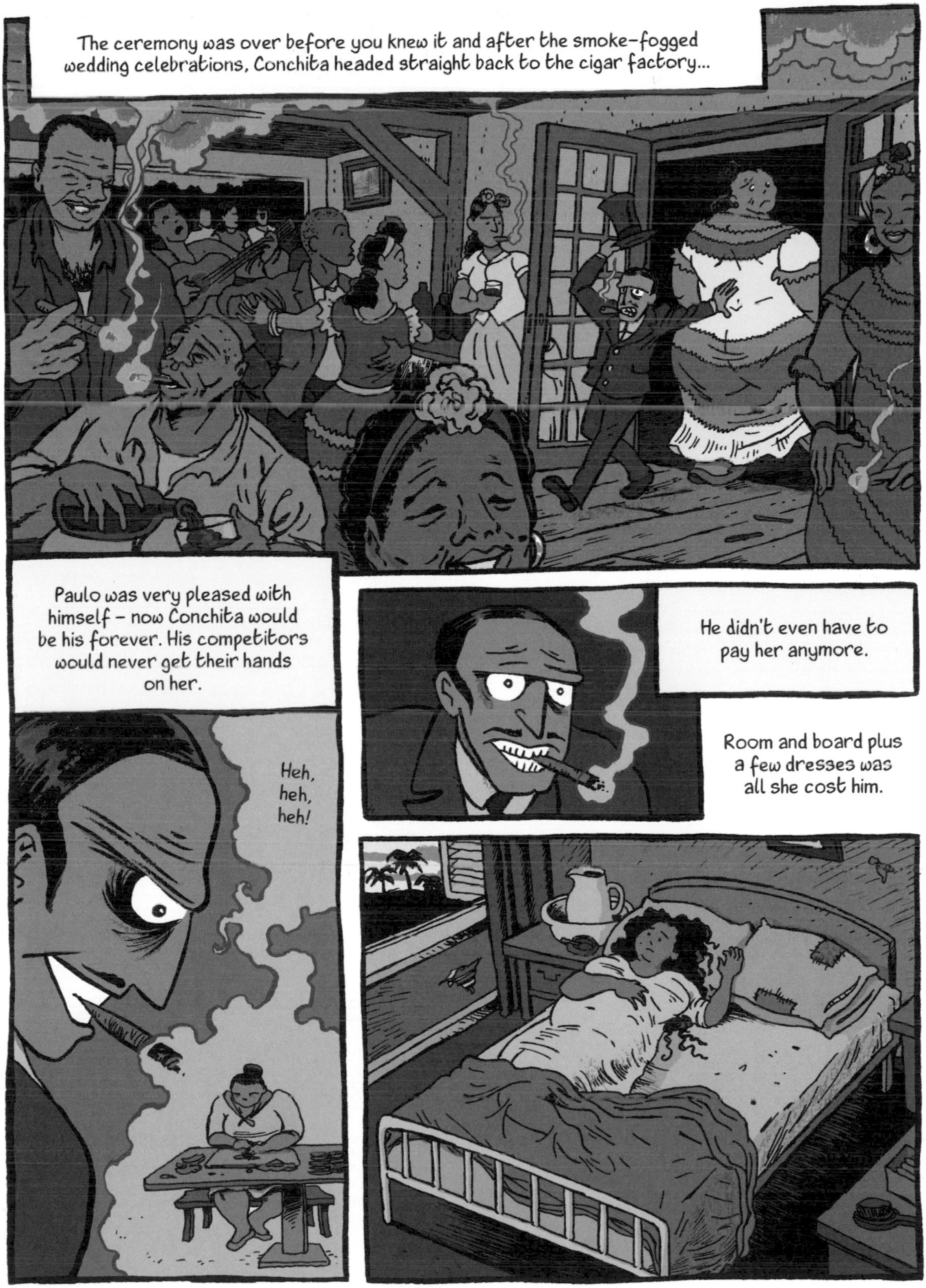
The ceremony was over before you knew it and after the smoke-fogged wedding celebrations, Conchita headed straight back to the cigar factory...
Paulo was very pleased with himself – now Conchita would be his forever. His competitors would never get their hands on her.
He didn't even have to pay her anymore.
Heh, heh, heh!
Room and board plus a few dresses was all she cost him.

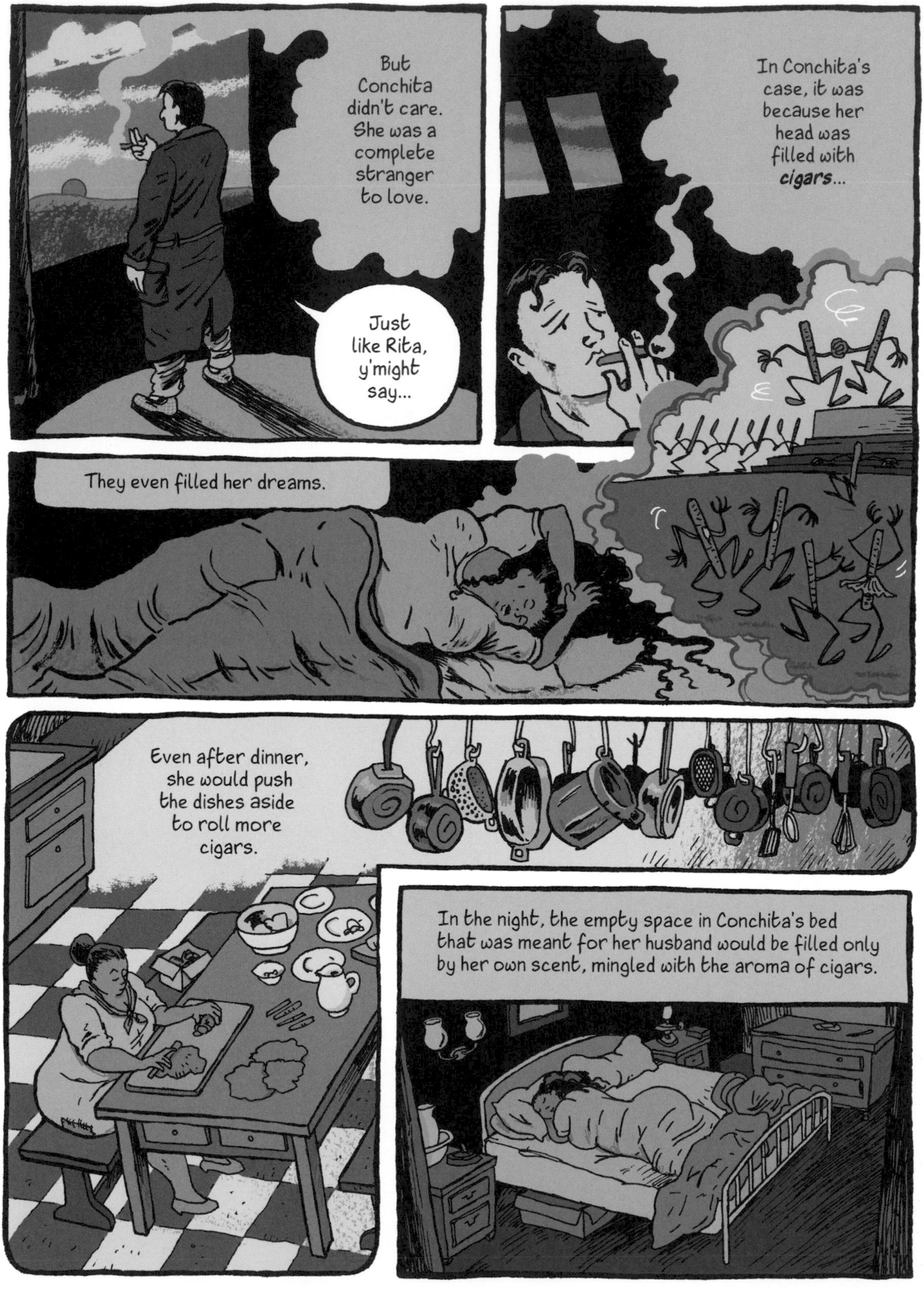
But Conchita didn't care. She was a complete stranger to love.
Just like Rita, y'might say...
In Conchita's case, it was because her head was filled with **cigars**...
They even filled her dreams.
Even after dinner, she would push the dishes aside to roll more cigars.
In the night, the empty space in Conchita's bed that was meant for her husband would be filled only by her own scent, mingled with the aroma of cigars.

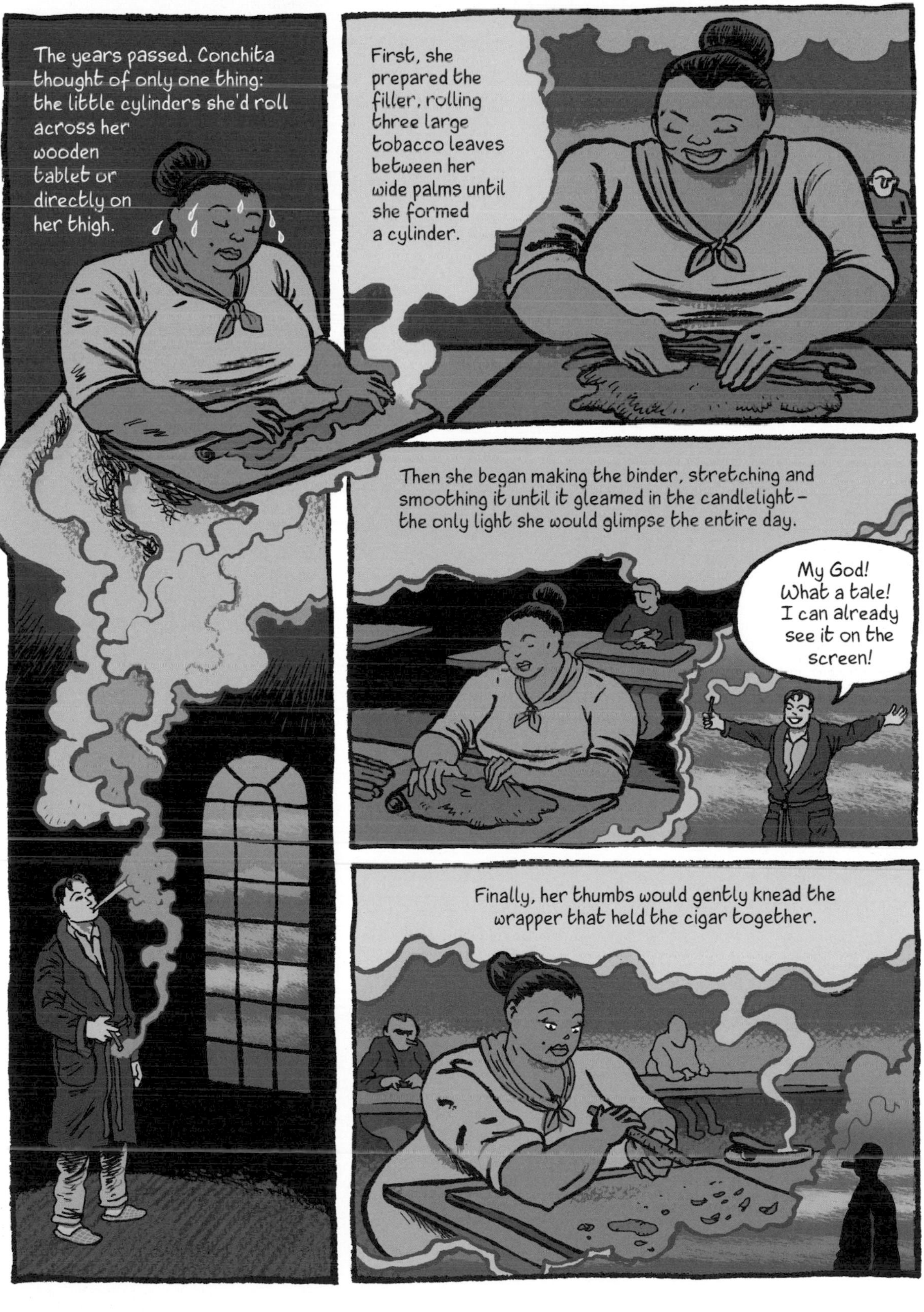
The years passed. Conchita thought of only one thing: the little cylinders she'd roll across her wooden tablet or directly on her thigh.
First, she prepared the filler, rolling three large tobacco leaves between her wide palms until she formed a cylinder.
Then she began making the binder, stretching and smoothing it until it gleamed in the candlelight – the only light she would glimpse the entire day.
My God! What a tale! I can already see it on the screen!
Finally, her thumbs would gently knead the wrapper that held the cigar together.

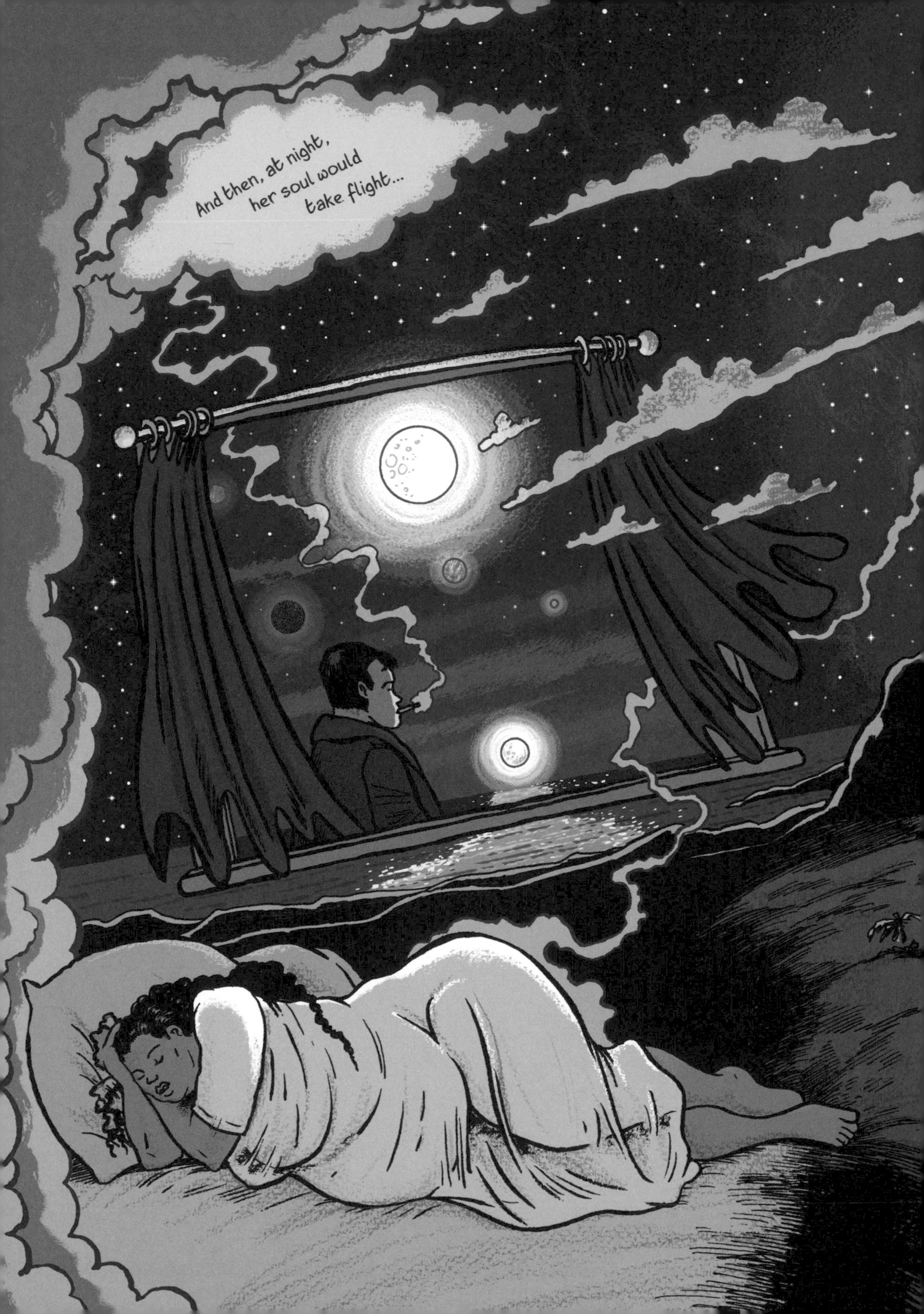
And then, at night, her soul would take flight...

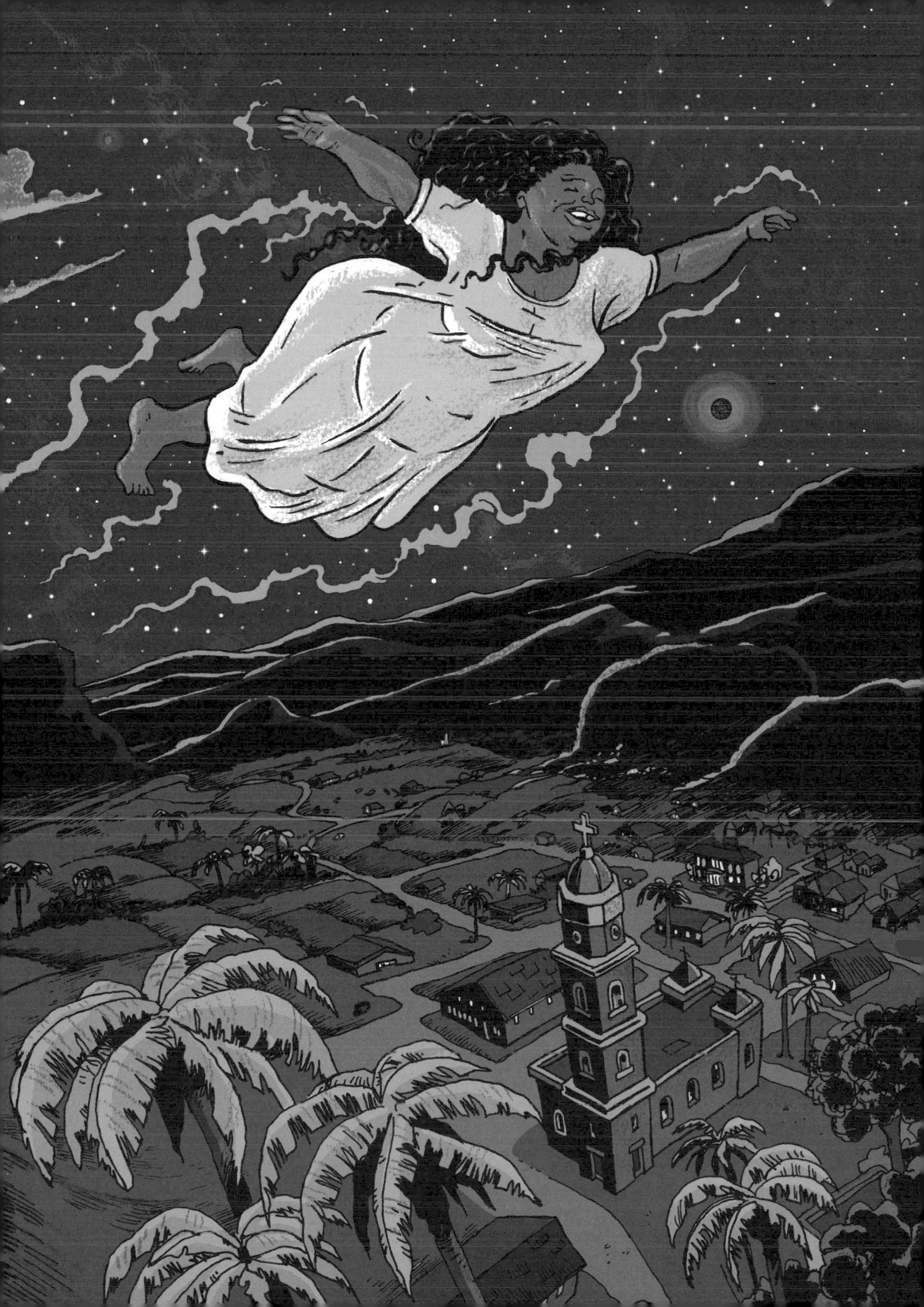

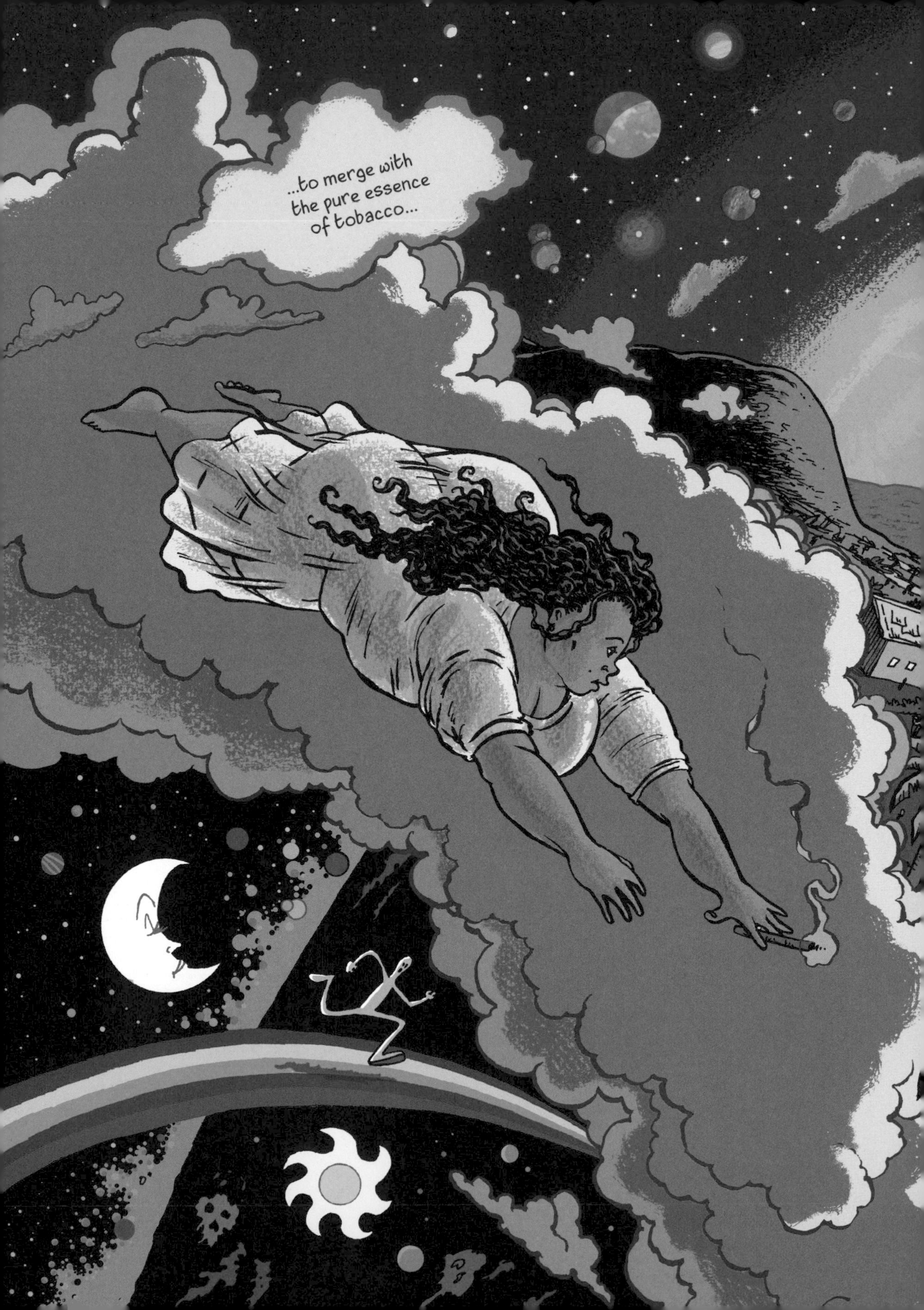
...to merge with
the pure essence
of tobacco...

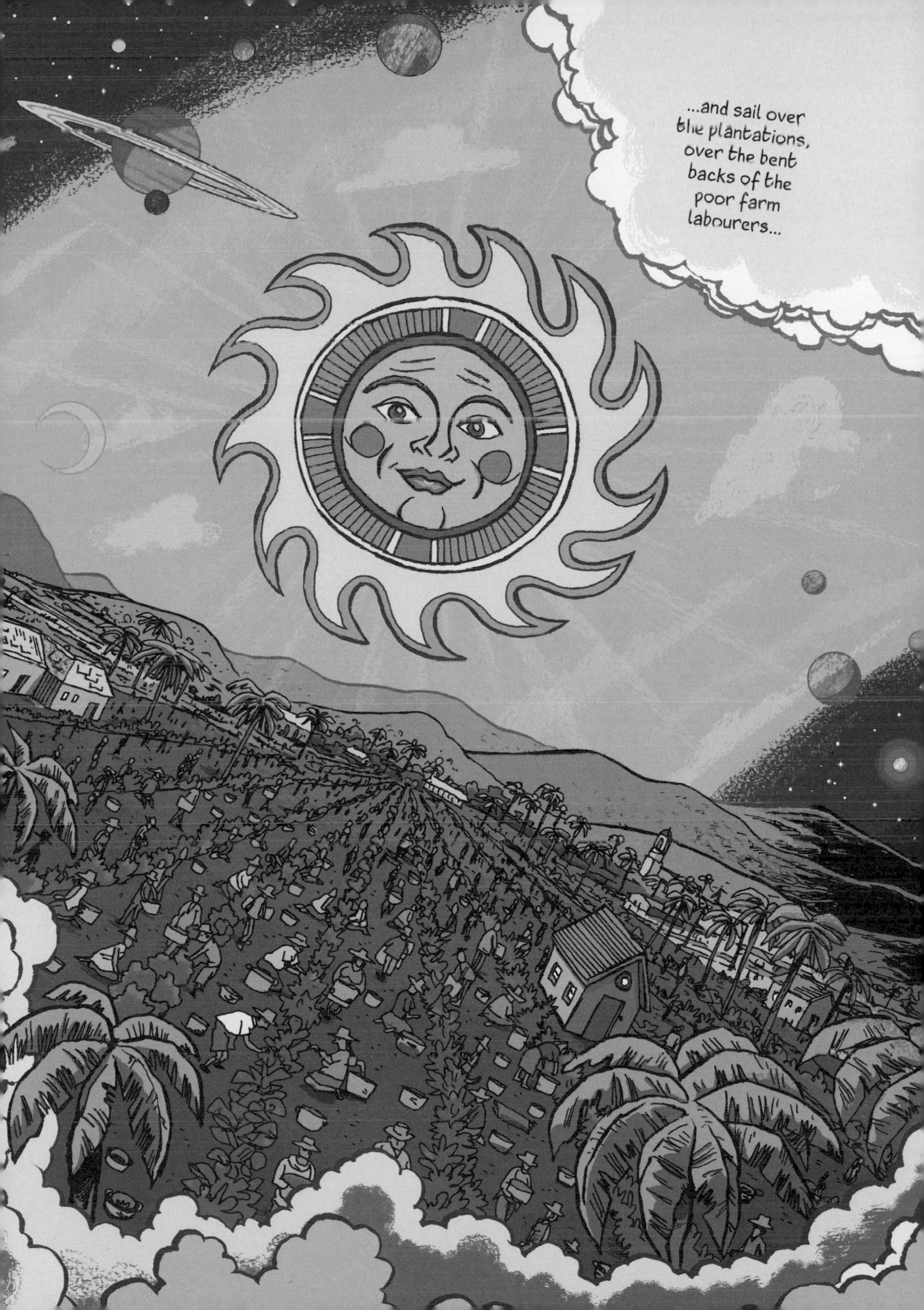
...and sail over the plantations, over the bent backs of the poor farm labourers...

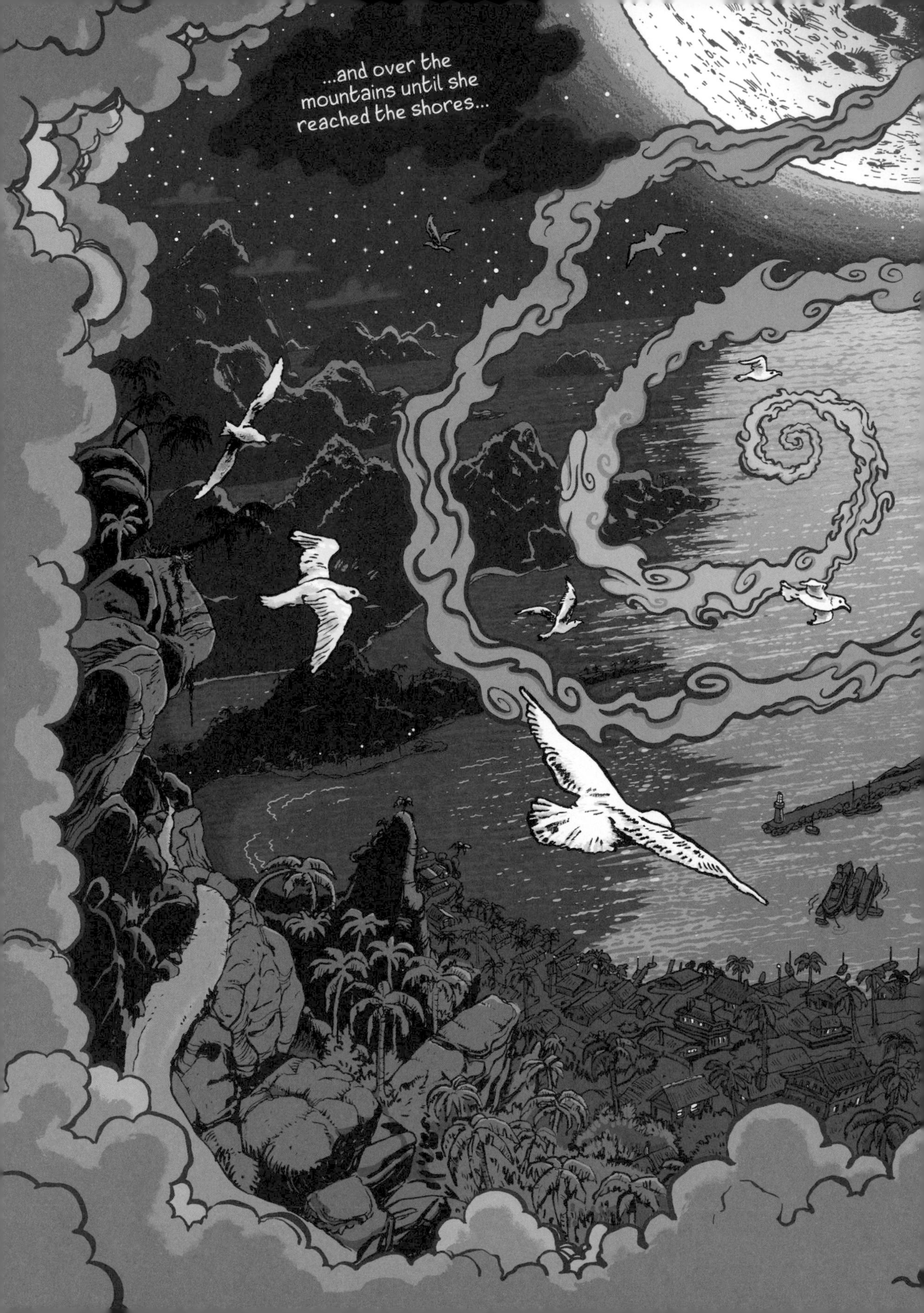
...and over the mountains until she reached the shores...

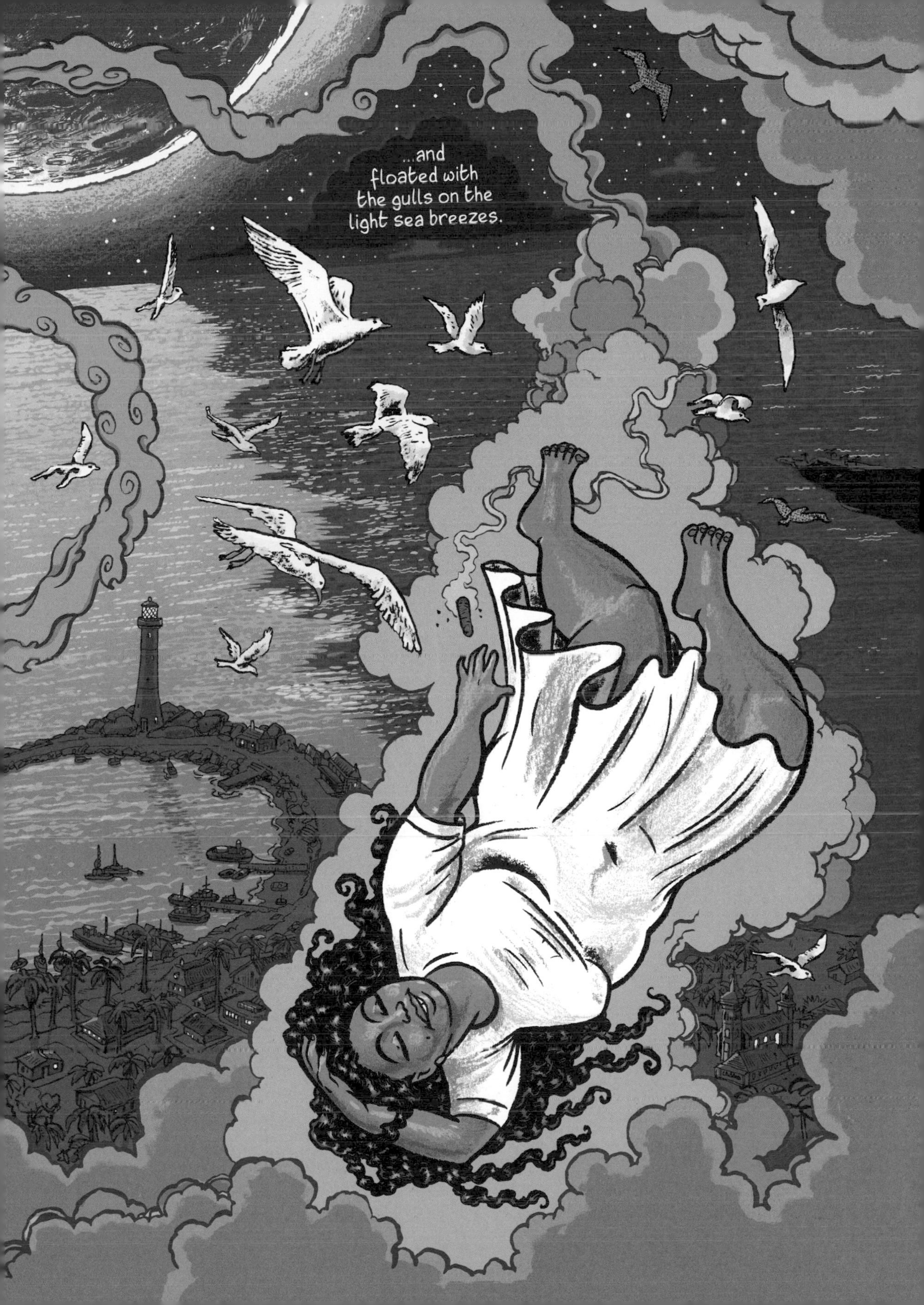
...and floated with the gulls on the light sea breezes.

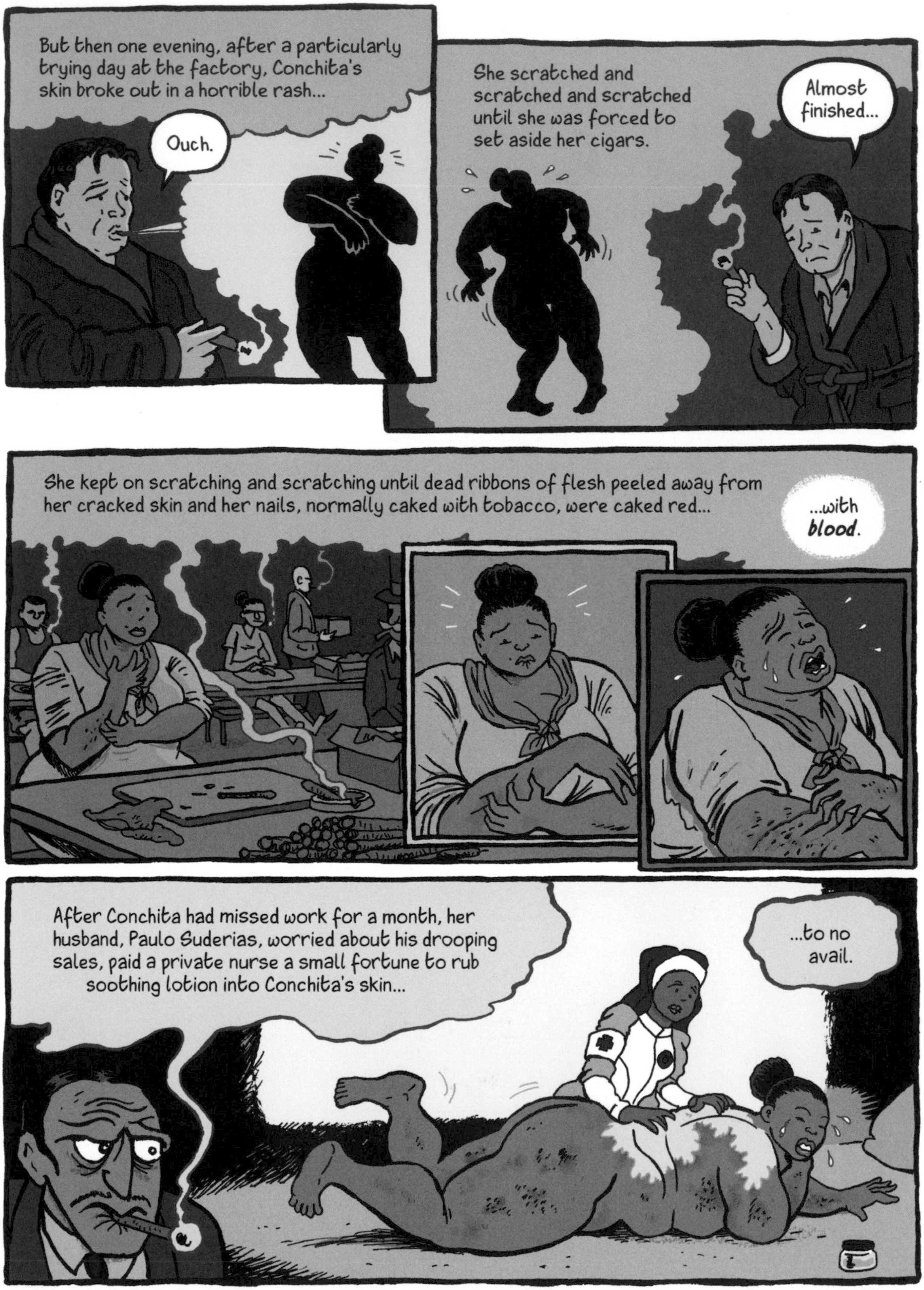
But then one evening, after a particularly trying day at the factory, Conchita's skin broke out in a horrible rash...
Ouch.
She scratched and scratched and scratched until she was forced to set aside her cigars.
Almost finished...
She kept on scratching and scratching until dead ribbons of flesh peeled away from her cracked skin and her nails, normally caked with tobacco, were caked red...
...with *blood*.
After Conchita had missed work for a month, her husband, Paulo Suderias, worried about his drooping sales, paid a private nurse a small fortune to rub soothing lotion into Conchita's skin...
...to no avail.

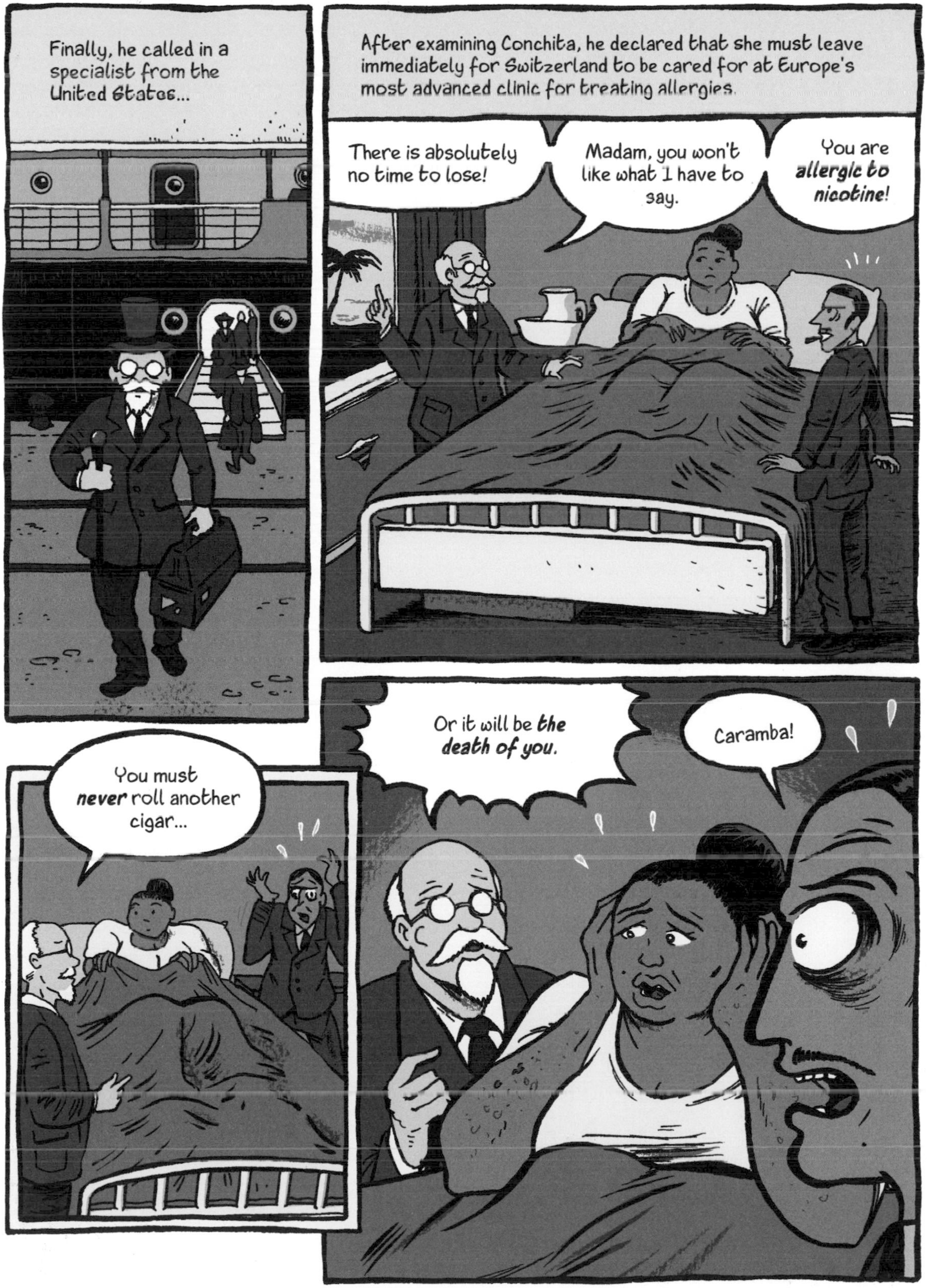
Finally, he called in a specialist from the United States...
After examining Conchita, he declared that she must leave immediately for Switzerland to be cared for at Europe's most advanced clinic for treating allergies.
There is absolutely no time to lose!
Madam, you won't like what I have to say.
You are allergic to nicotine!
You must never roll another cigar...
Or it will be the death of you.
Caramba!

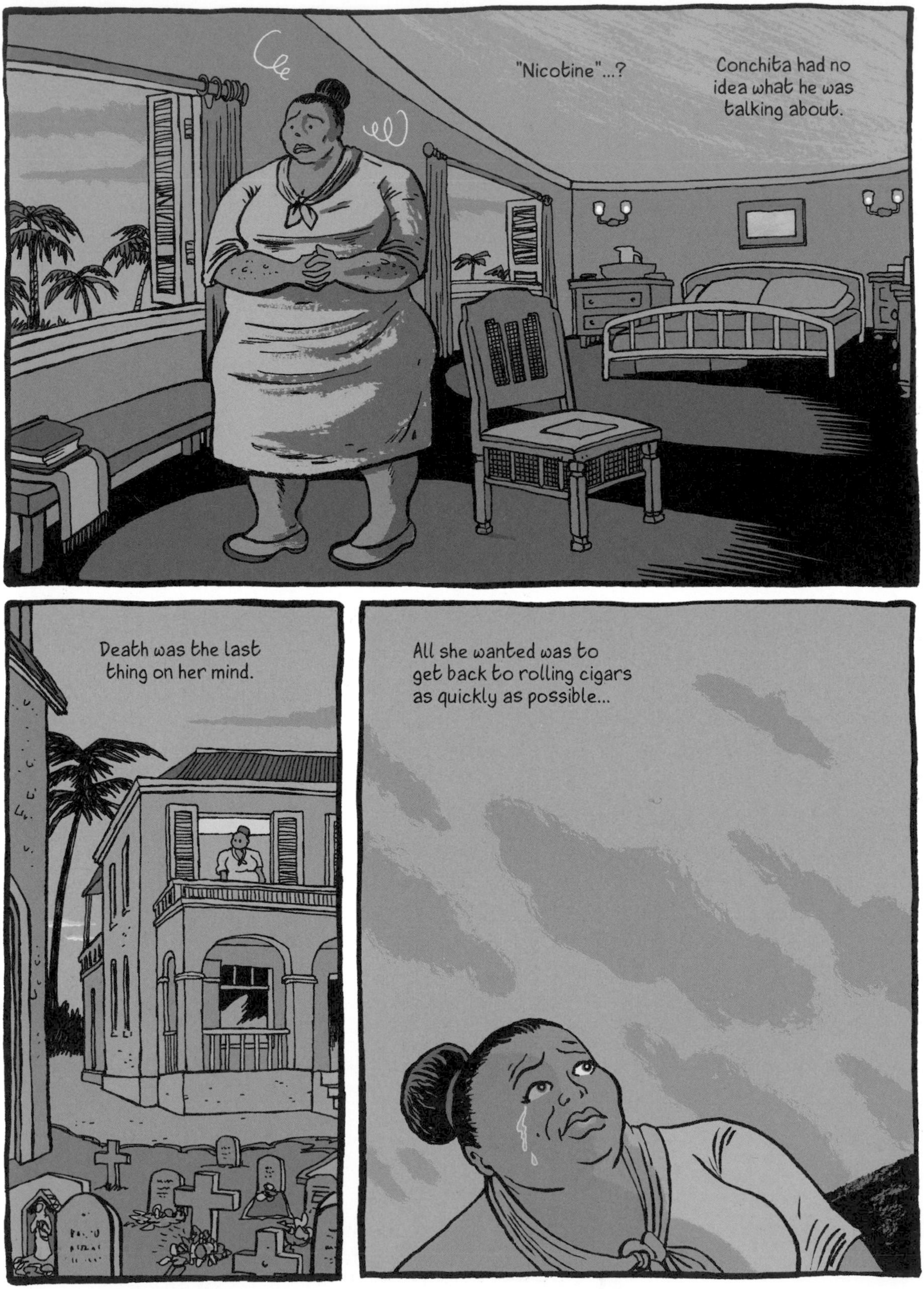
"Nicotine"...?
Conchita had no idea what he was talking about.
Death was the last thing on her mind.
All she wanted was to get back to rolling cigars as quickly as possible...

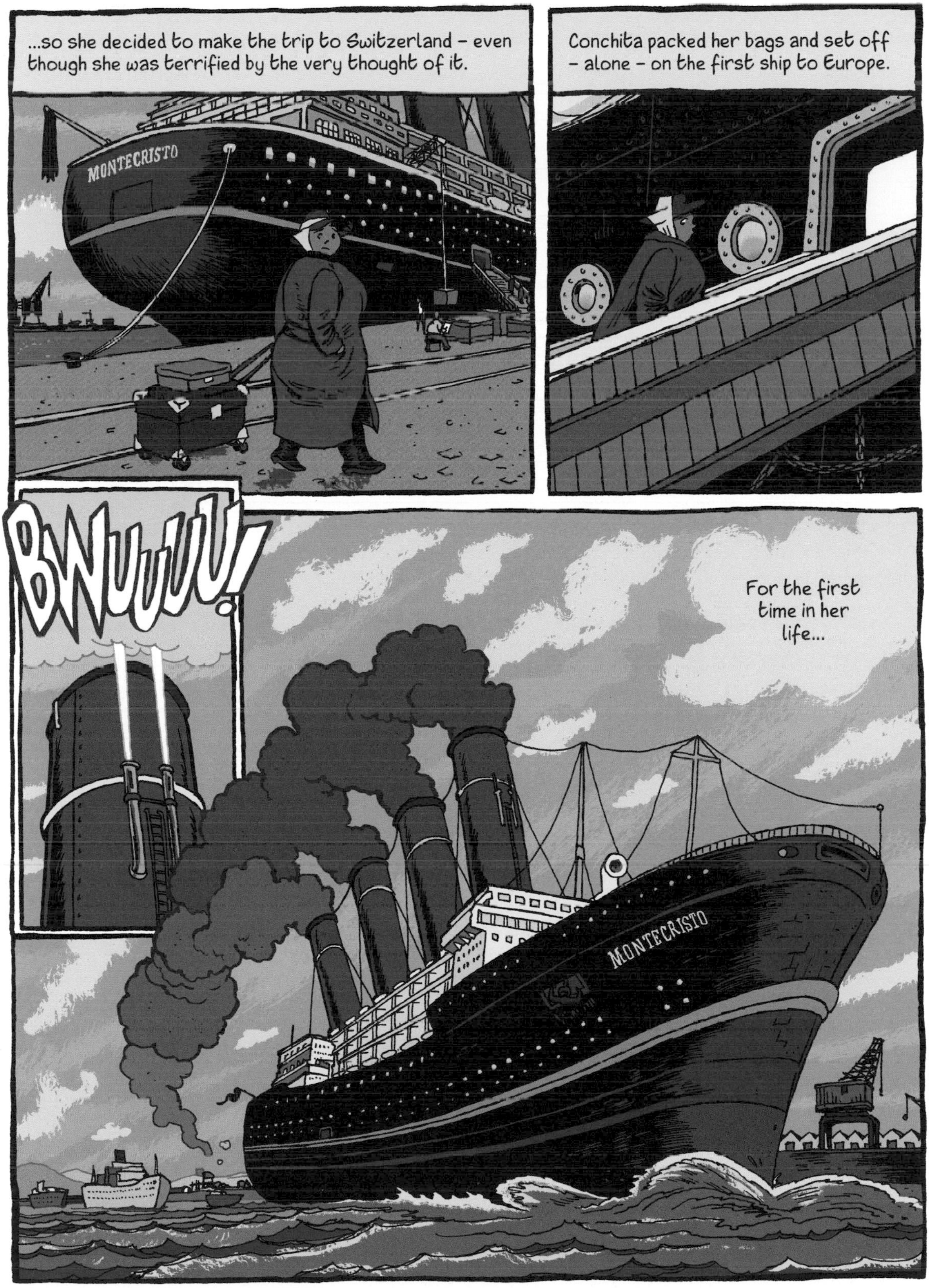
...so she decided to make the trip to Switzerland – even though she was terrified by the very thought of it.
MONTECRISTO
Conchita packed her bags and set off – alone – on the first ship to Europe.
BWUUUU!
For the first time in her life...
MONTECRISTO

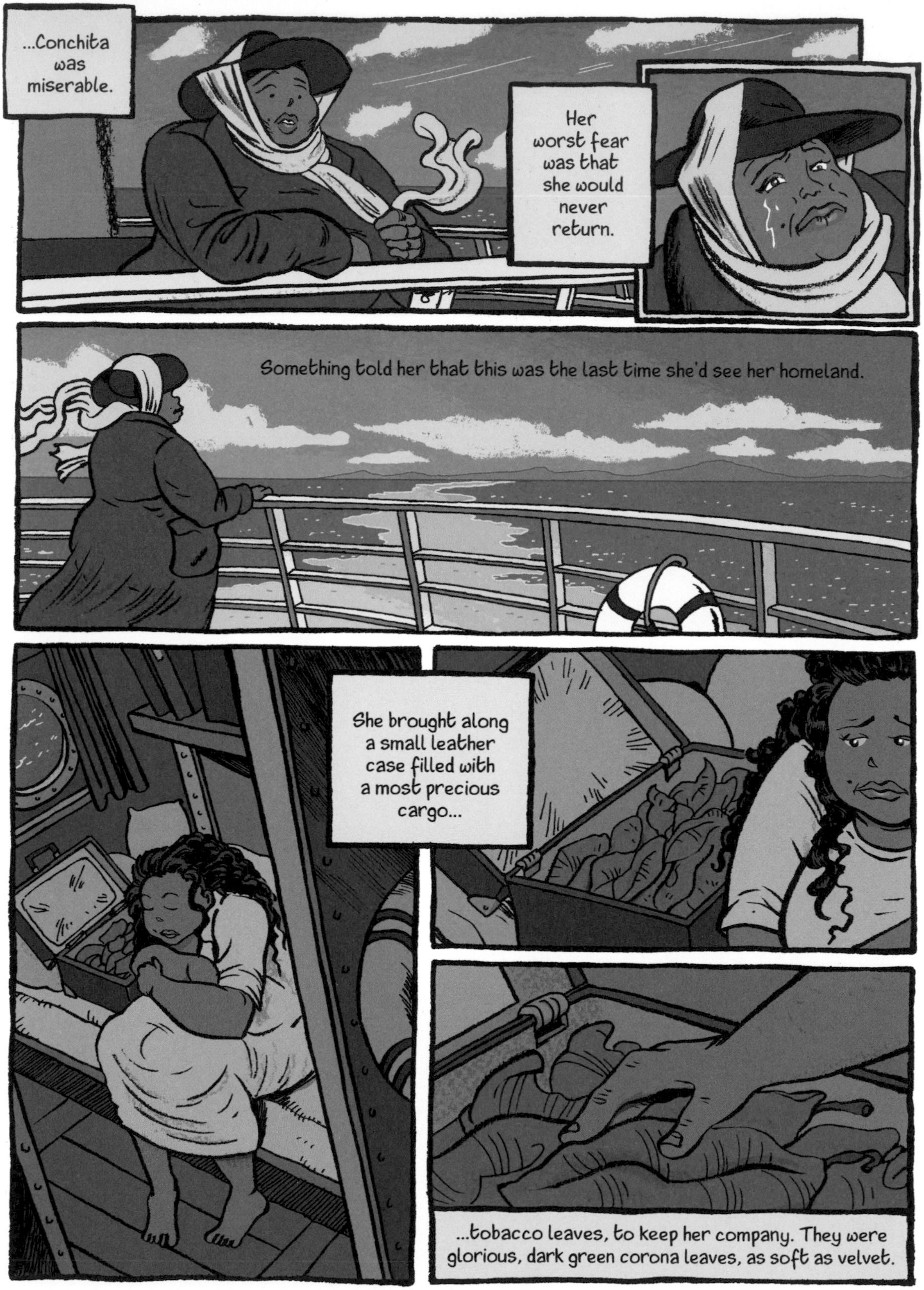

...Conchita was miserable.
Her worst fear was that she would never return.
Something told her that this was the last time she'd see her homeland.
She brought along a small leather case filled with a most precious cargo...
...tobacco leaves, to keep her company. They were glorious, dark green corona leaves, as soft as velvet.

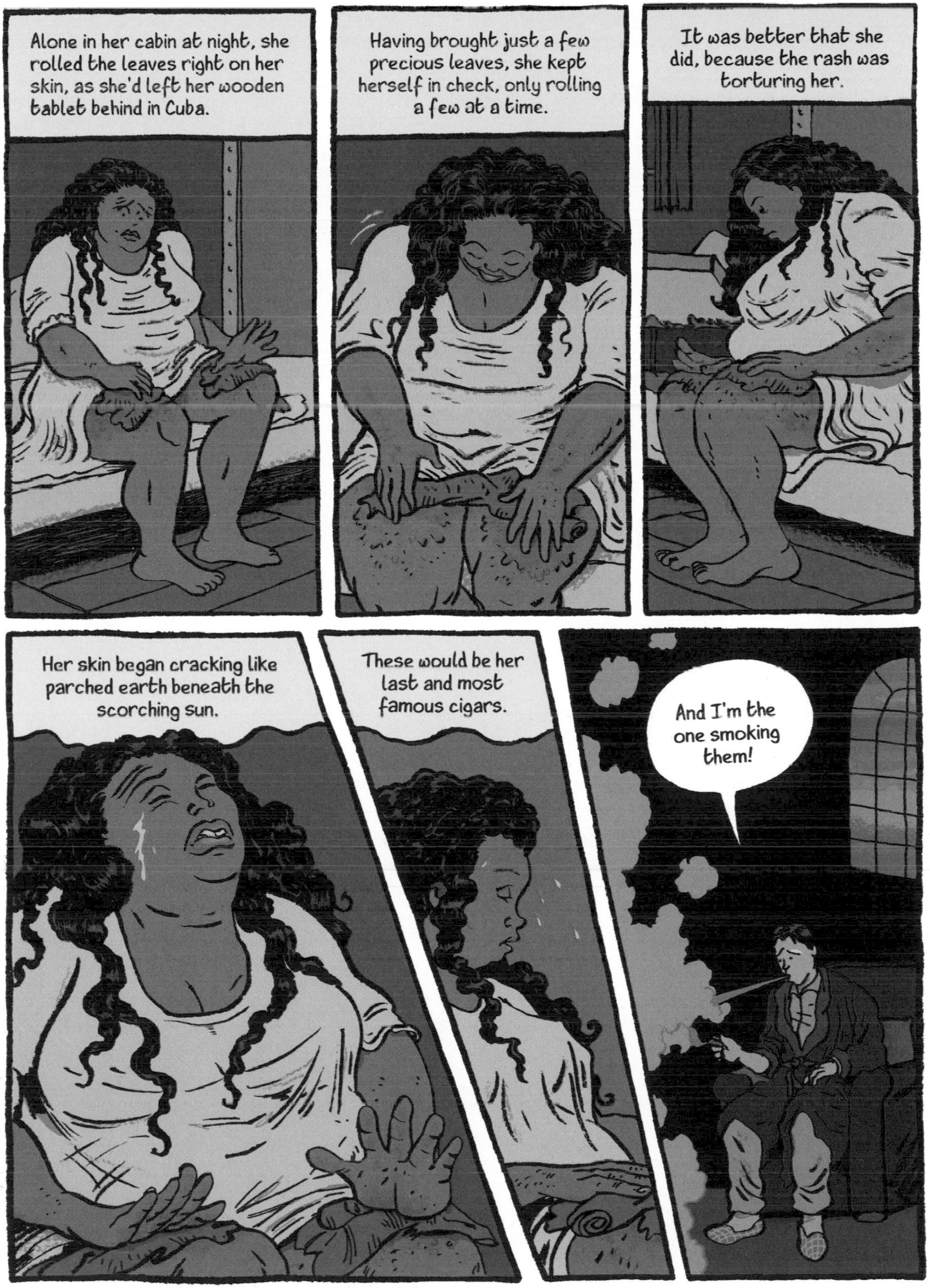
Alone in her cabin at night, she rolled the leaves right on her skin, as she'd left her wooden tablet behind in Cuba.
Having brought just a few precious leaves, she kept herself in check, only rolling a few at a time.
It was better that she did, because the rash was torturing her.
Her skin began cracking like parched earth beneath the scorching sun.
These would be her last and most famous cigars.
And I'm the one smoking them!

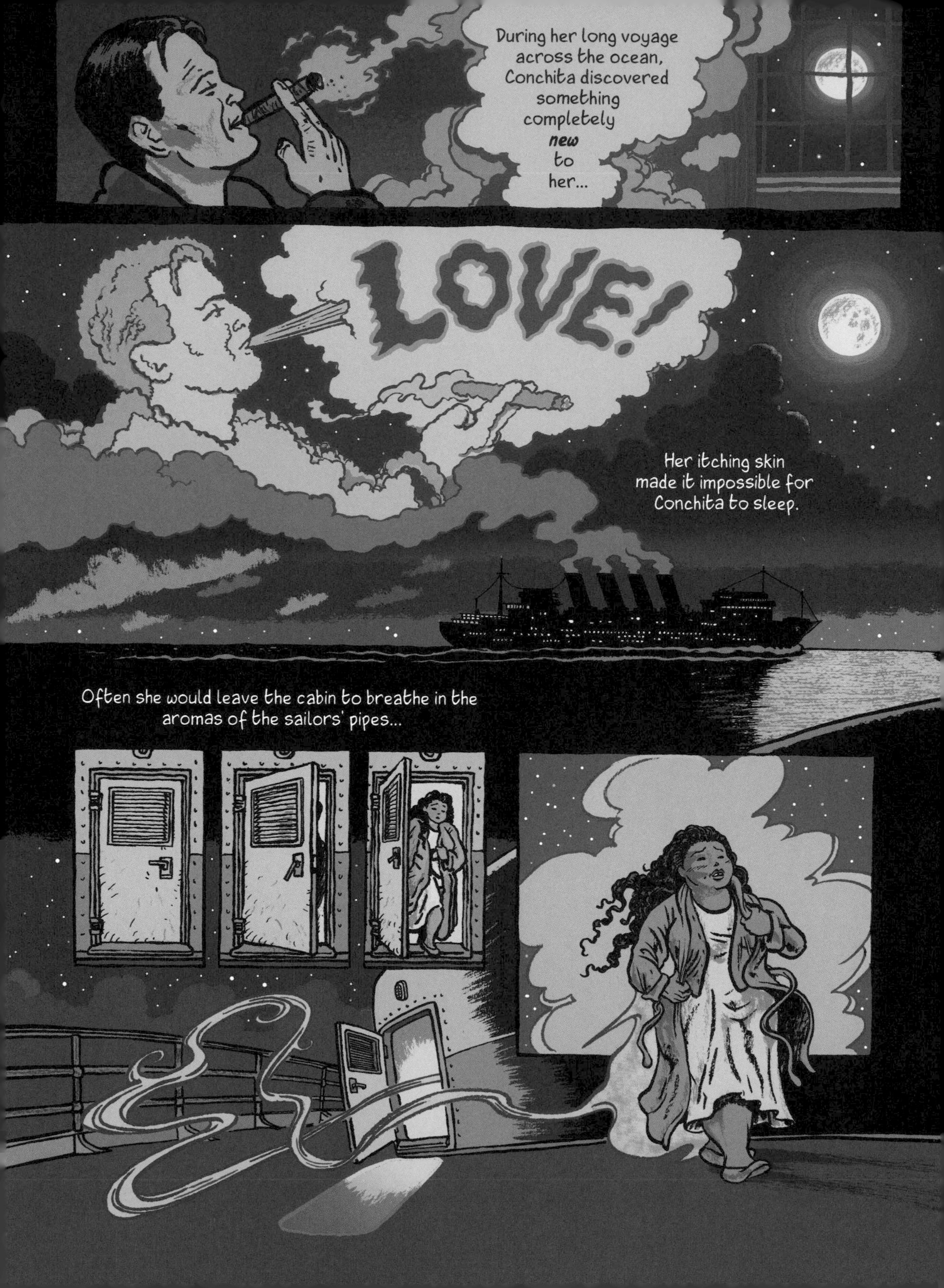
During her long voyage across the ocean, Conchita discovered something completely *new* to her...
LOVE!
Her itching skin made it impossible for Conchita to sleep.
Often she would leave the cabin to breathe in the aromas of the sailors' pipes...

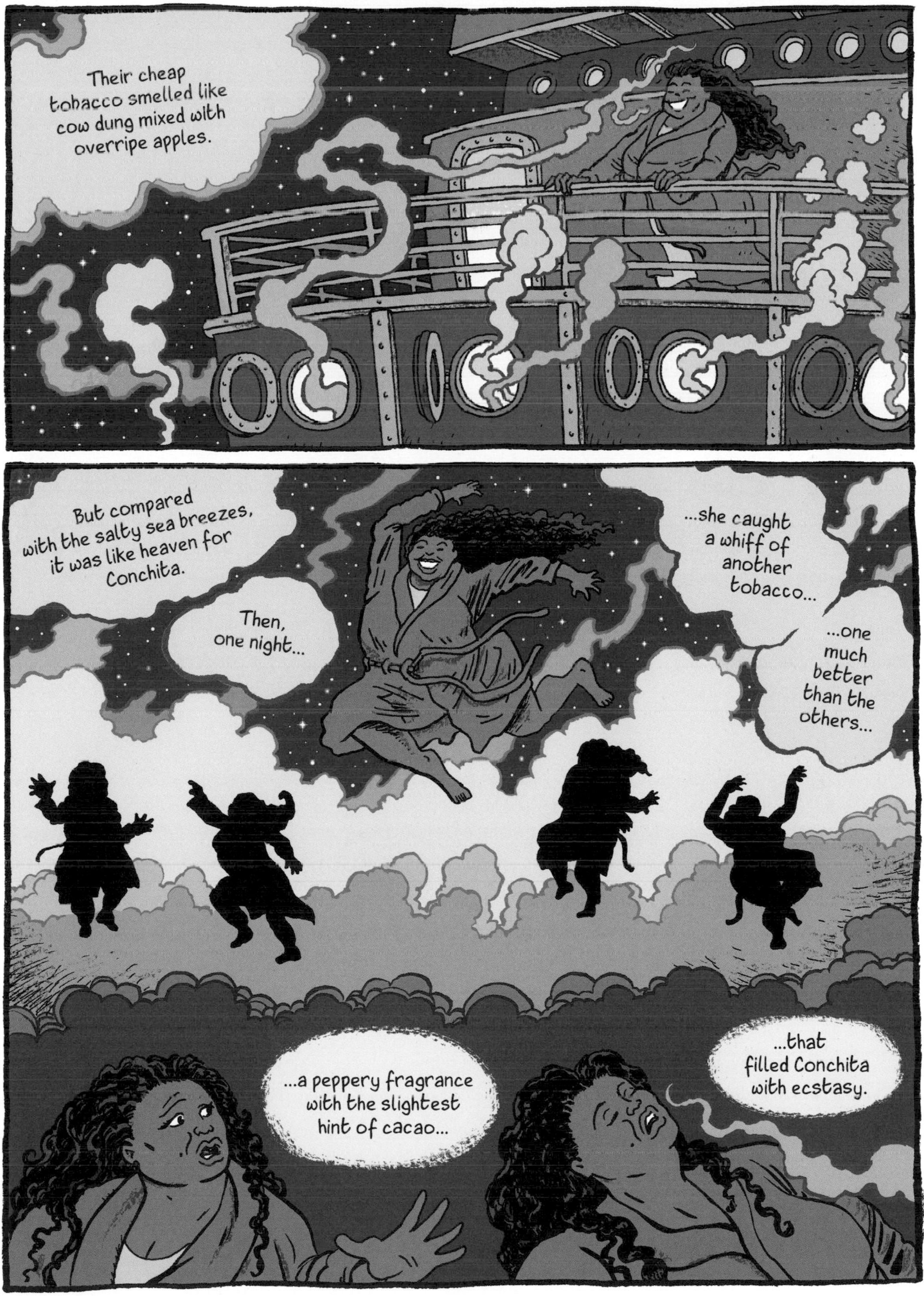

Their cheap tobacco smelled like cow dung mixed with overripe apples.
But compared with the salty sea breezes, it was like heaven for Conchita.
Then, one night...
...she caught a whiff of another tobacco...
...one much better than the others...
...a peppery fragrance with the slightest hint of cacao...
...that filled Conchita with ecstasy.

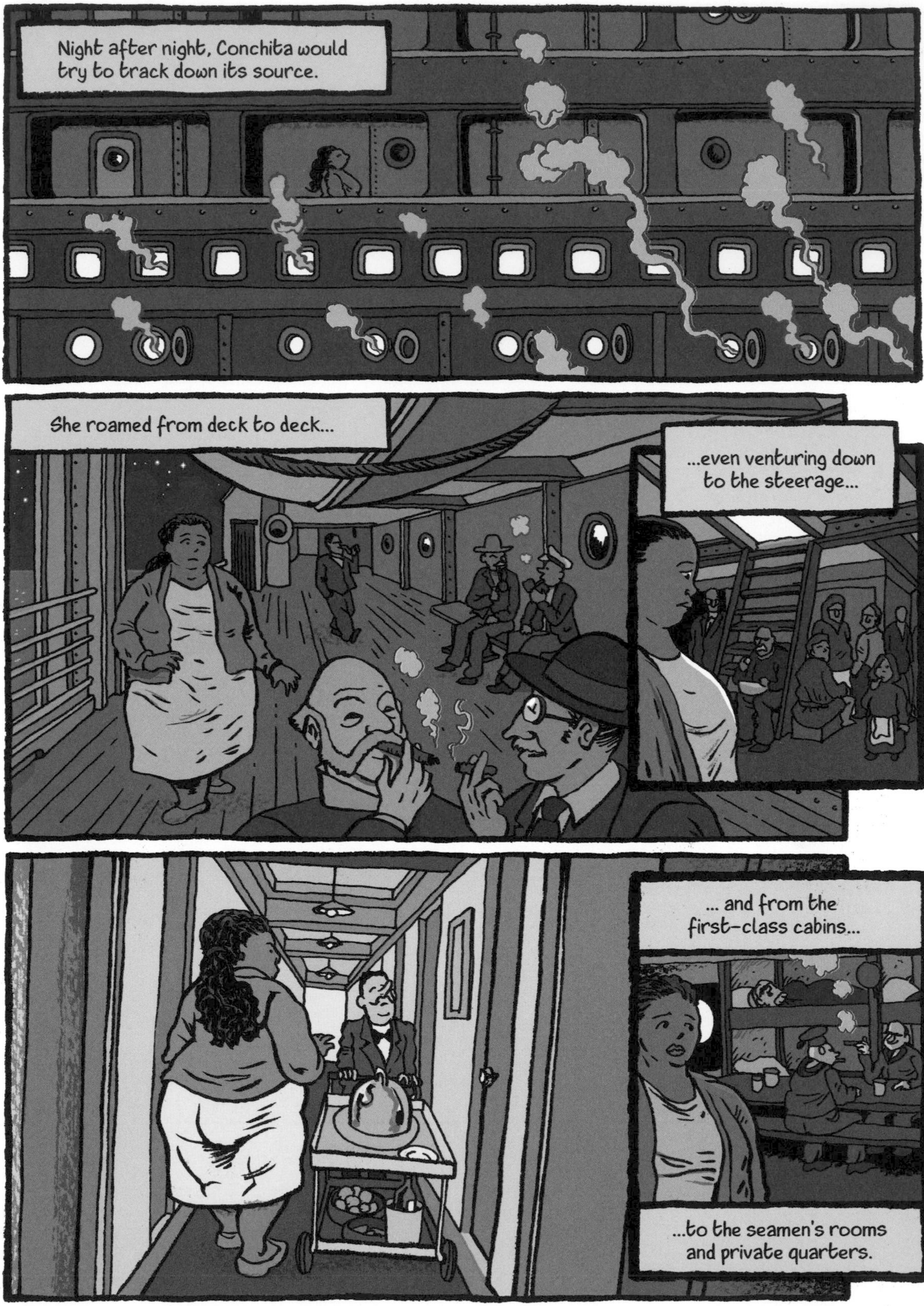
Night after night, Conchita would try to track down its source.
She roamed from deck to deck...
...even venturing down to the steerage...
... and from the first-class cabins...
...to the seamen's rooms and private quarters.

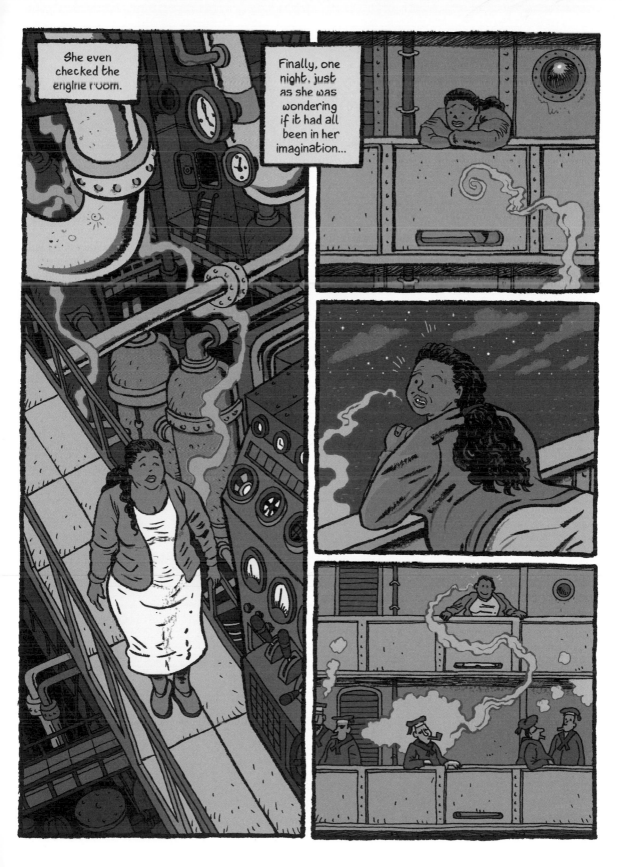

She even checked the engine room.

Finally, one night, just as she was wondering if it had all been in her imagination...

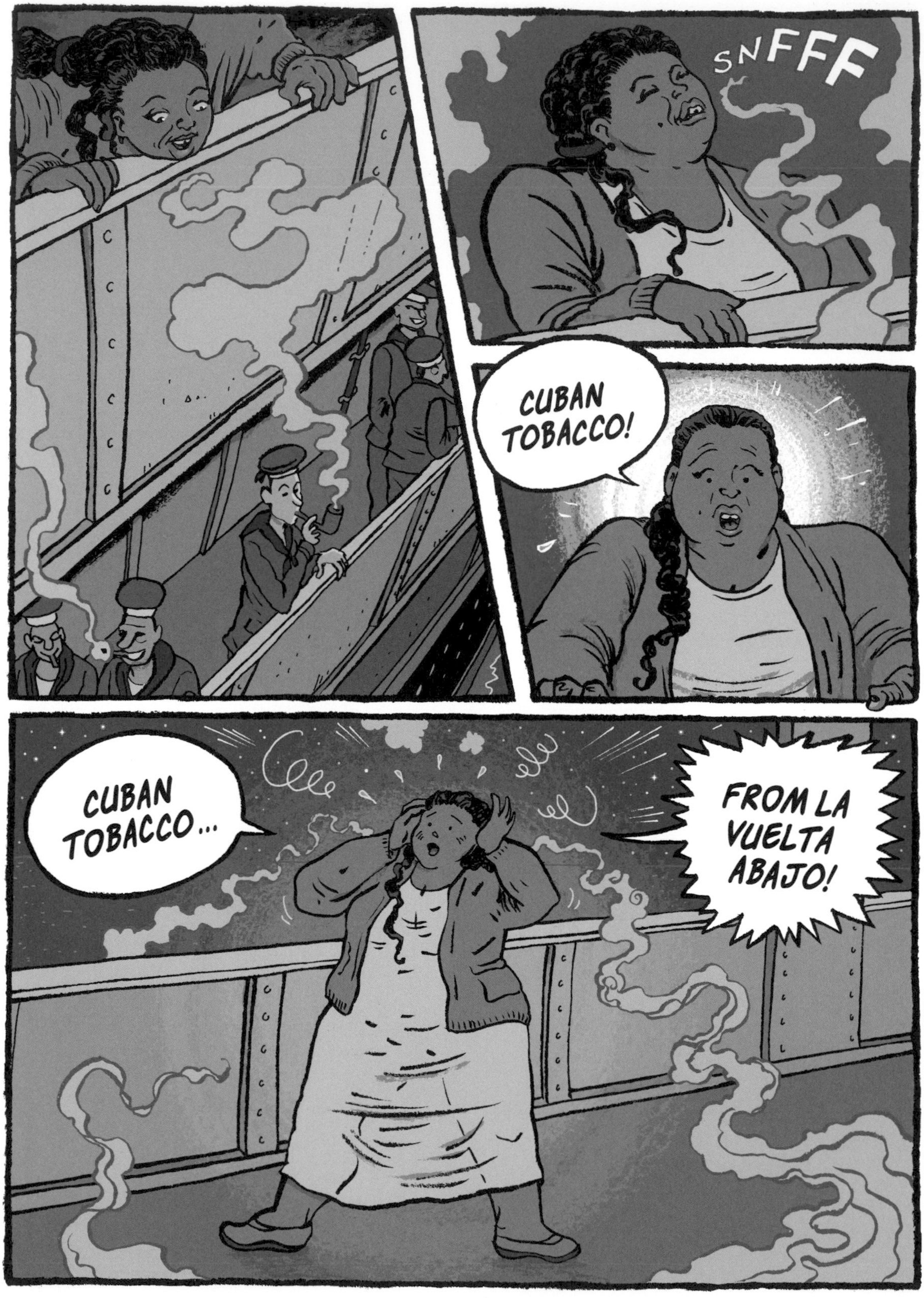
SNFFF
CUBAN TOBACCO!
CUBAN TOBACCO...
FROM LA VUELTA ABAJO!

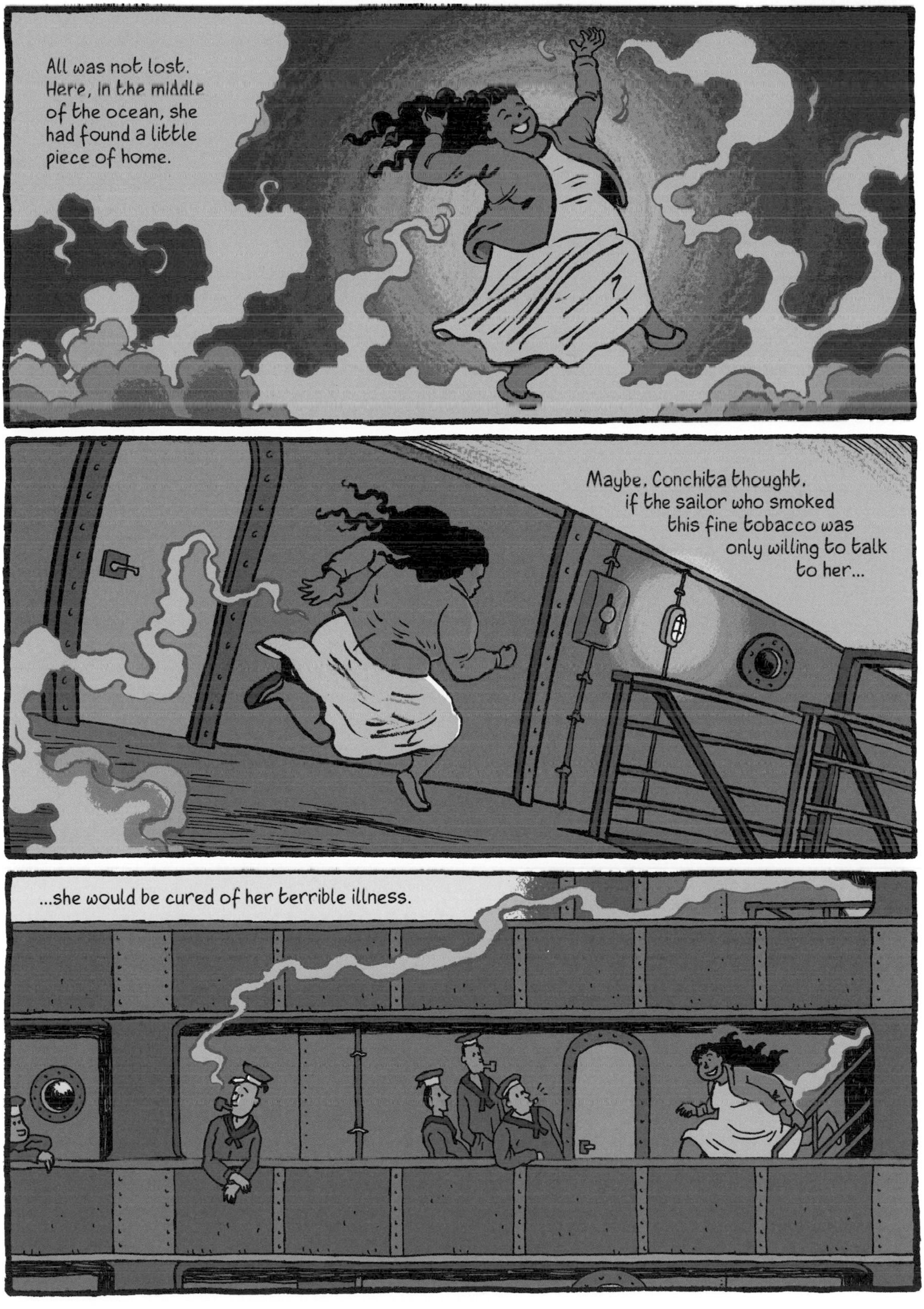
All was not lost. Here, in the middle of the ocean, she had found a little piece of home.
Maybe, Conchita thought, if the sailor who smoked this fine tobacco was only willing to talk to her...
...she would be cured of her terrible illness.

Hello, señor! Please excuse my intrusion – I could not help but notice that you are smoking a tobacco that I am most familiar with...

It fills my heart with such joy...

Oh! Señor!

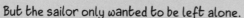

But the sailor only wanted to be left alone.

Much worse – he didn't want any females near him, especially a fat lady who seemed obsessed with rolling his fingers through her pudgy hands.

Go away.

Señor!

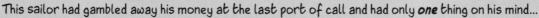

This sailor had gambled away his money at the last port of call and had only *one* thing on his mind...

Damn!

...getting some of it back.

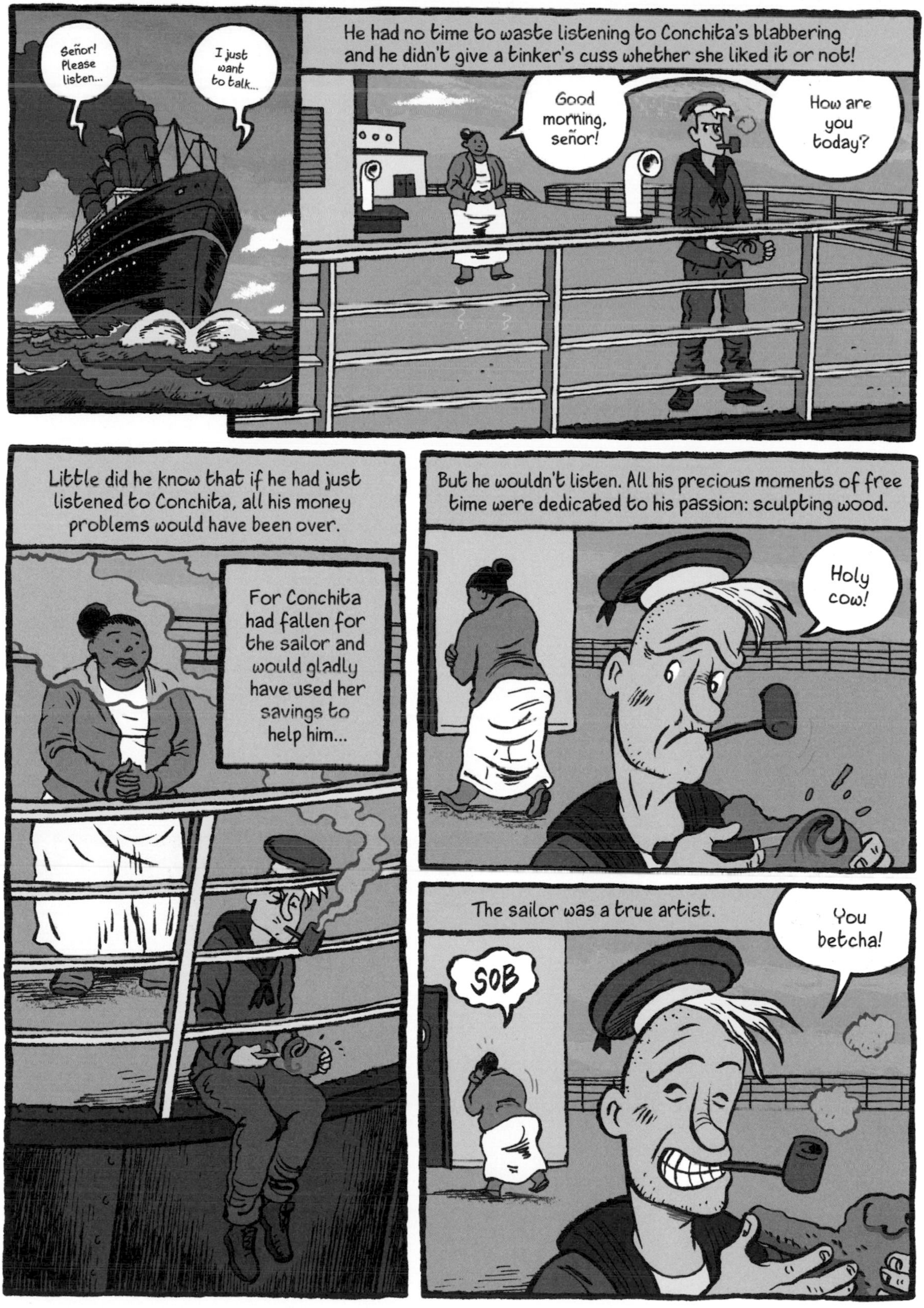
Señor! Please listen...
I just want to talk...
He had no time to waste listening to Conchita's blabbering and he didn't give a tinker's cuss whether she liked it or not!
Good morning, señor!
How are you today?
Little did he know that if he had just listened to Conchita, all his money problems would have been over.
For Conchita had fallen for the sailor and would gladly have used her savings to help him...
But he wouldn't listen. All his precious moments of free time were dedicated to his passion: sculpting wood.
Holy cow!
The sailor was a true artist.
SOB
You betcha!

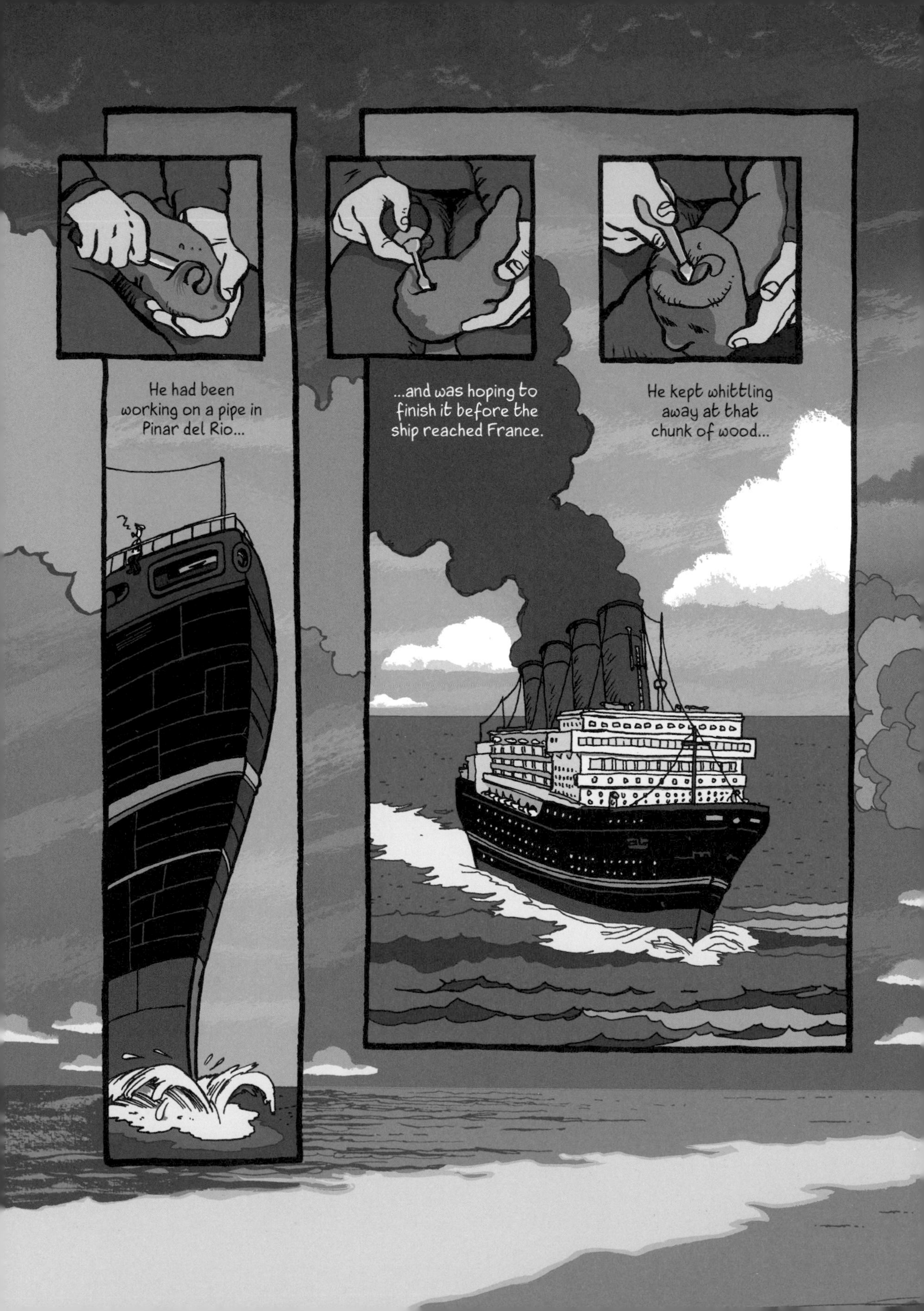

He had been working on a pipe in Pinar del Rio...
...and was hoping to finish it before the ship reached France.
He kept whittling away at that chunk of wood...

...and slowly... slowly, it began taking the shape of a sailor's head.

The sailor was hoping to sell this pipe, this little work of art, to pay off his gambling debts.

For the rest of the trip, he refused to acknowledge Conchita's presence.

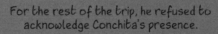

Finally, she gave up hope of him ever talking to her.

Despite the excruciating pain it caused her, she spent the remaining days of the voyage rolling her final cigars...

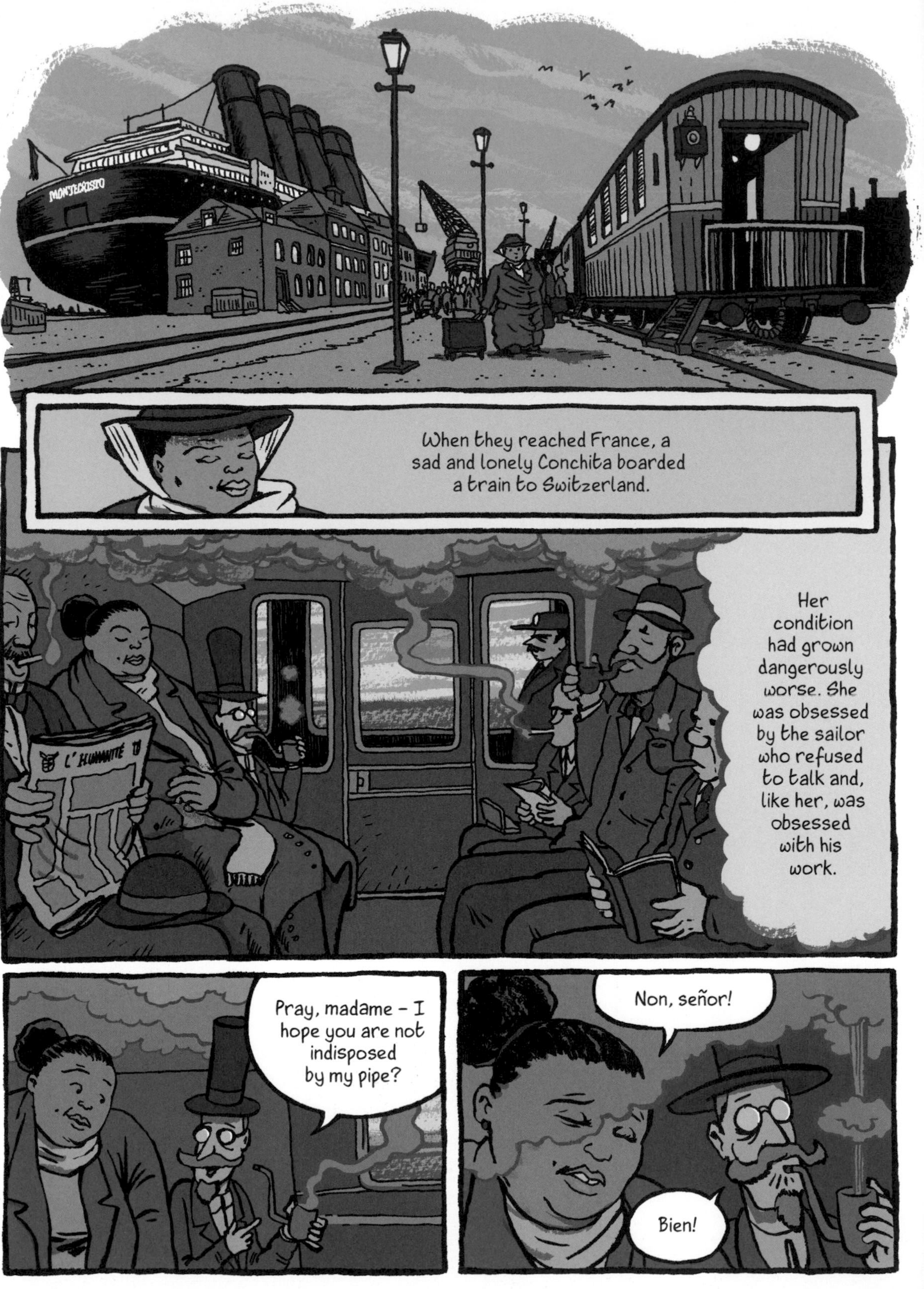
MONTECRISTO
When they reached France, a sad and lonely Conchita boarded a train to Switzerland.
L'HUMANITÉ
Her condition had grown dangerously worse. She was obsessed by the sailor who refused to talk and, like her, was obsessed with his work.
Pray, madame – I hope you are not indisposed by my pipe?
Non, señor!
Bien!

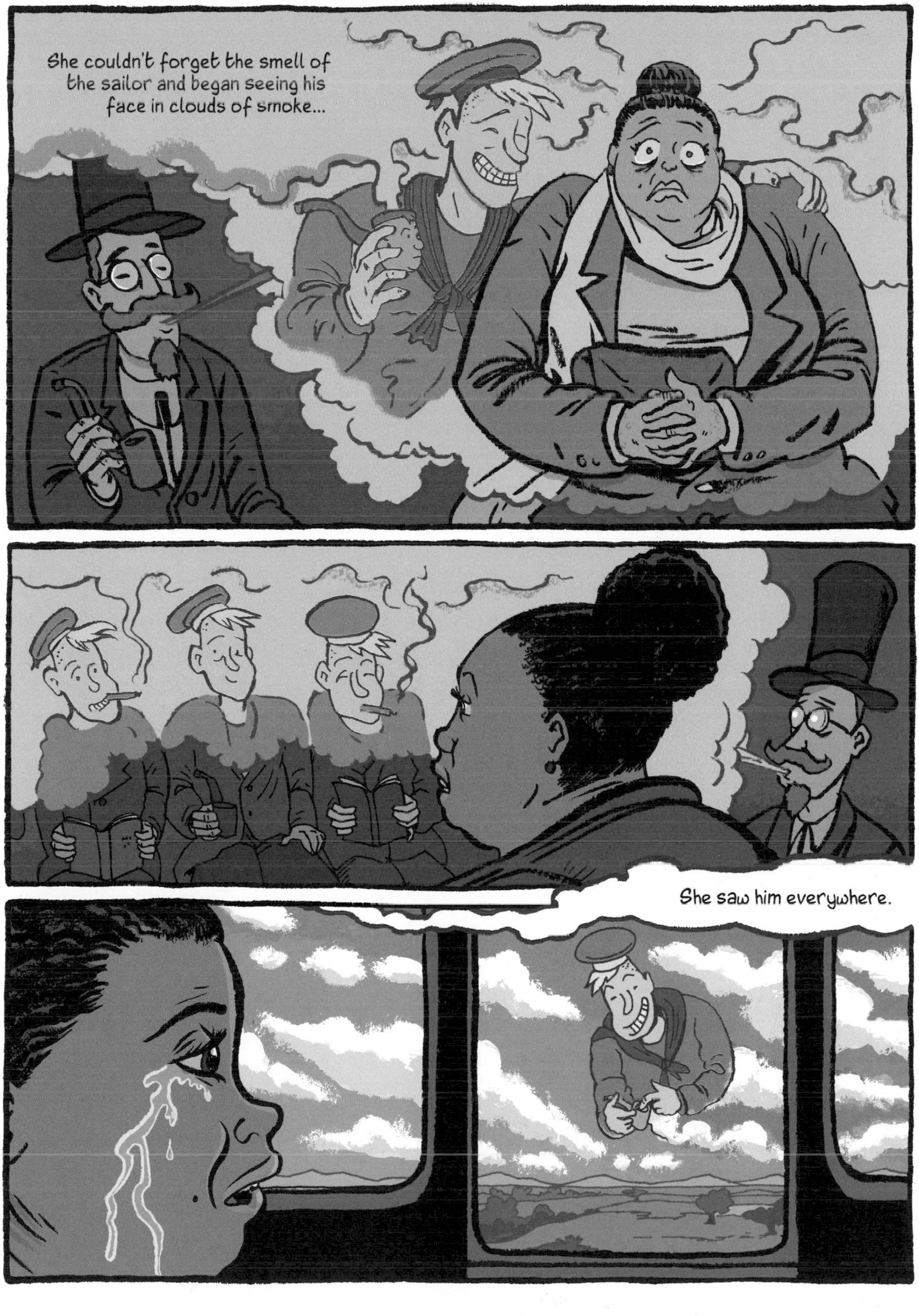
She couldn't forget the smell of the sailor and began seeing his face in clouds of smoke...
She saw him everywhere.

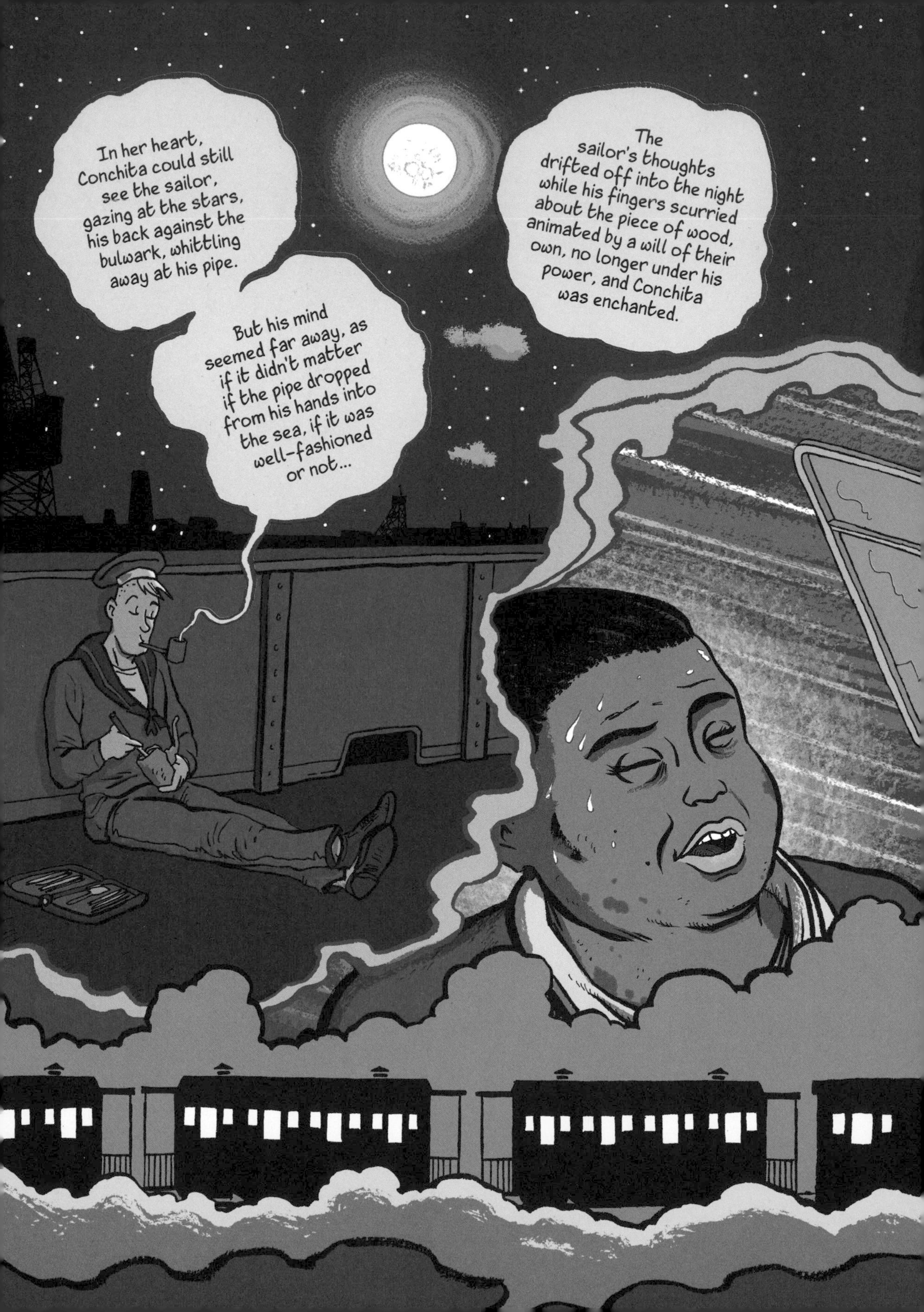
In her heart, Conchita could still see the sailor, gazing at the stars, his back against the bulwark, whittling away at his pipe.
But his mind seemed far away, as if it didn't matter if the pipe dropped from his hands into the sea, if it was well-fashioned or not...
The sailor's thoughts drifted off into the night while his fingers scurried about the piece of wood, animated by a will of their own, no longer under his power, and Conchita was enchanted.

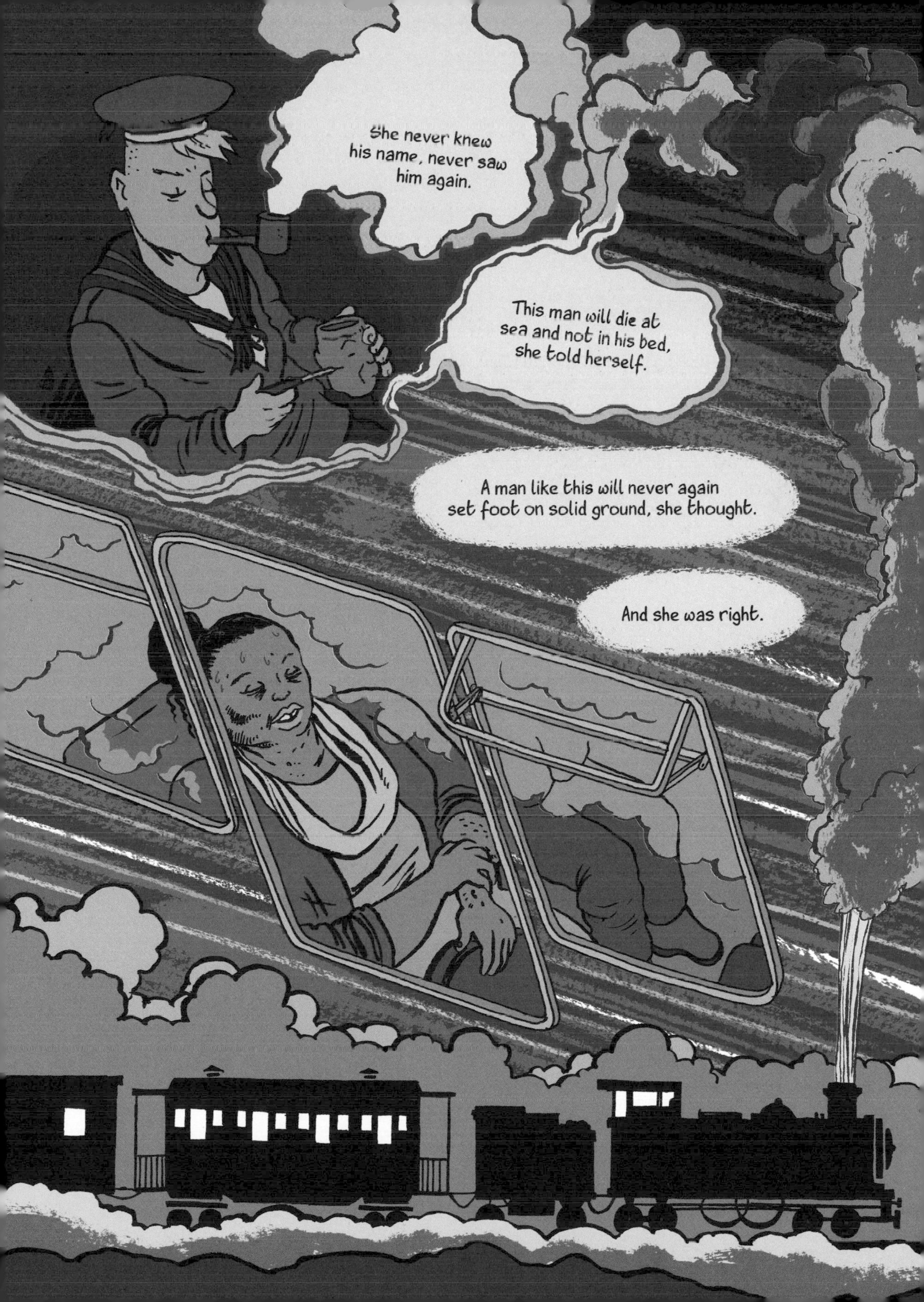
She never knew his name, never saw him again.
This man will die at sea and not in his bed, she told herself.
A man like this will never again set foot on solid ground, she thought.
And she was right.

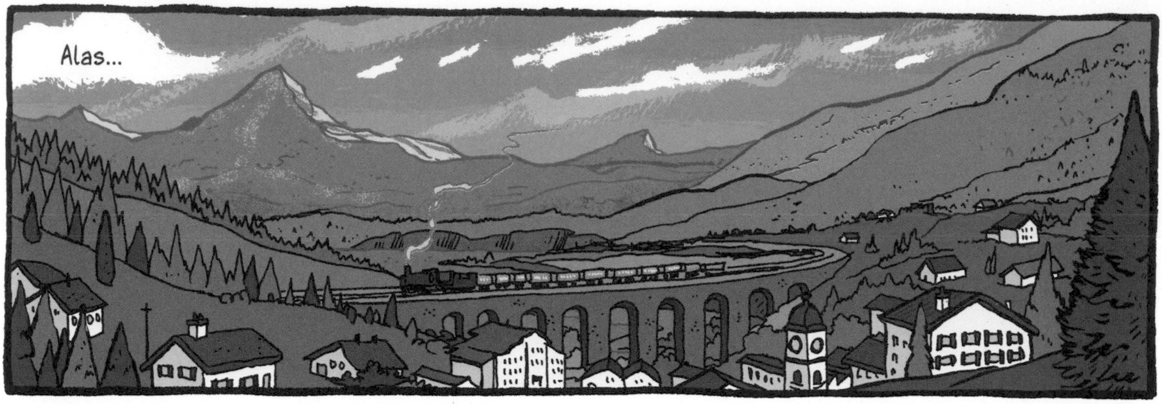
Alas...

Conchita did not live to see Switzerland.

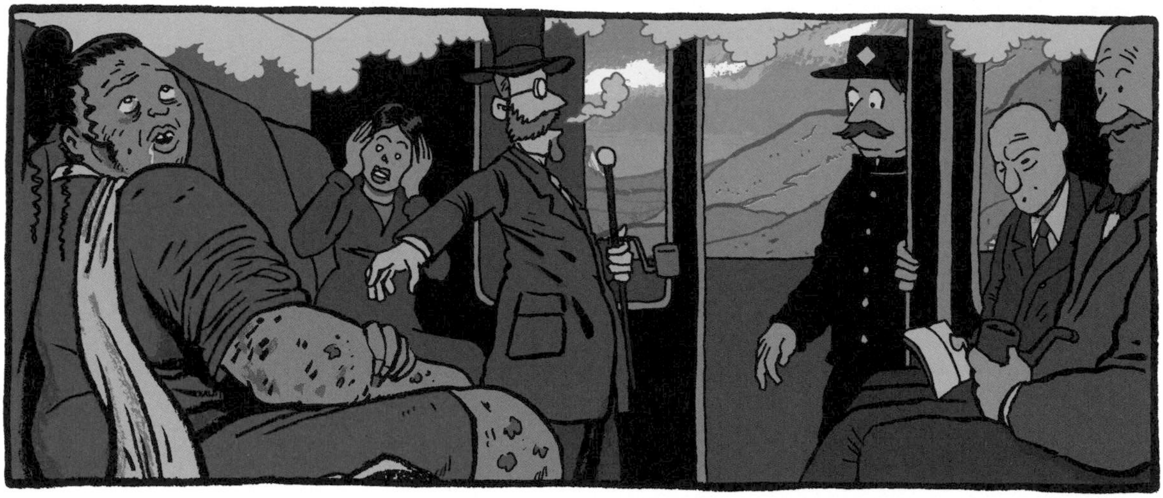

Yet it was there, far away from Cuba, that she would be laid to rest.

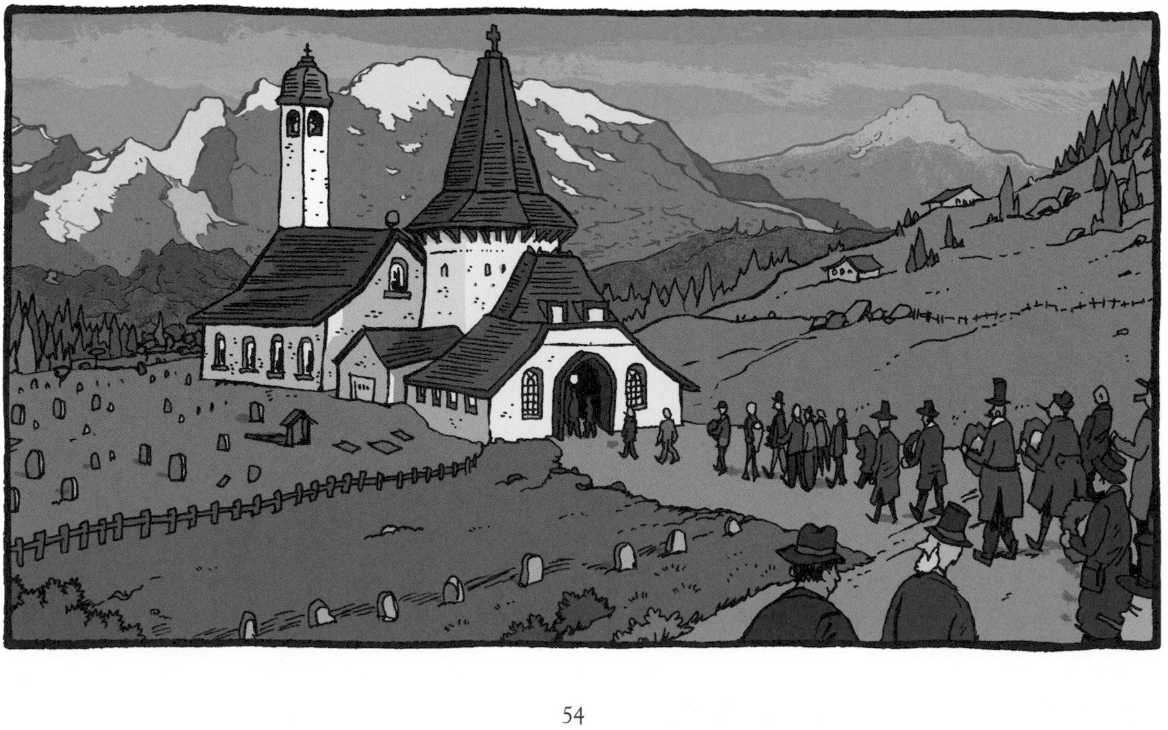

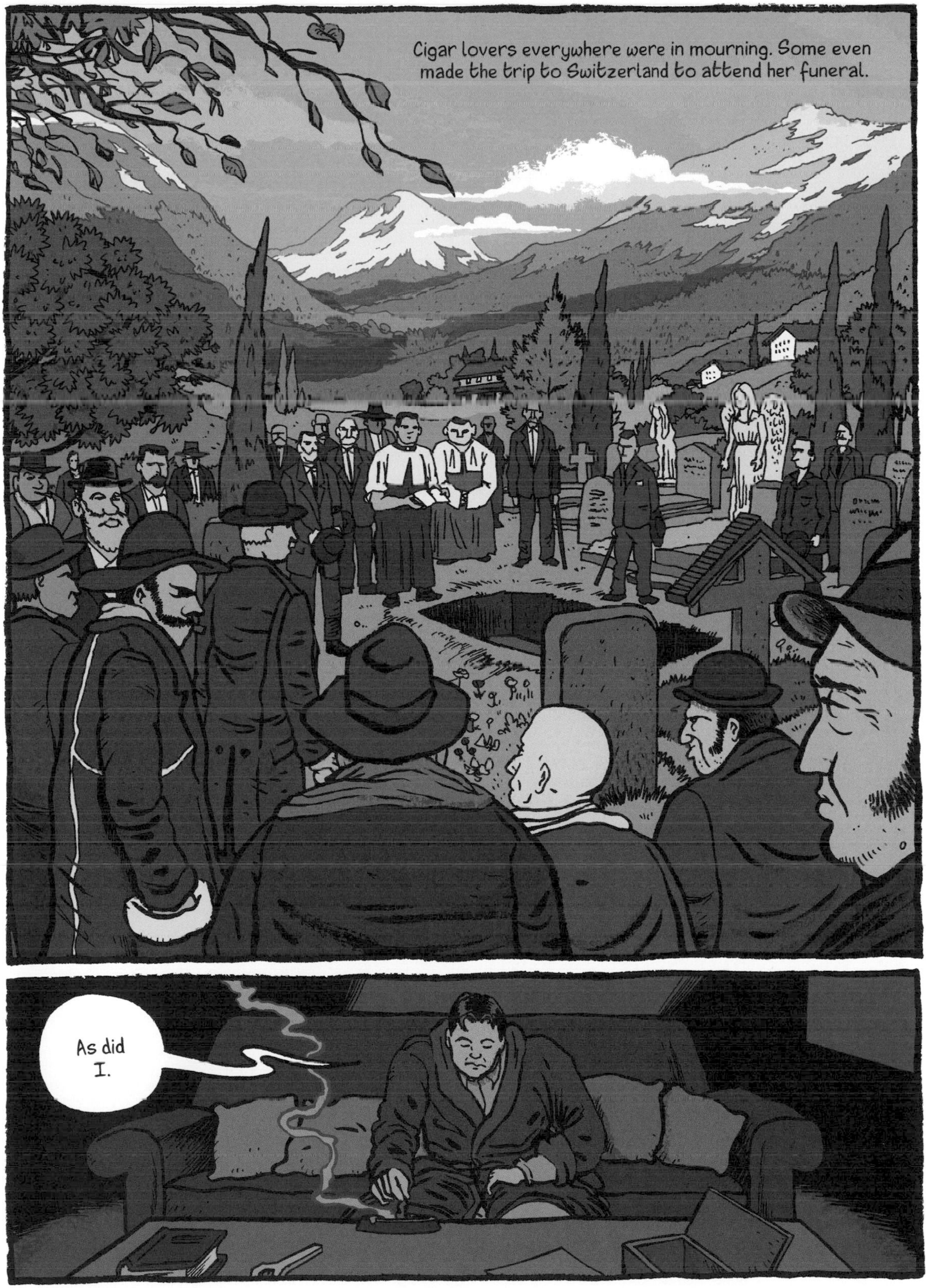
Cigar lovers everywhere were in mourning. Some even made the trip to Switzerland to attend her funeral.
As did I.

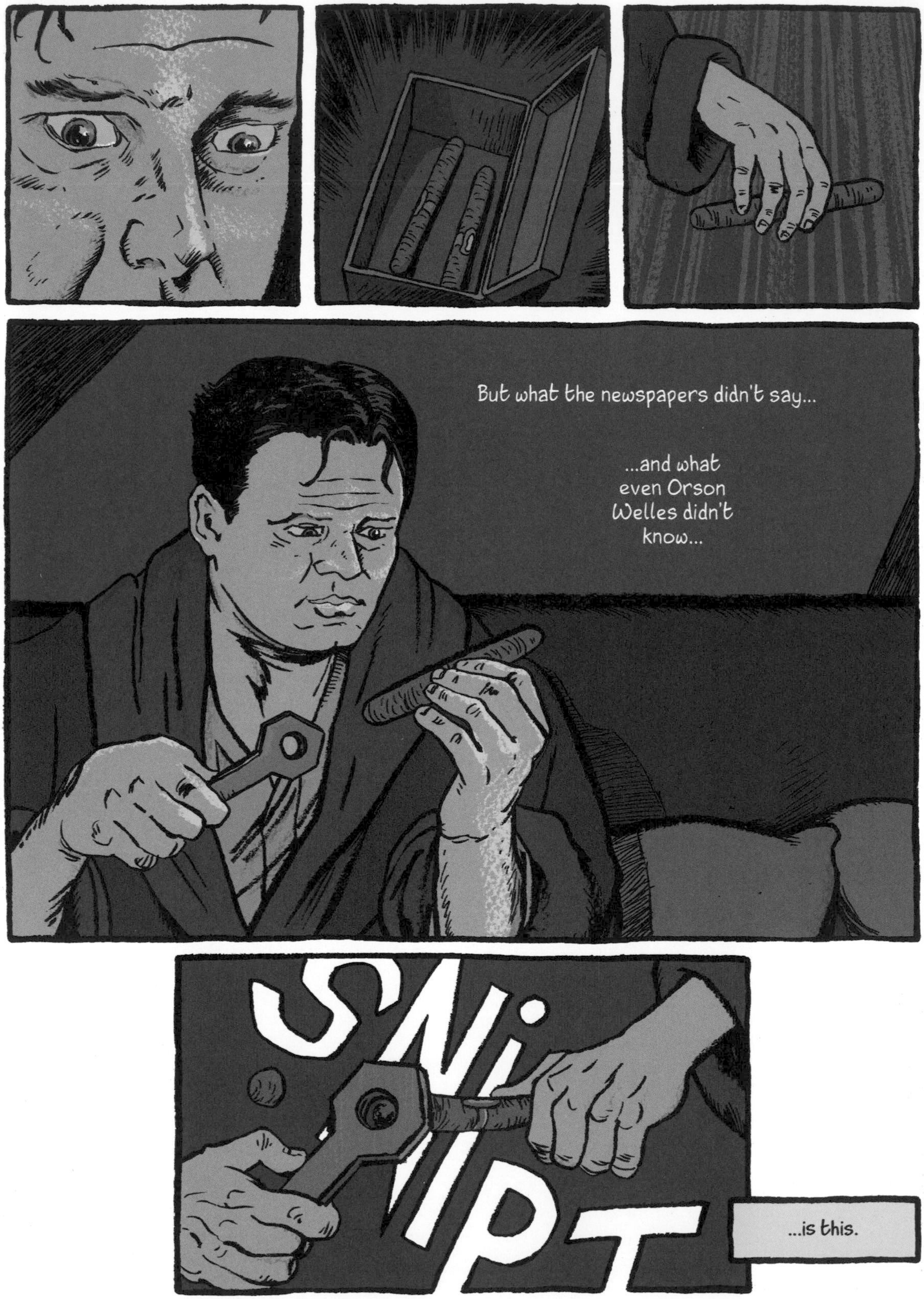

But what the newspapers didn't say...
...and what even Orson Welles didn't know...
SNIIPT
...is this.

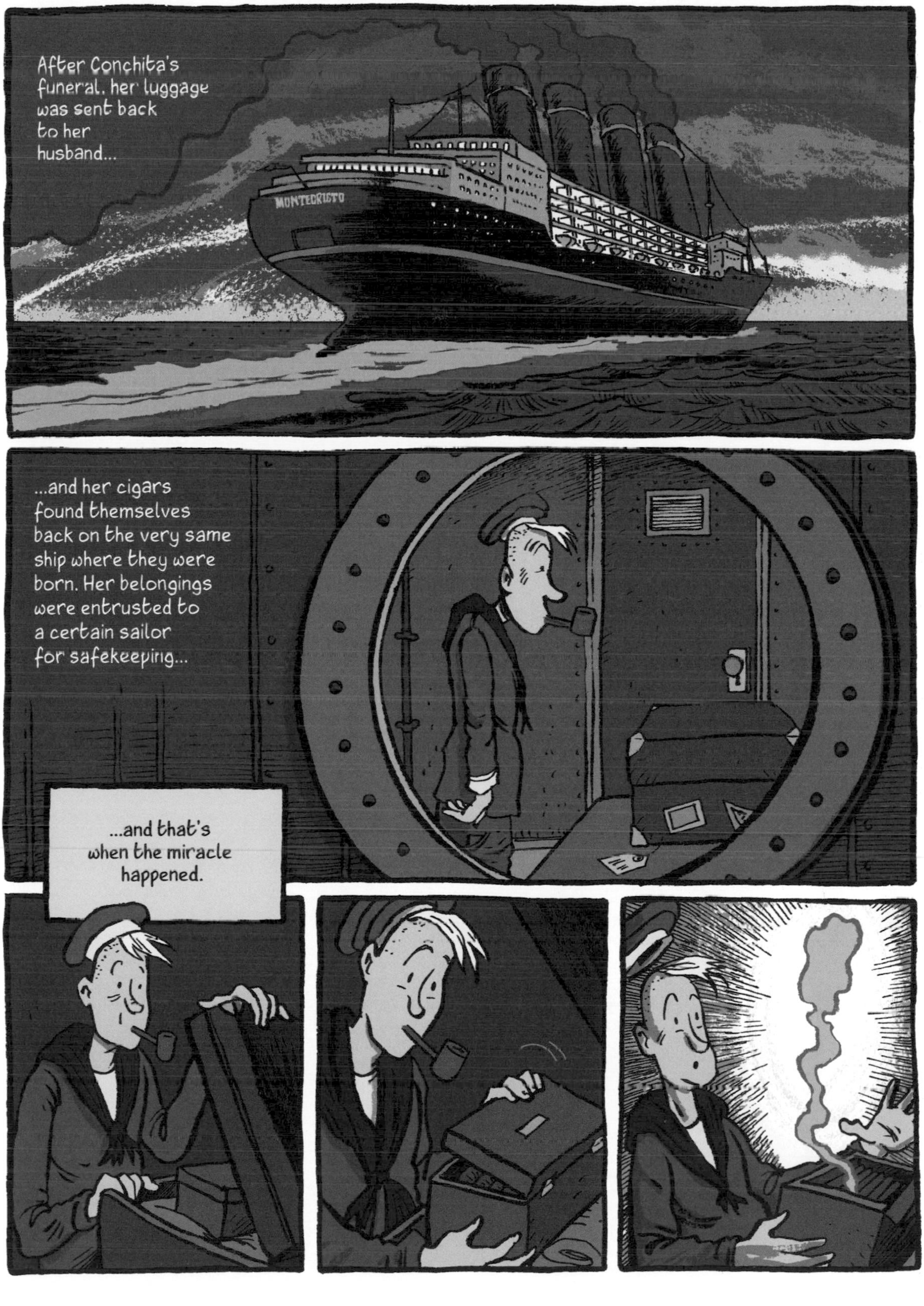
After Conchita's funeral, her luggage was sent back to her husband...
MONTECRISTO
...and her cigars found themselves back on the very same ship where they were born. Her belongings were entrusted to a certain sailor for safekeeping...
...and that's when the miracle happened.

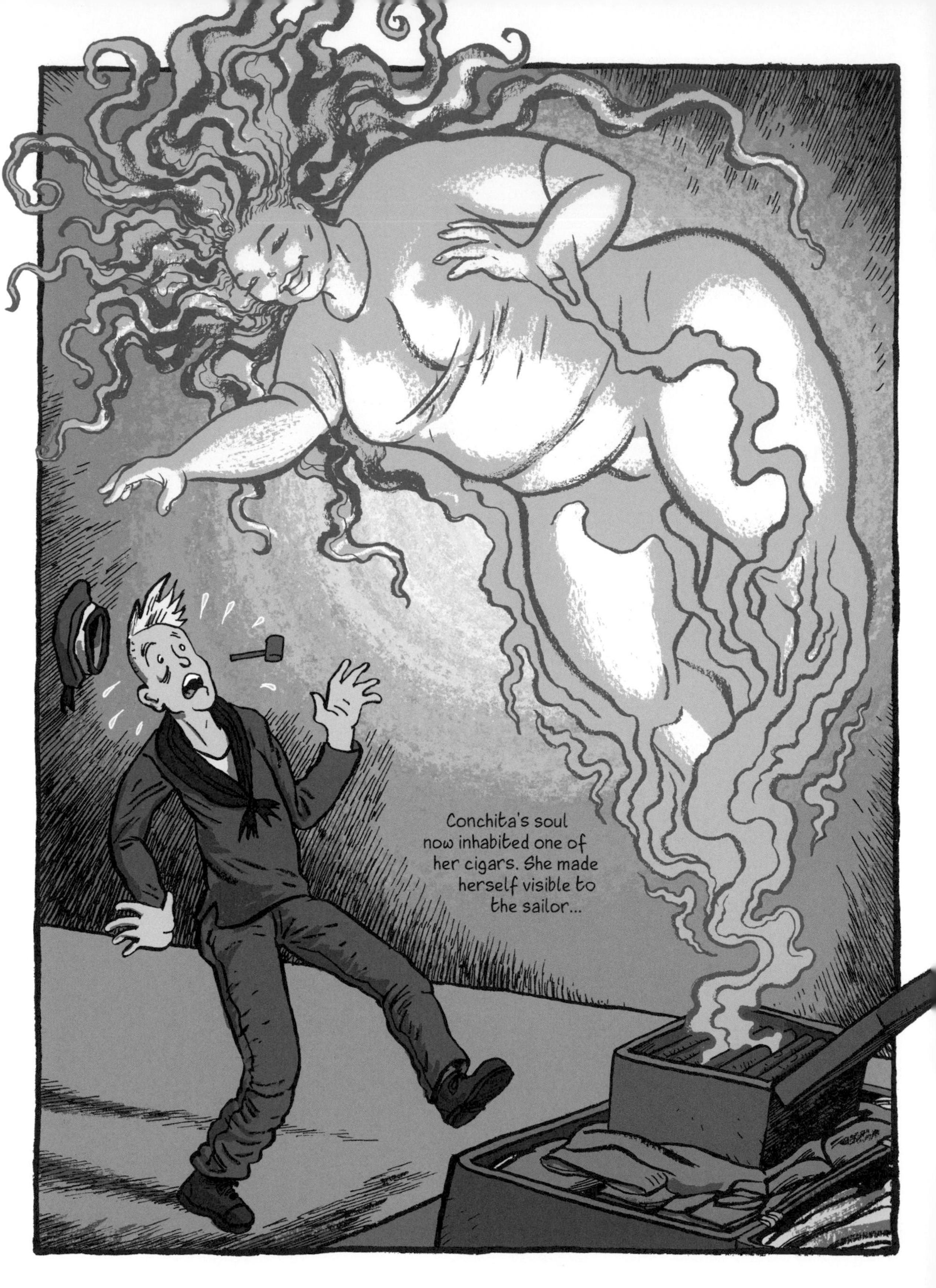
Conchita's soul now inhabited one of her cigars. She made herself visible to the sailor...

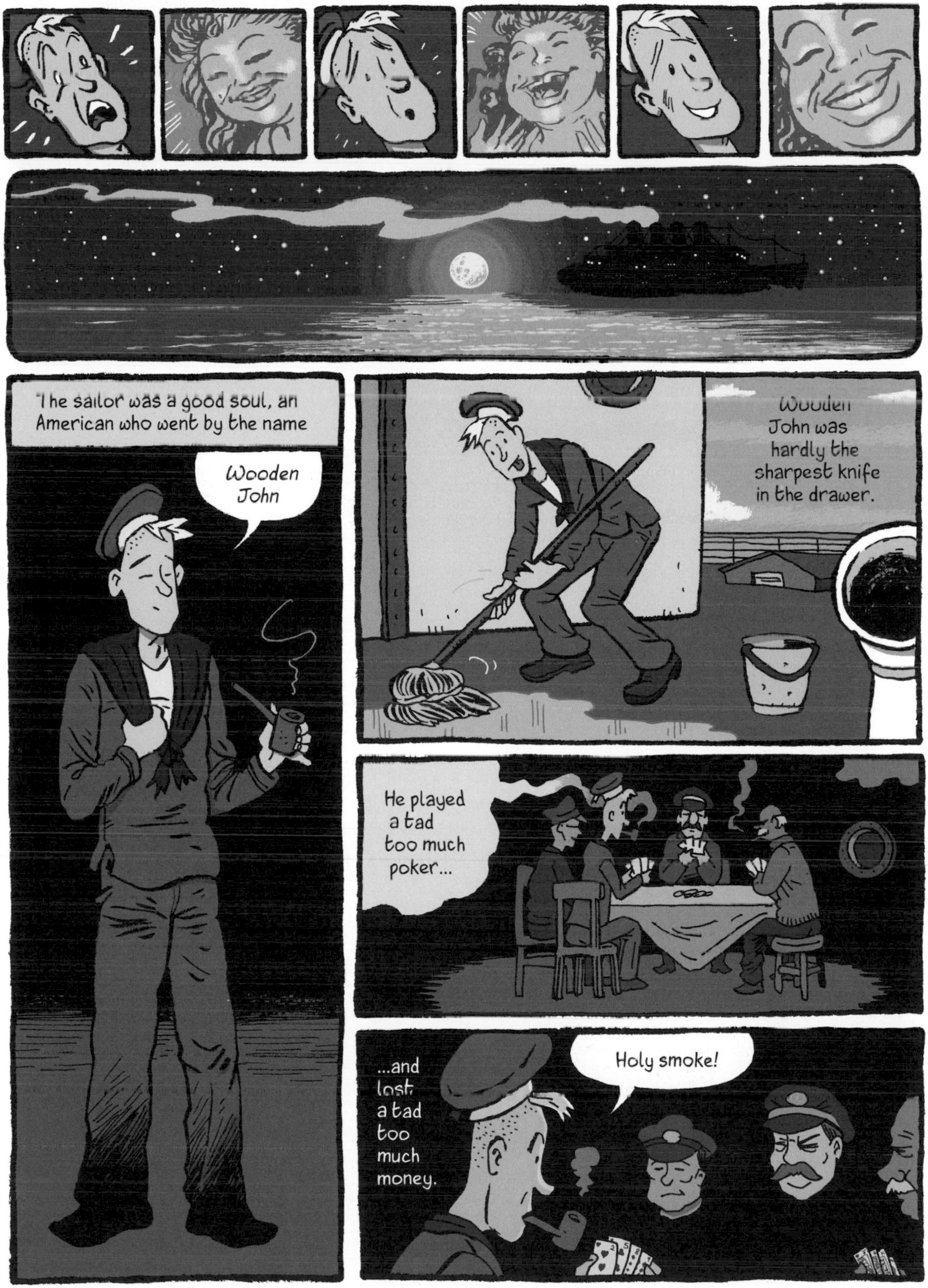
The sailor was a good soul, an American who went by the name
Wooden John
Wooden John was hardly the sharpest knife in the drawer.
He played a tad too much poker...
...and lost a tad too much money.
Holy smoke!

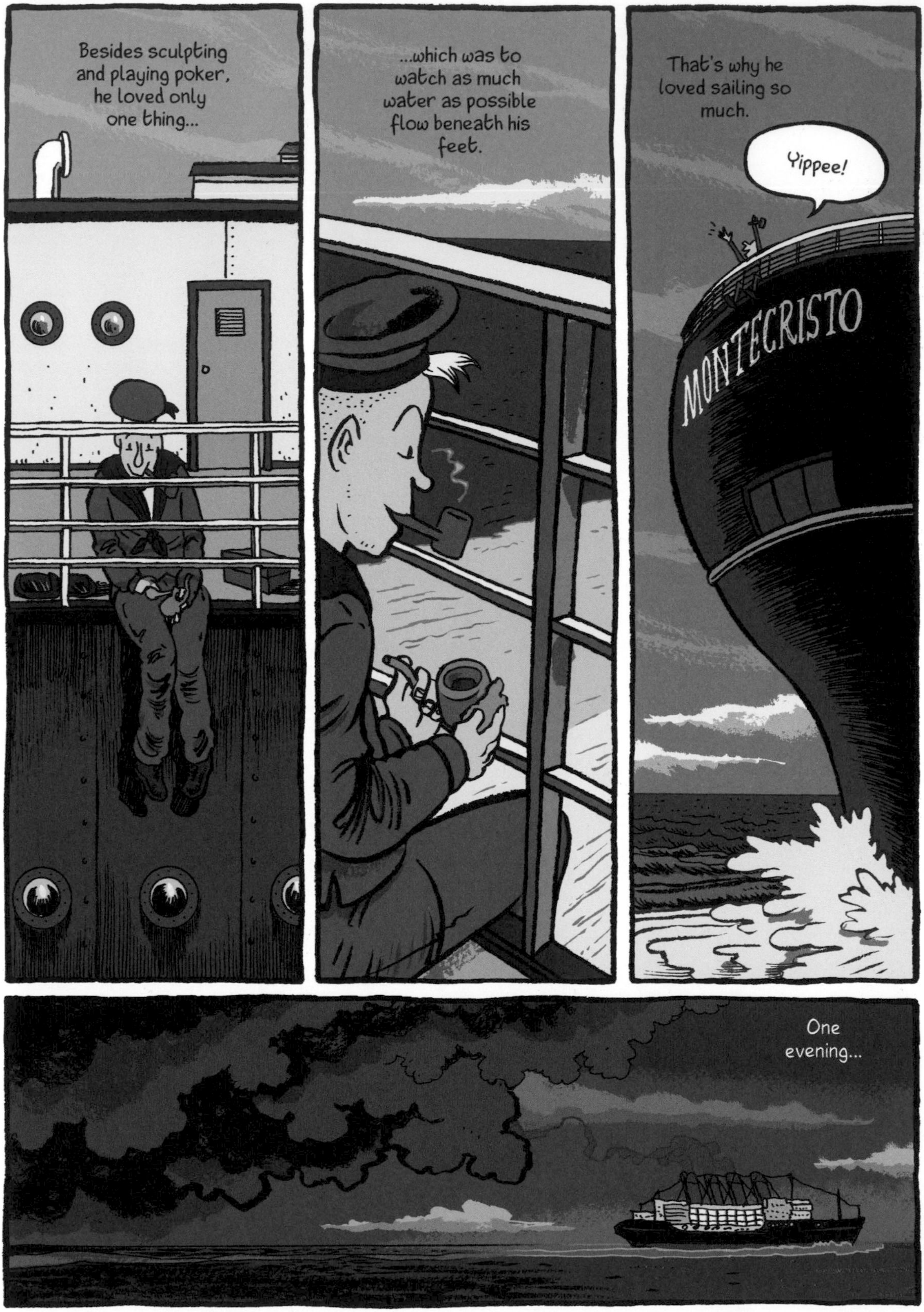
Besides sculpting and playing poker, he loved only one thing...
...which was to watch as much water as possible flow beneath his feet.
That's why he loved sailing so much.
Yippee!
MONTECRISTO
One evening...

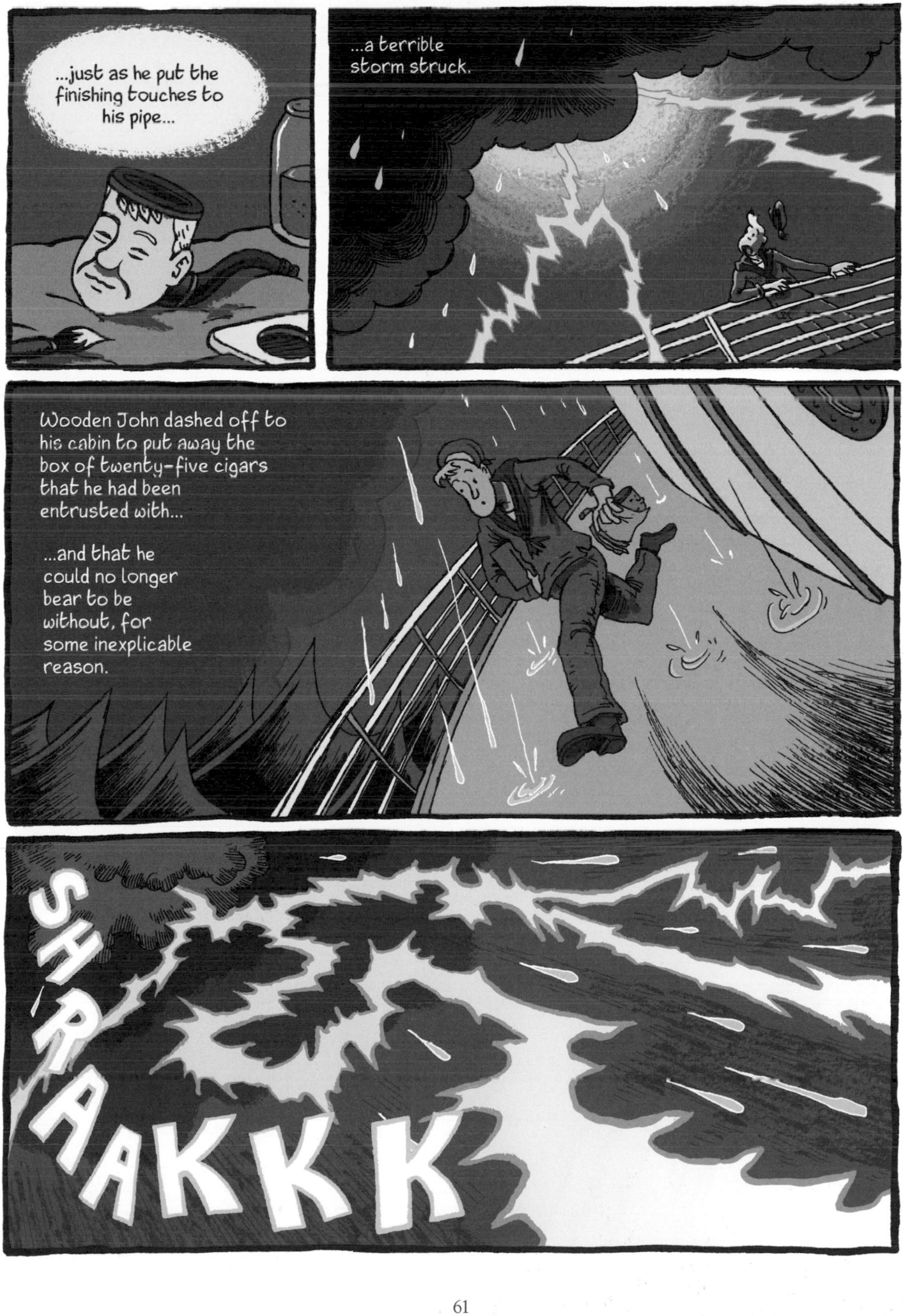
...just as he put the finishing touches to his pipe...
...a terrible storm struck.
Wooden John dashed off to his cabin to put away the box of twenty-five cigars that he had been entrusted with...
...and that he could no longer bear to be without, for some inexplicable reason.
SHRAAKKK

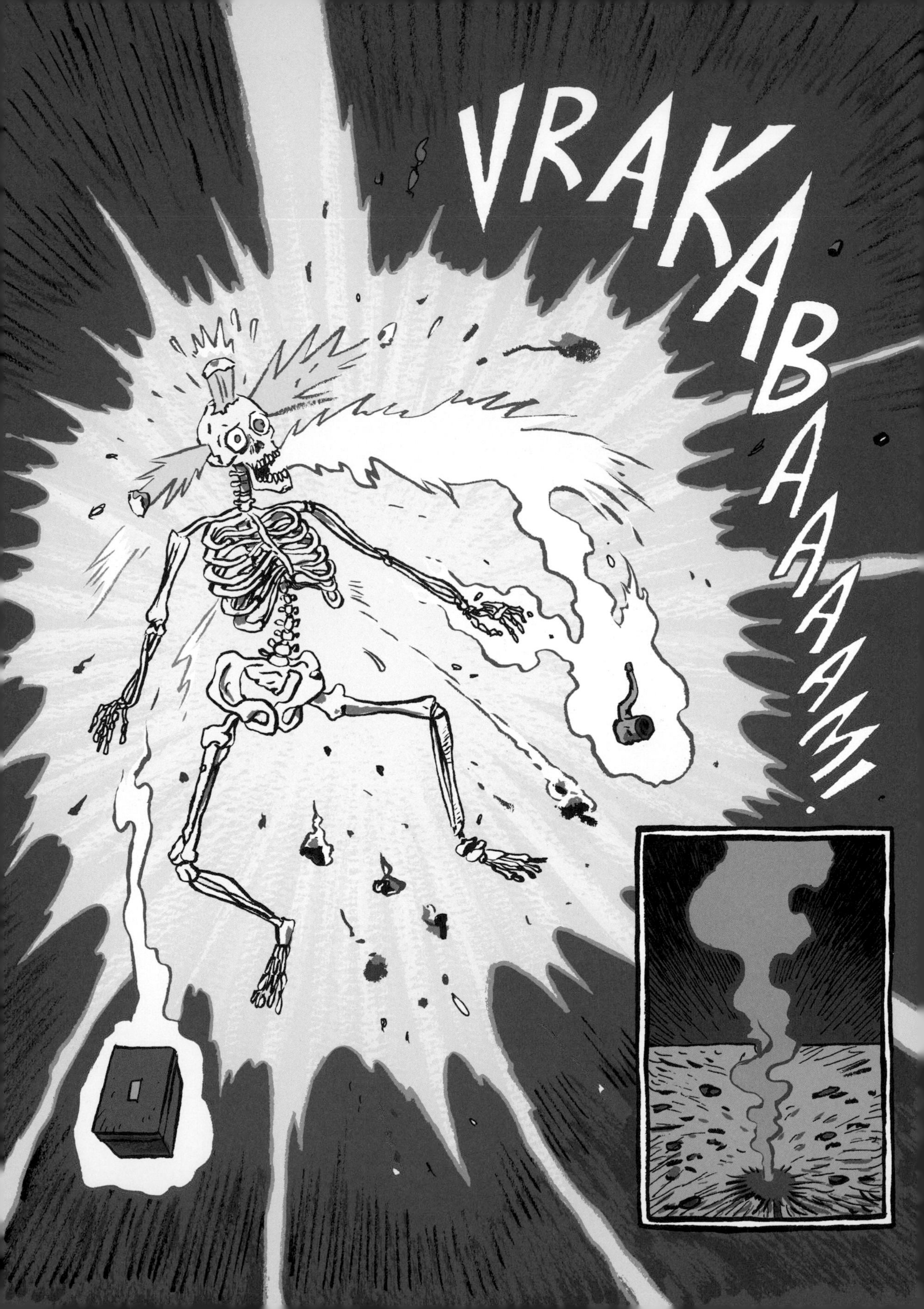
VRAKABAAAAAAM!

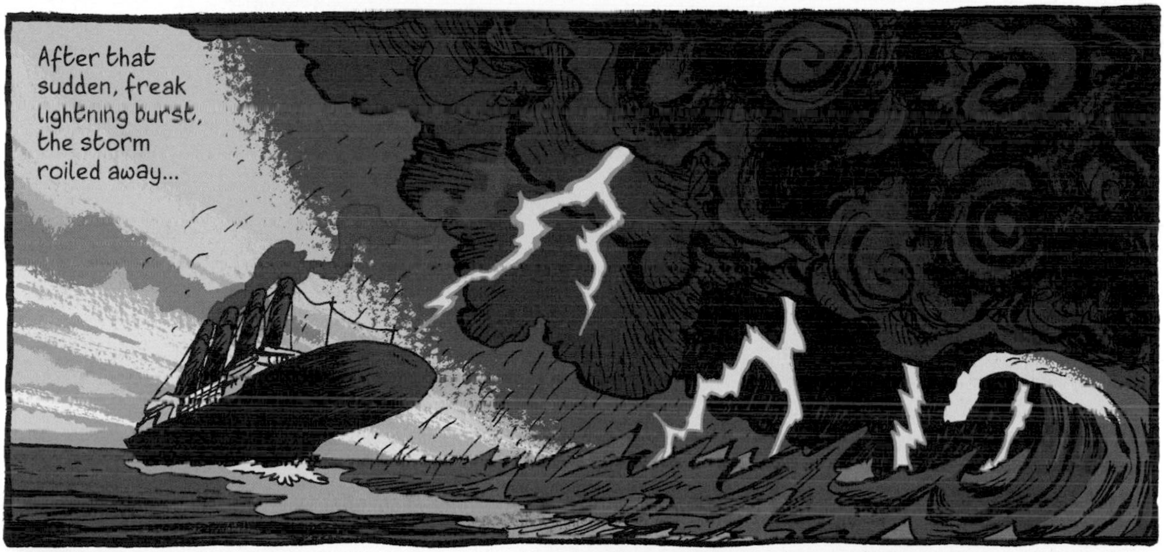
After that sudden, freak lightning burst, the storm roiled away...

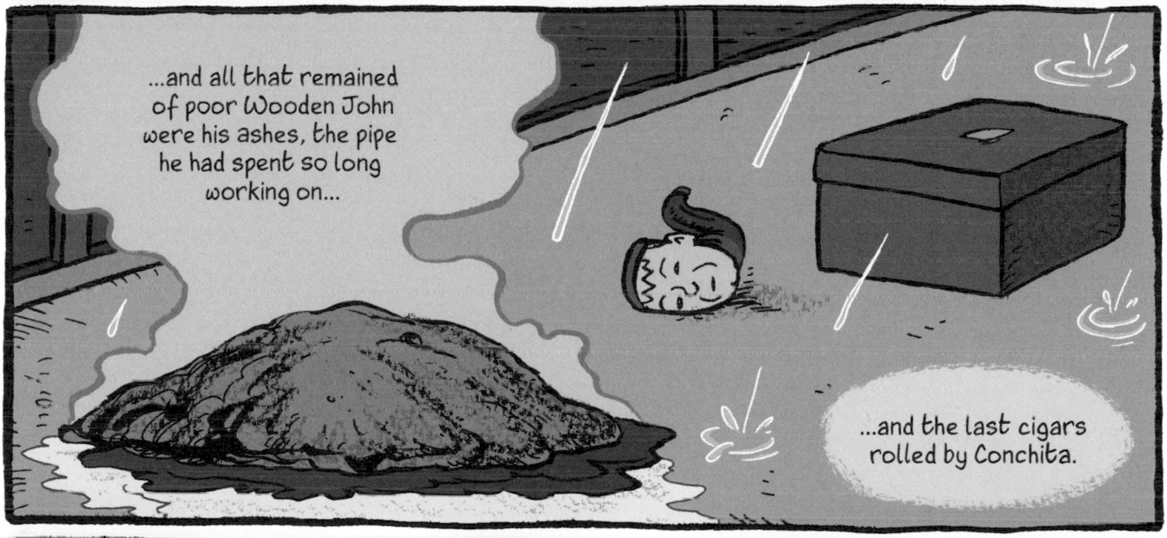
...and all that remained of poor Wooden John were his ashes, the pipe he had spent so long working on...
...and the last cigars rolled by Conchita.

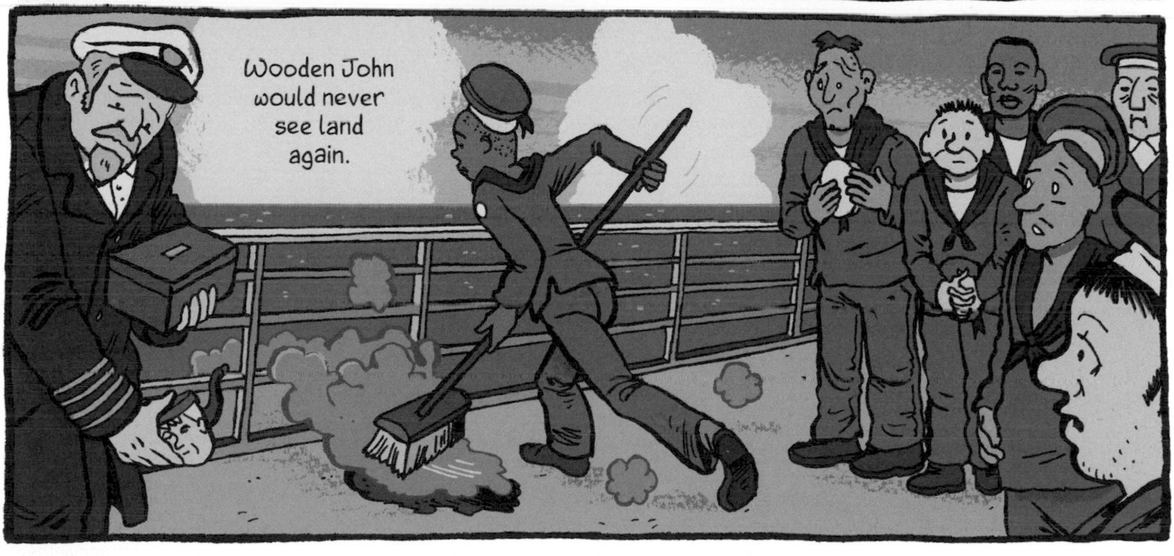
Wooden John would never see land again.

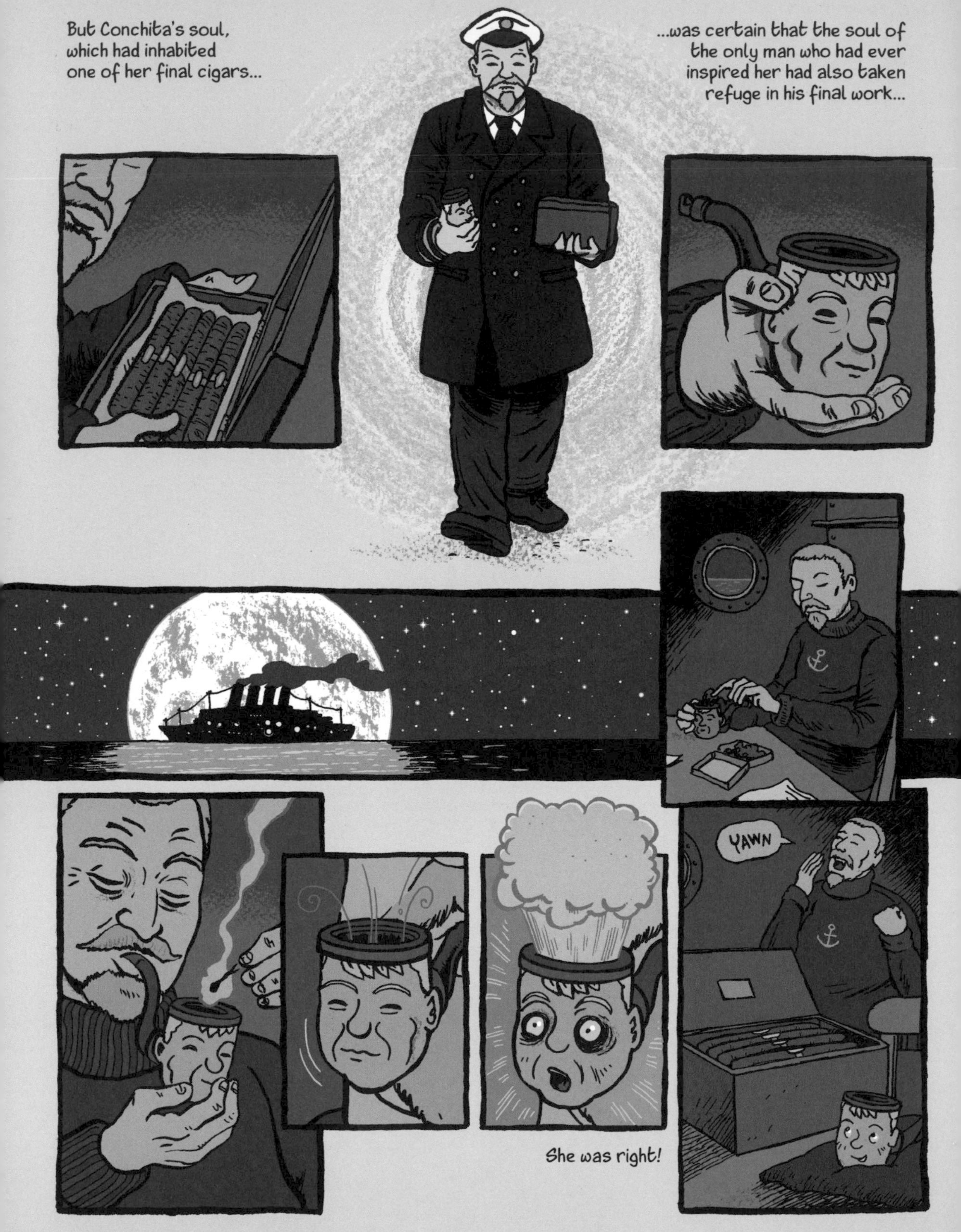
But Conchita's soul, which had inhabited one of her final cigars...
...was certain that the soul of the only man who had ever inspired her had also taken refuge in his final work...
YAWN
She was right!

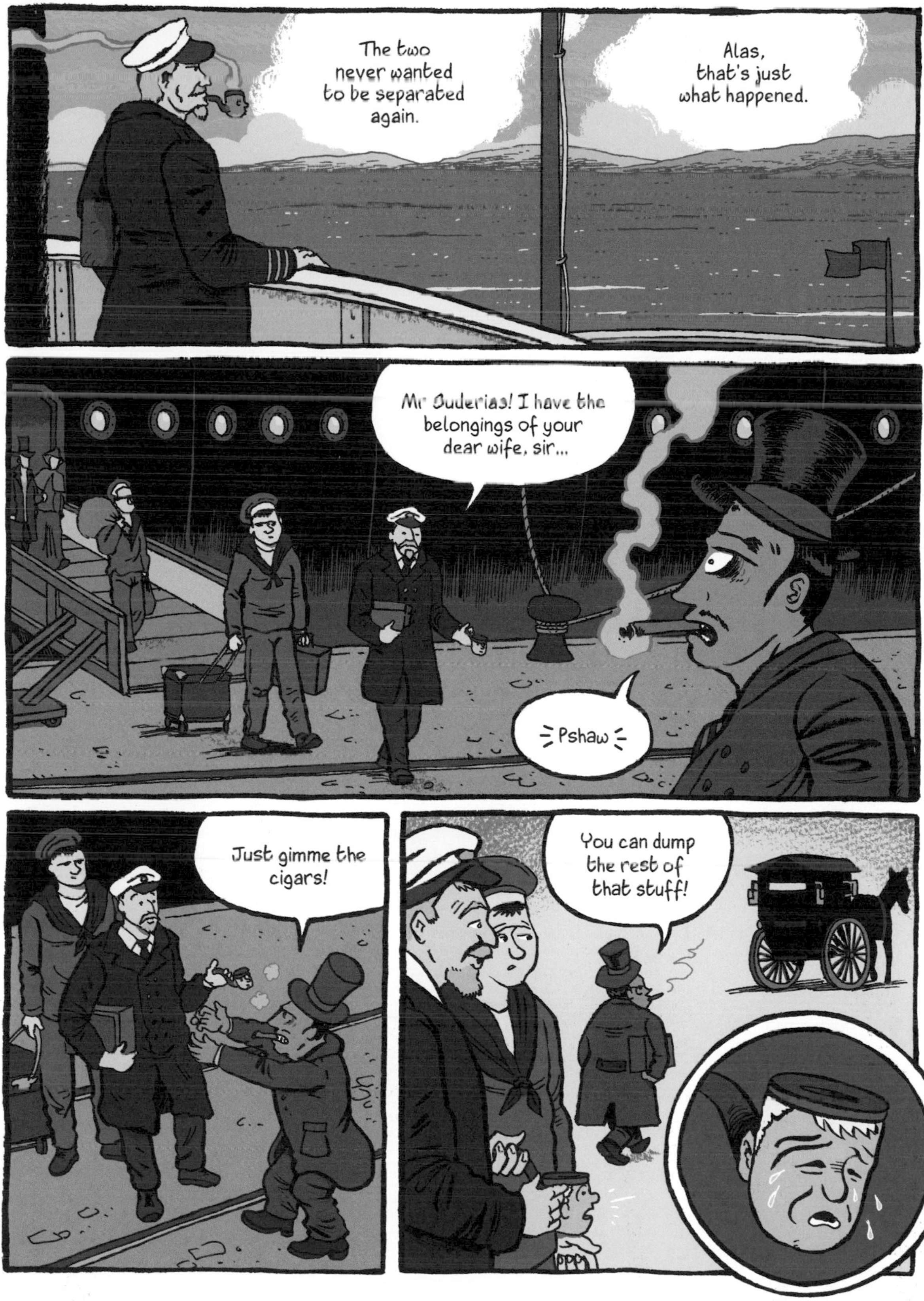
The two never wanted to be separated again.
Alas, that's just what happened.
Mr Ouderias! I have the belongings of your dear wife, sir...
Pshaw
Just gimme the cigars!
You can dump the rest of that stuff!

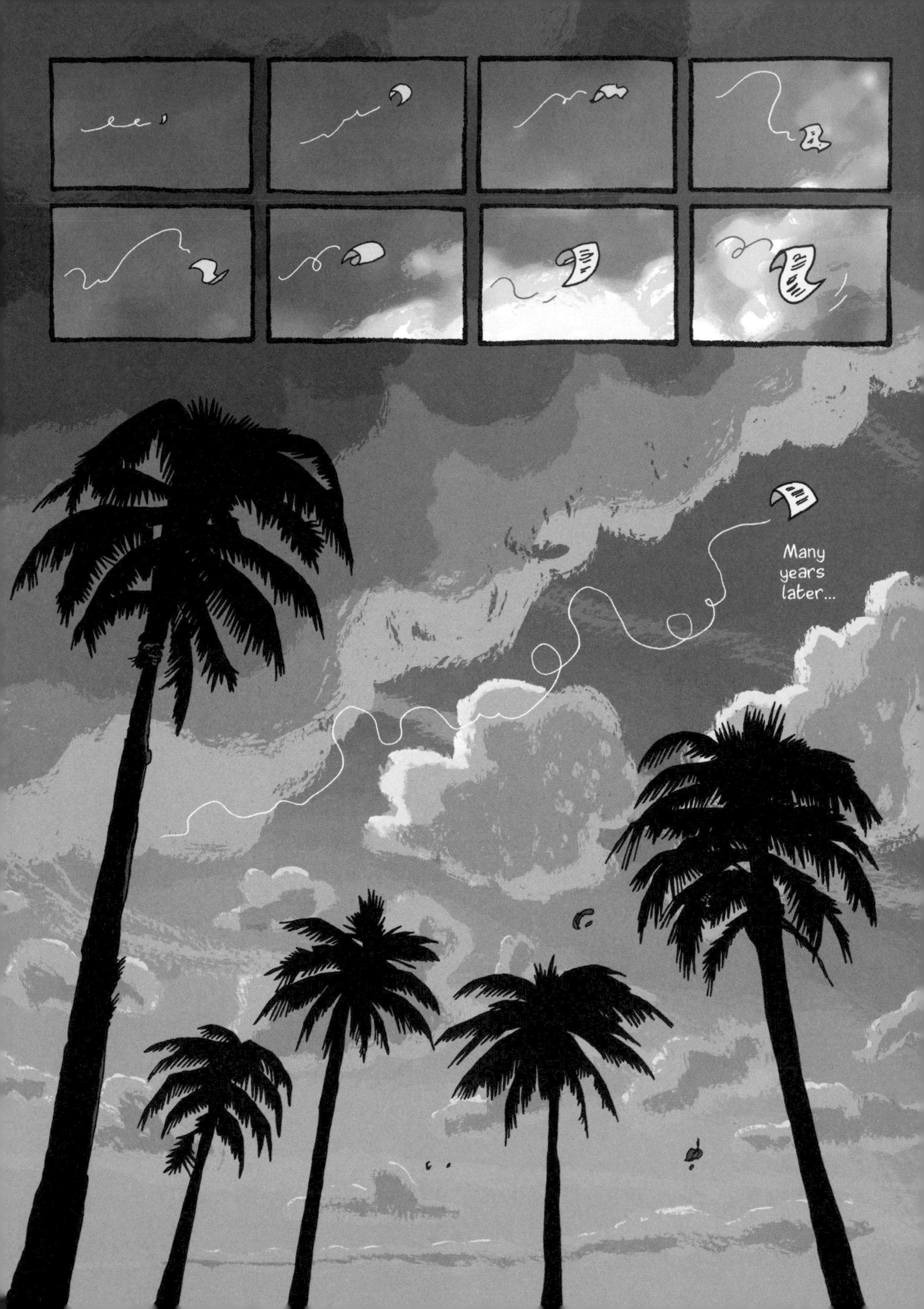
Many years later...

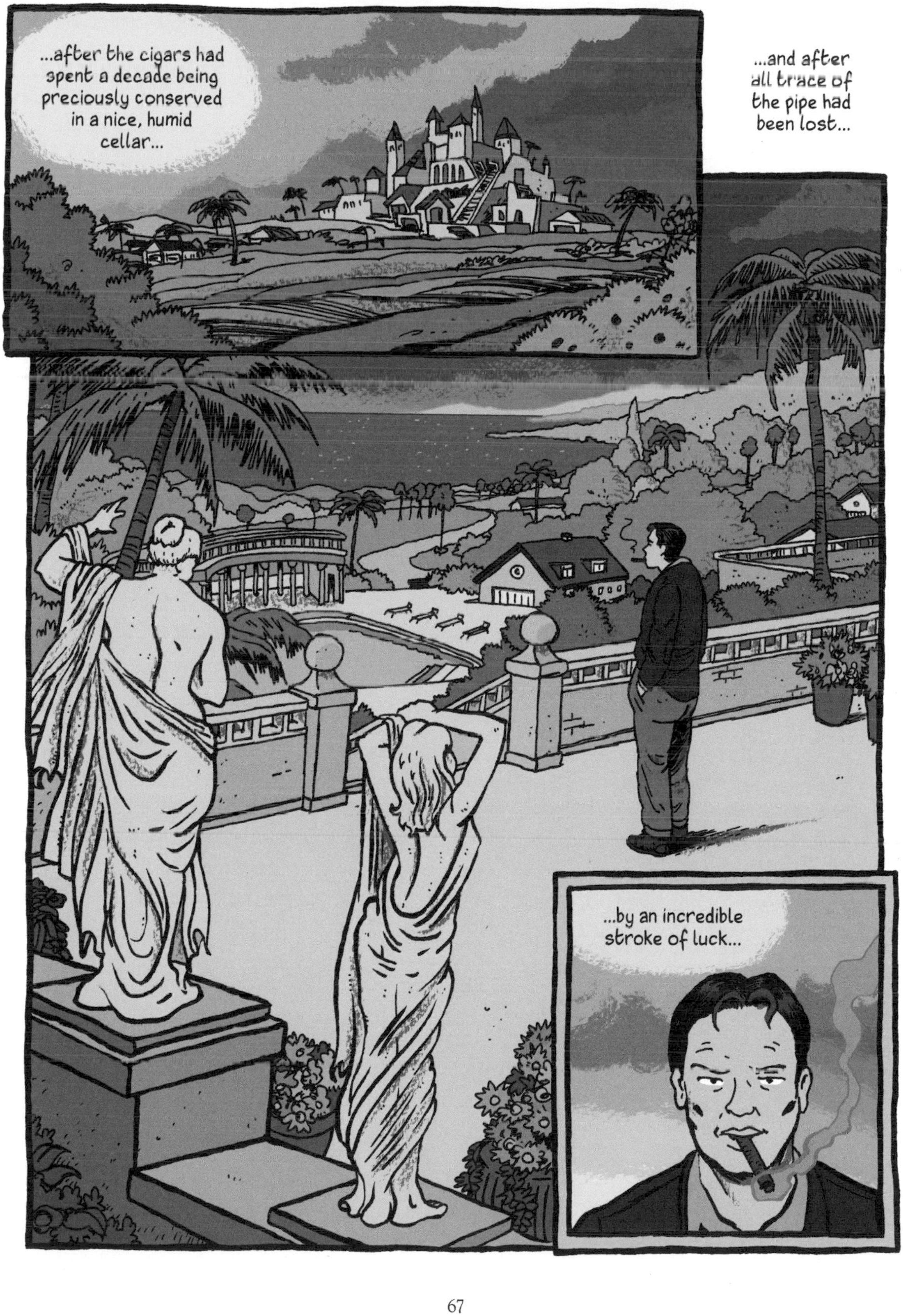
...after the cigars had spent a decade being preciously conserved in a nice, humid cellar...
...and after all trace of the pipe had been lost...
...by an incredible stroke of luck...

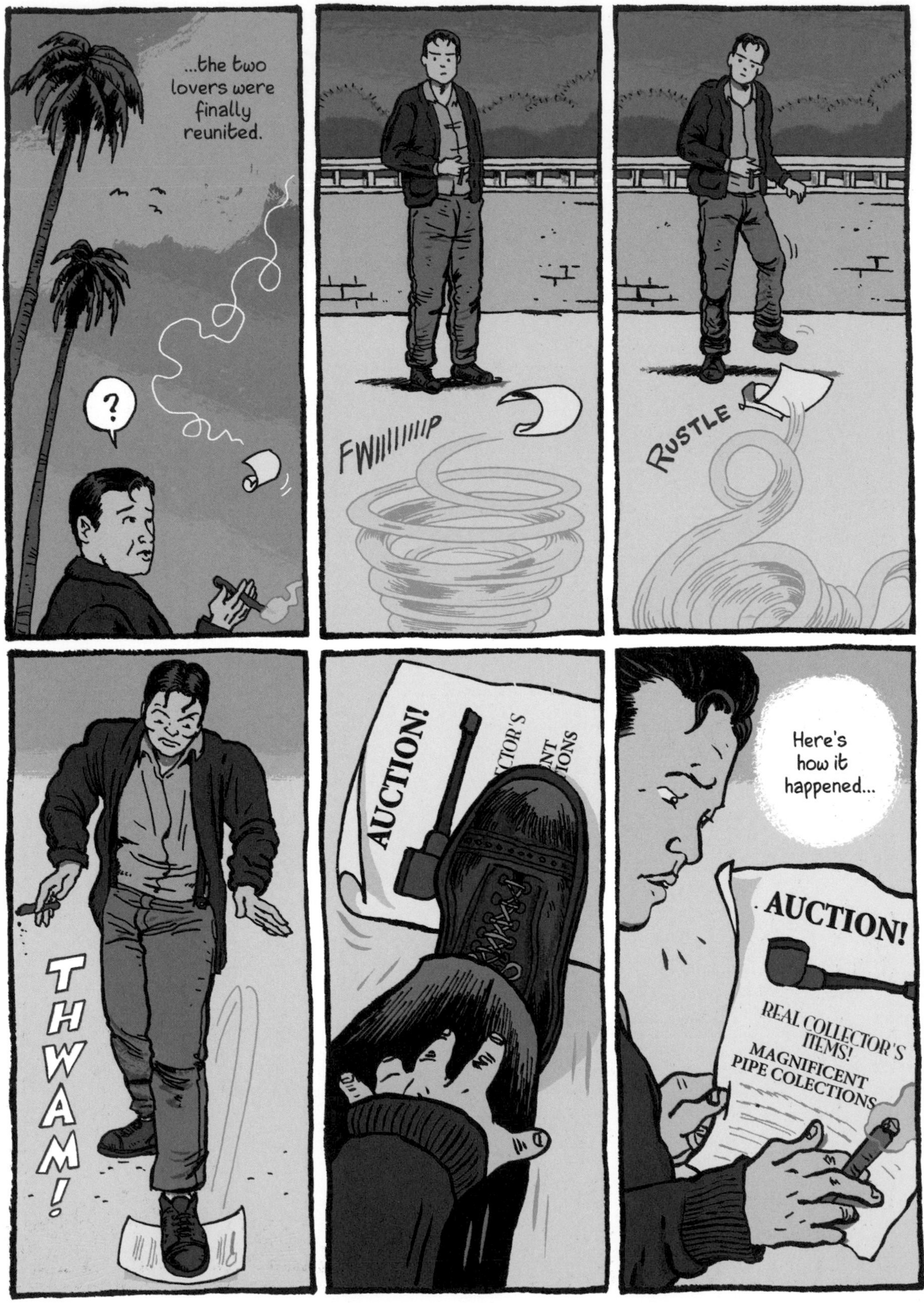
...the two lovers were finally reunited.
?
FWIIIIIIP
RUSTLE
THWAM!
AUCTION!
Here's how it happened...
AUCTION!
REAL COLLECTOR'S ITEMS!
MAGNIFICENT PIPE COLECTIONS

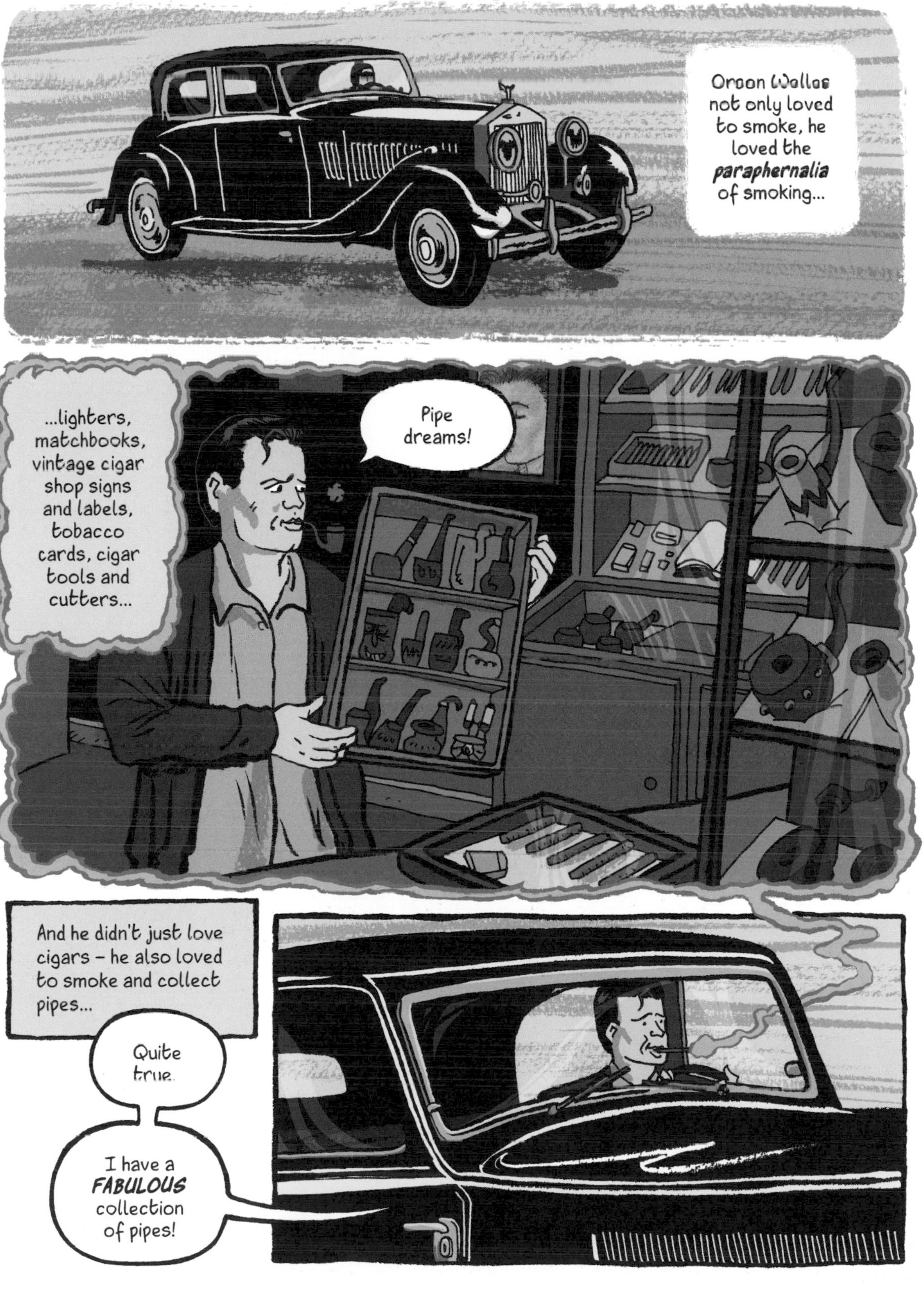
Orson Welles not only loved to smoke, he loved the ***paraphernalia*** of smoking...
...lighters, matchbooks, vintage cigar shop signs and labels, tobacco cards, cigar tools and cutters...
Pipe dreams!
And he didn't just love cigars – he also loved to smoke and collect pipes...
Quite true.
I have a ***FABULOUS*** collection of pipes!

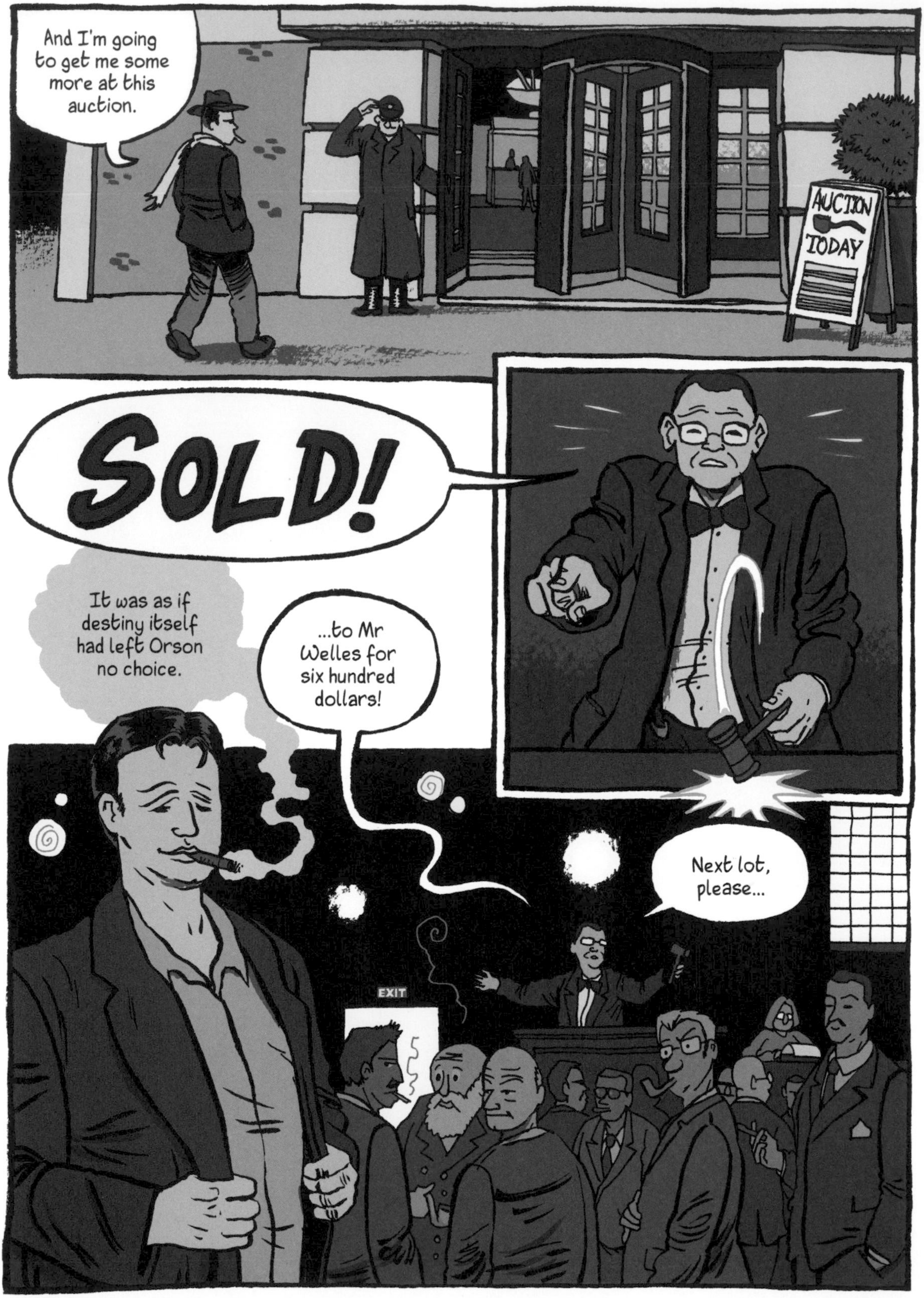
And I'm going to get me some more at this auction.
AUCTION TODAY
SOLD!
It was as if destiny itself had left Orson no choice.
...to Mr Welles for six hundred dollars!
Next lot, please...
EXIT

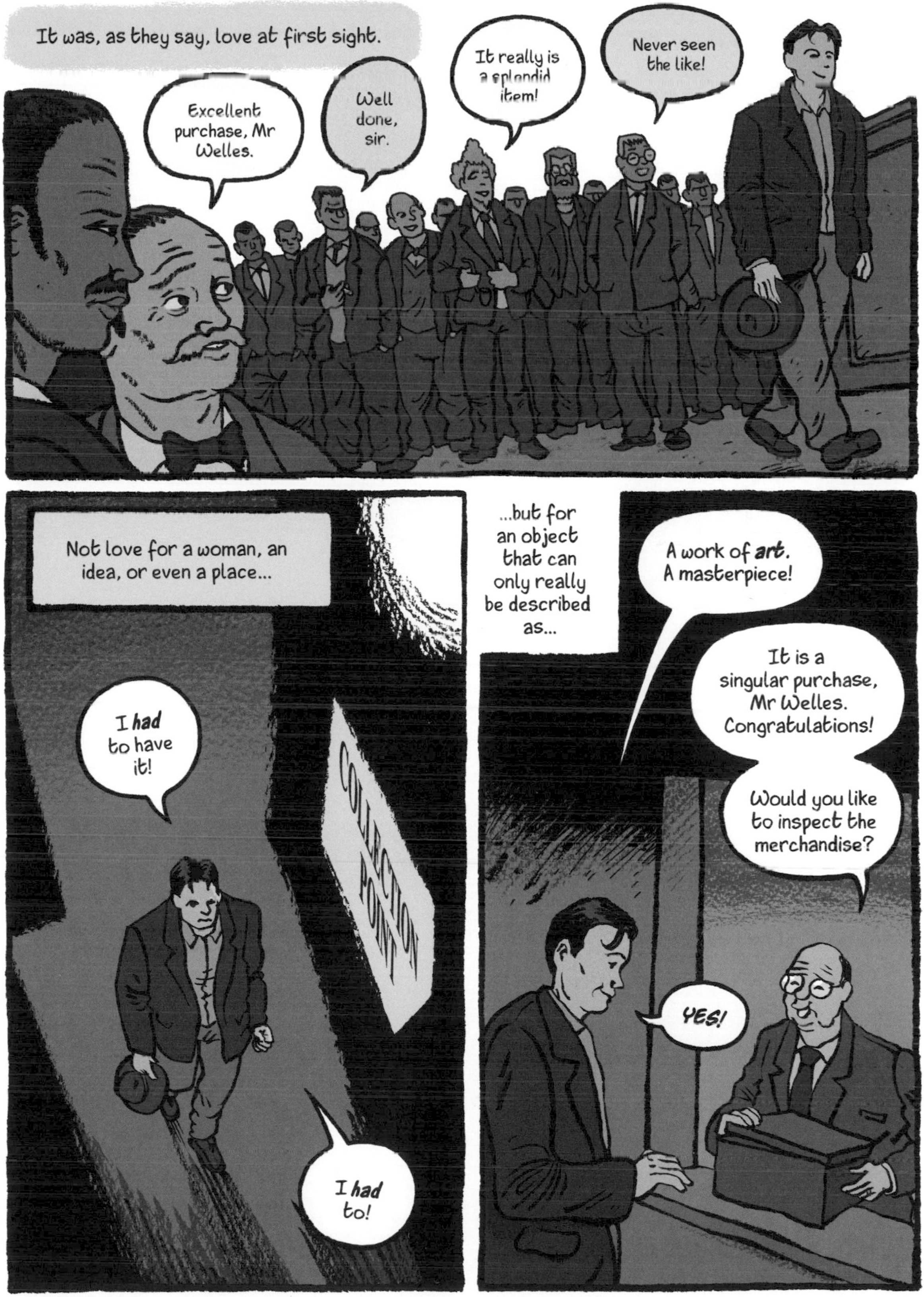
It was, as they say, love at first sight.
Excellent purchase, Mr Welles.
Well done, sir.
It really is a splendid item!
Never seen the like!
Not love for a woman, an idea, or even a place...
I *had* to have it!
COLLECTION POINT
I *had* to!
...but for an object that can only really be described as...
A work of **art**. A masterpiece!
It is a singular purchase, Mr Welles. Congratulations!
Would you like to inspect the merchandise?
YES!

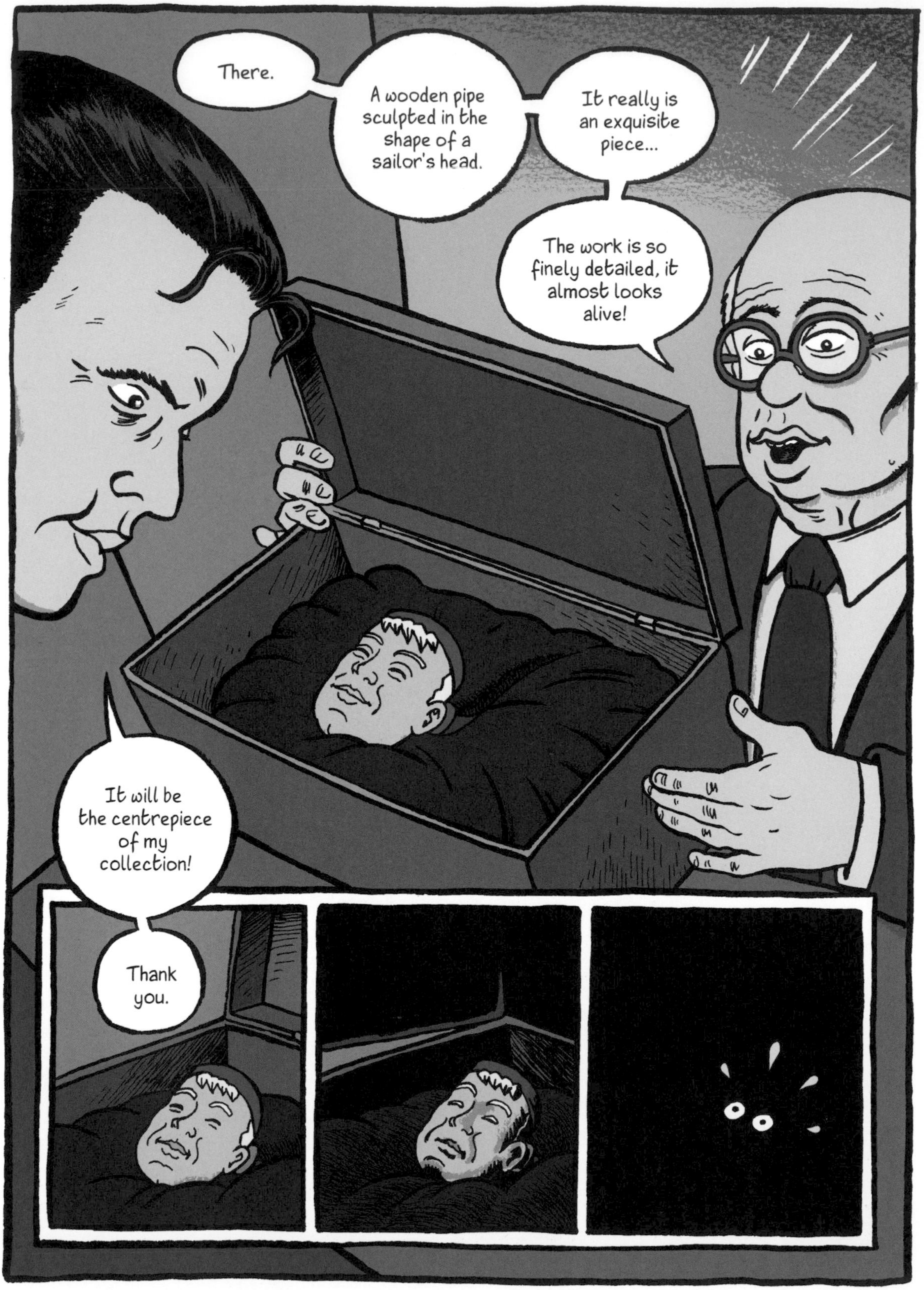
There.
A wooden pipe sculpted in the shape of a sailor's head.
It really is an exquisite piece...
The work is so finely detailed, it almost looks alive!
It will be the centrepiece of my collection!
Thank you.

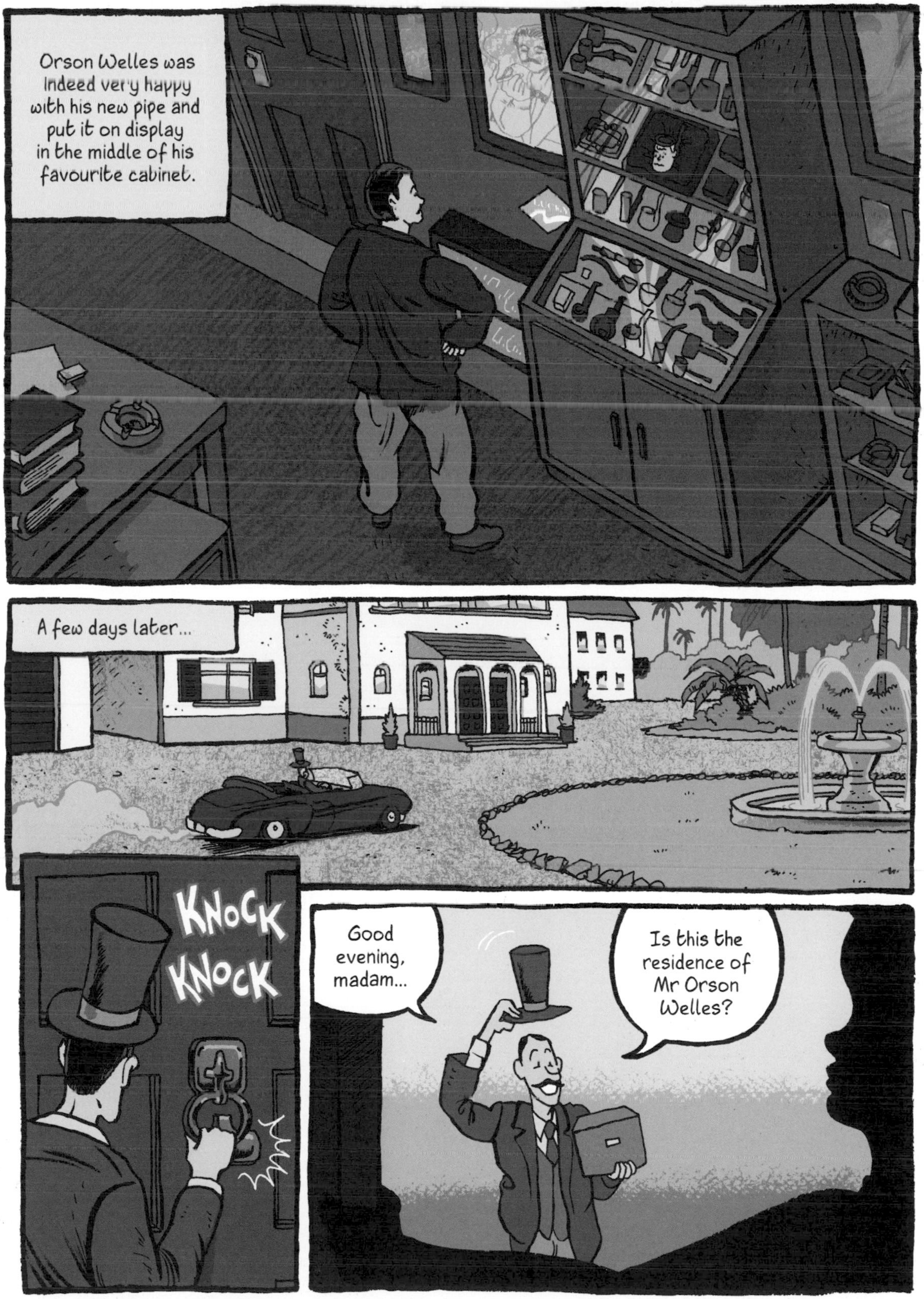
Orson Welles was indeed very happy with his new pipe and put it on display in the middle of his favourite cabinet.
A few days later...
KNOCK KNOCK
Good evening, madam...
Is this the residence of Mr Orson Welles?

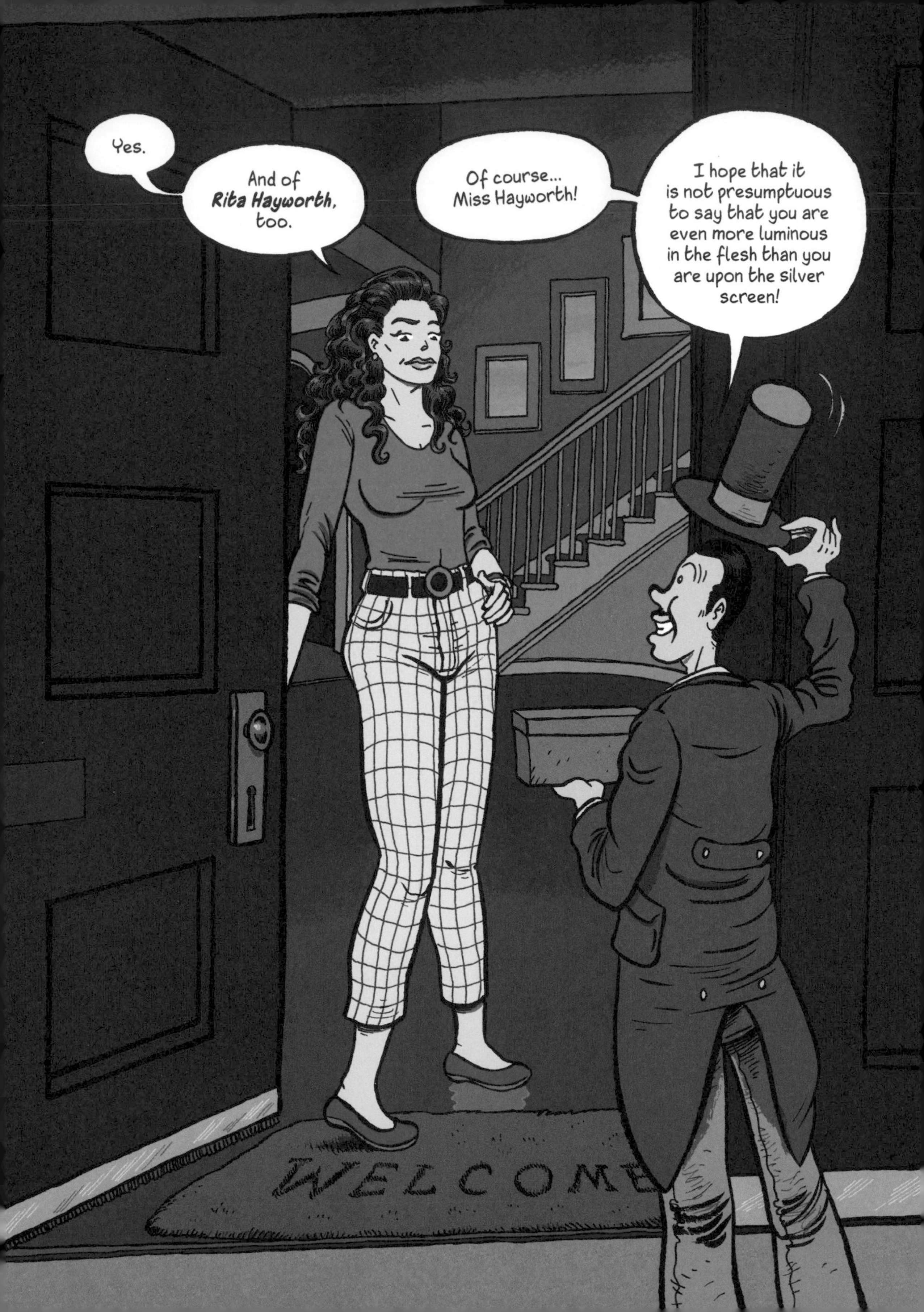
Yes.
And of Rita Hayworth, too.
Of course... Miss Hayworth!
I hope that it is not presumptuous to say that you are even more luminous in the flesh than you are upon the silver screen!
WELCOME

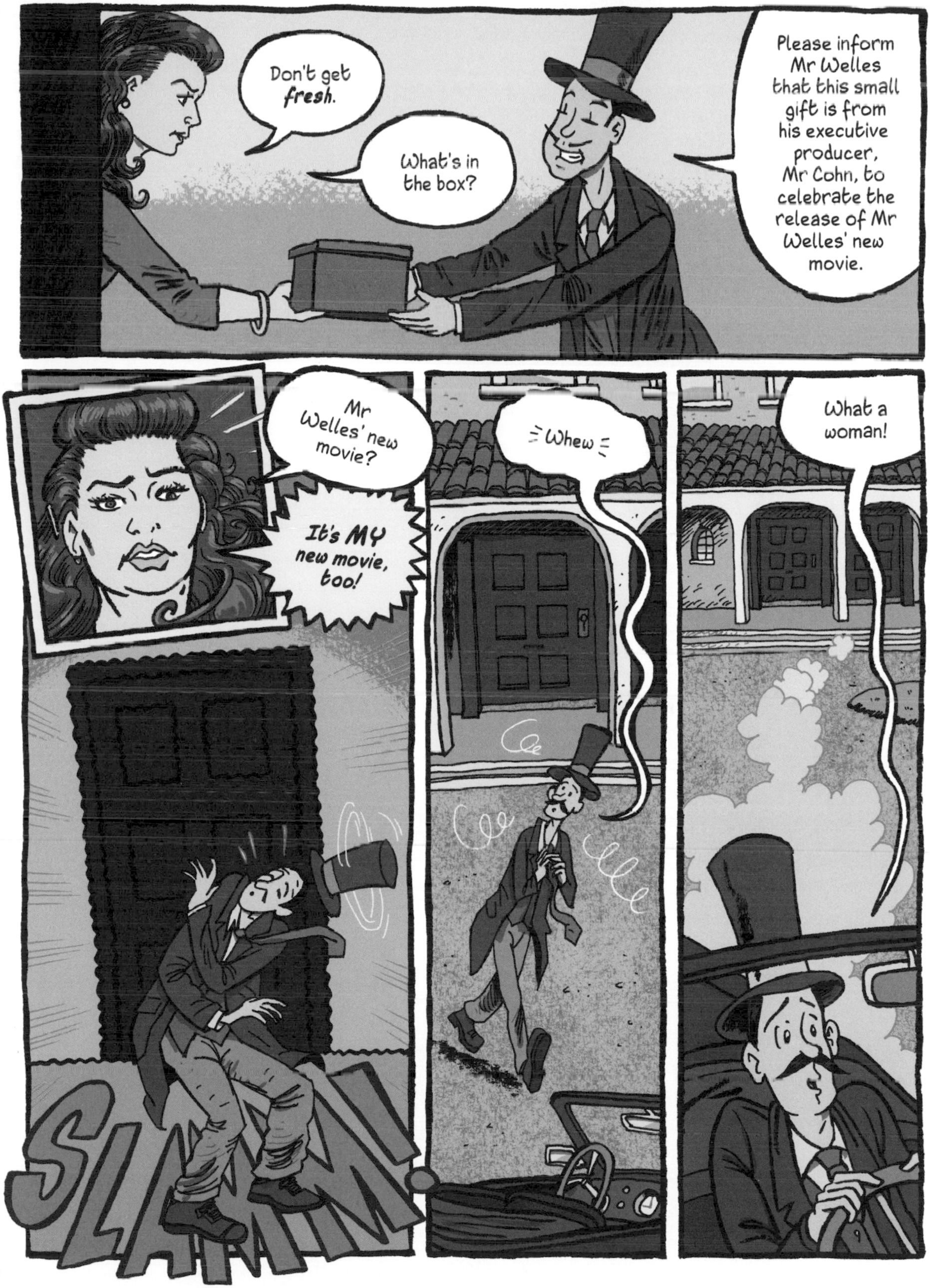
Don't get *fresh*.
What's in the box?
Please inform Mr Welles that this small gift is from his executive producer, Mr Cohn, to celebrate the release of Mr Welles' new movie.
Mr Welles' new movie?
It's MY new movie, too!
SLAM!
Whew
What a woman!

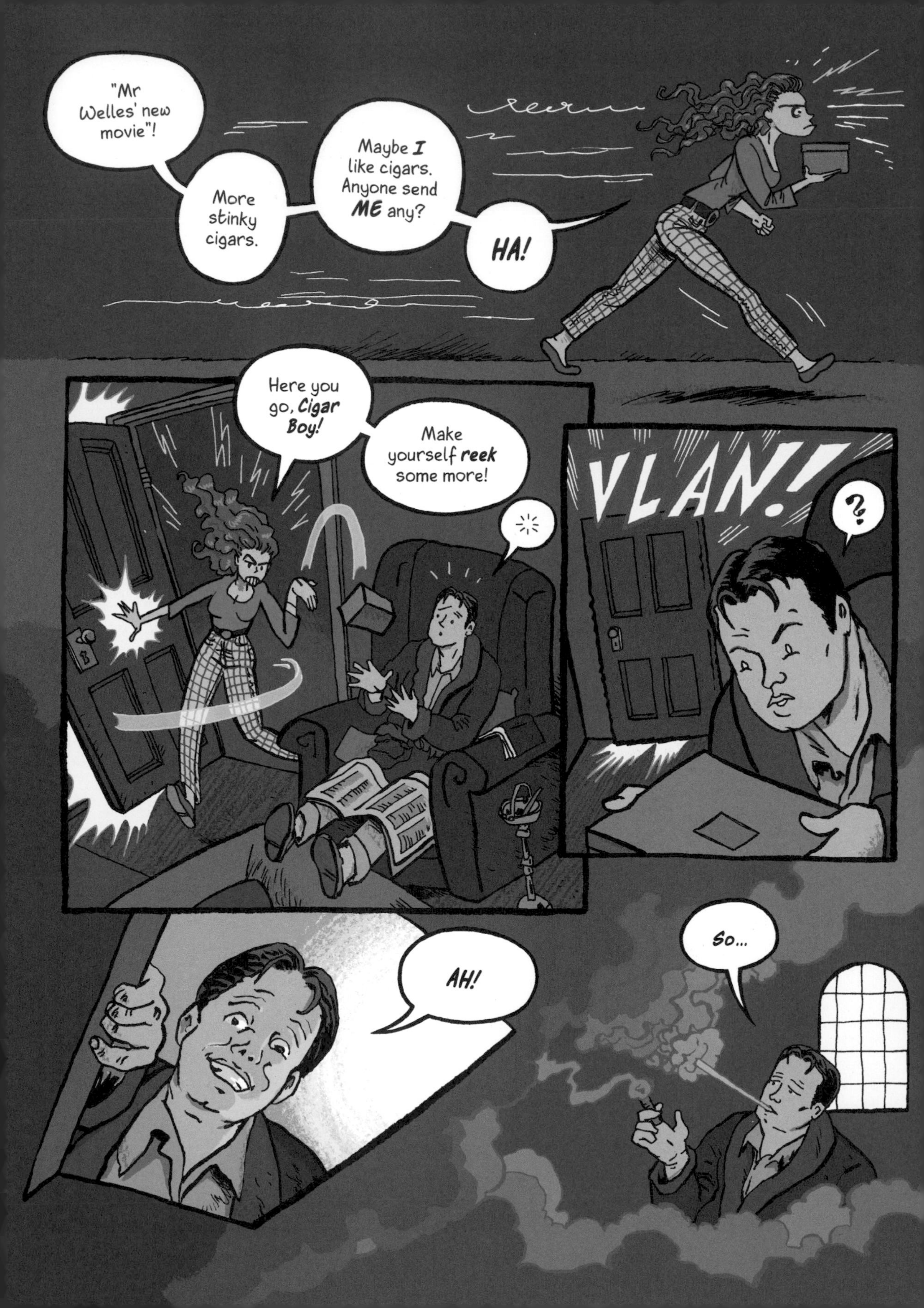
"Mr Welles' new movie"!
More stinky cigars.
Maybe I like cigars. Anyone send ME any?
HA!
Here you go, Cigar Boy!
Make yourself reek some more!
VLAN!
?
AH!
So...

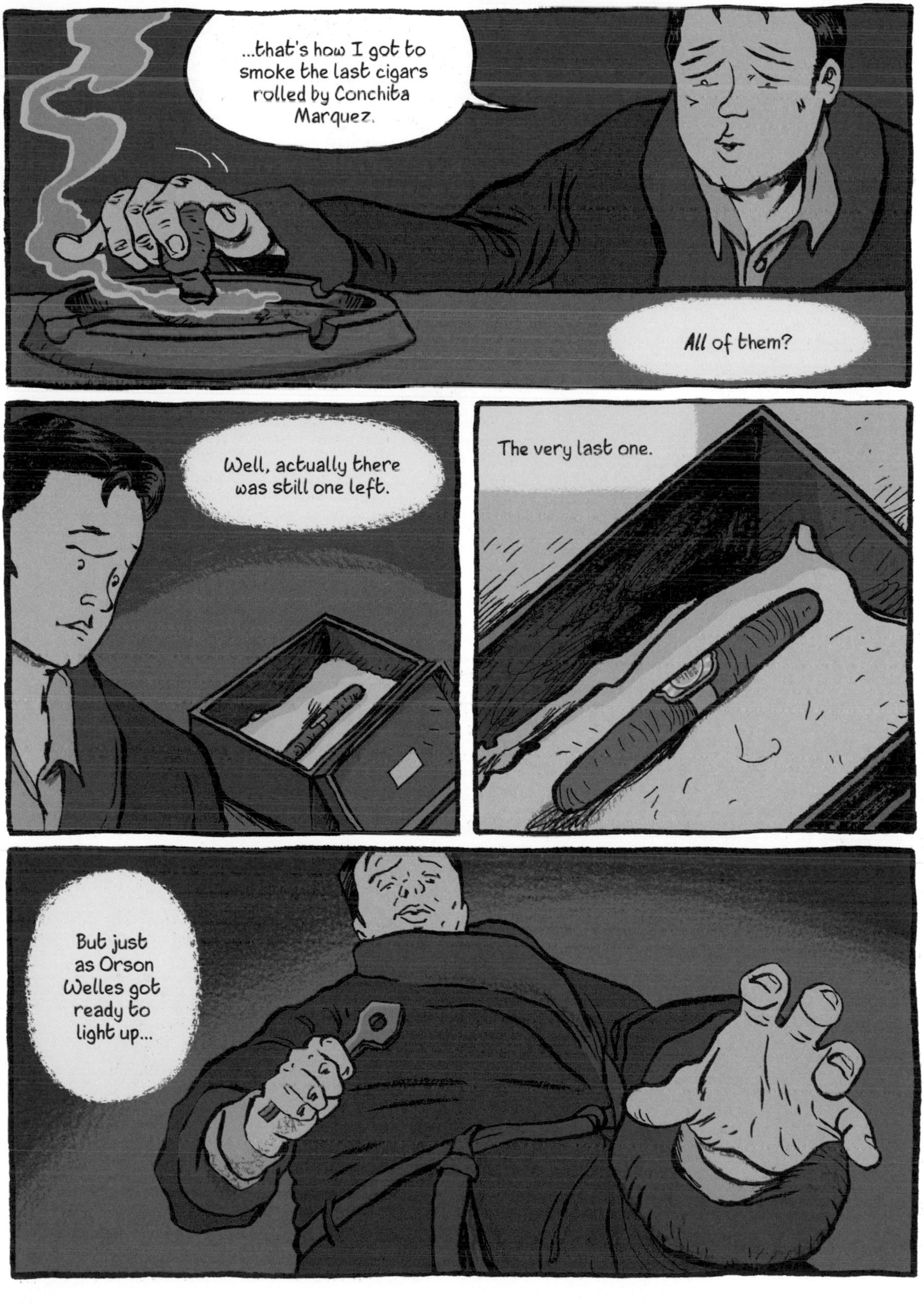
...that's how I got to smoke the last cigars rolled by Conchita Marquez.
All of them?
Well, actually there was still one left.
The very last one.
But just as Orson Welles got ready to light up...

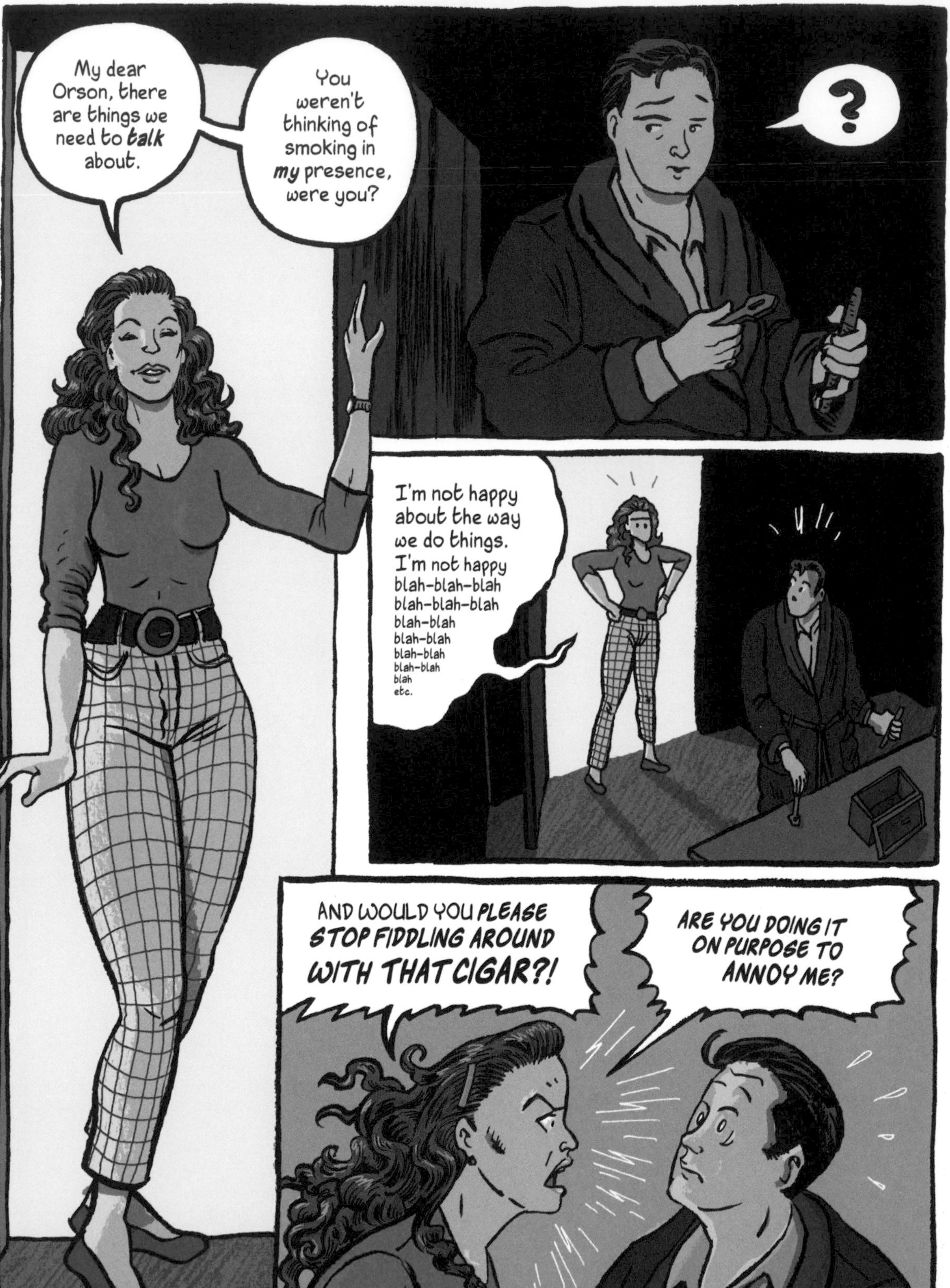
My dear Orson, there are things we need to talk about.
You weren't thinking of smoking in my presence, were you?
?
I'm not happy about the way we do things. I'm not happy blah-blah-blah blah-blah-blah blah-blah blah-blah blah-blah blah-blah blah etc.
AND WOULD YOU PLEASE STOP FIDDLING AROUND WITH THAT CIGAR?!
ARE YOU DOING IT ON PURPOSE TO ANNOY ME?

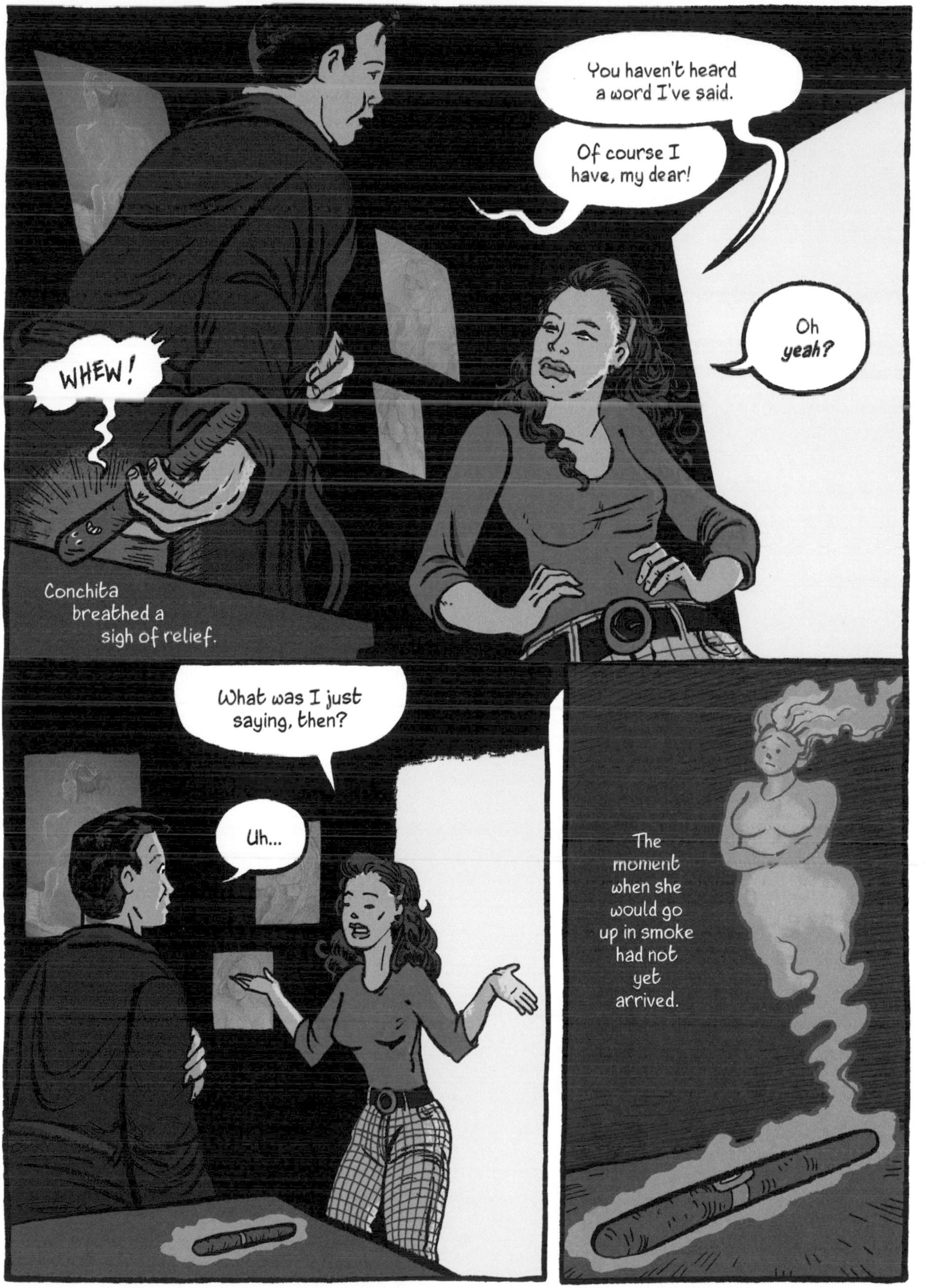
You haven't heard a word I've said.
Of course I have, my dear!
Oh yeah?
WHEW!
Conchita breathed a sigh of relief.
What was I just saying, then?
Uh...
The moment when she would go up in smoke had not yet arrived.

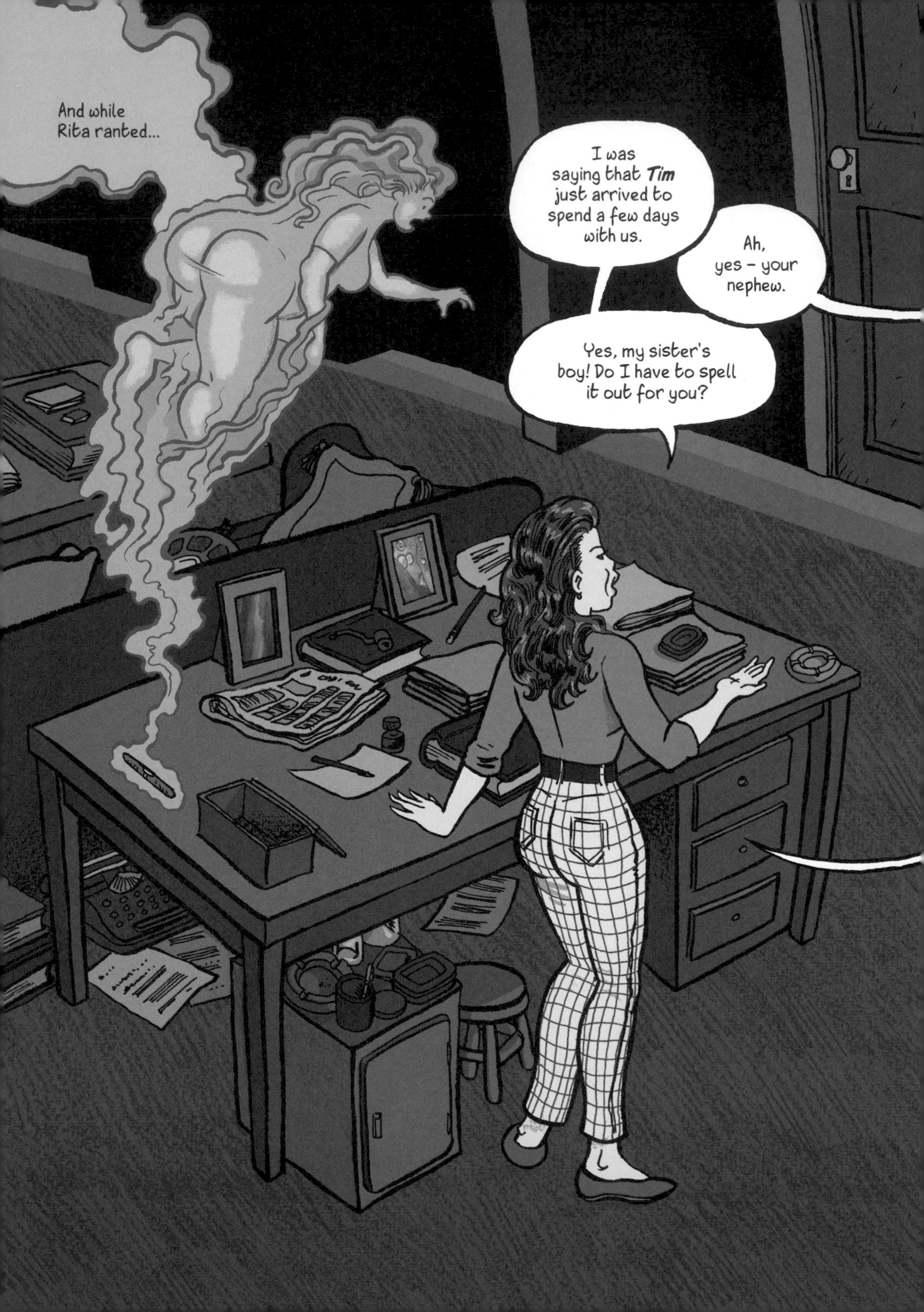
And while Rita ranted...
I was saying that *Tim* just arrived to spend a few days with us.
Ah, yes – your nephew.
Yes, my sister's boy! Do I have to spell it out for you?

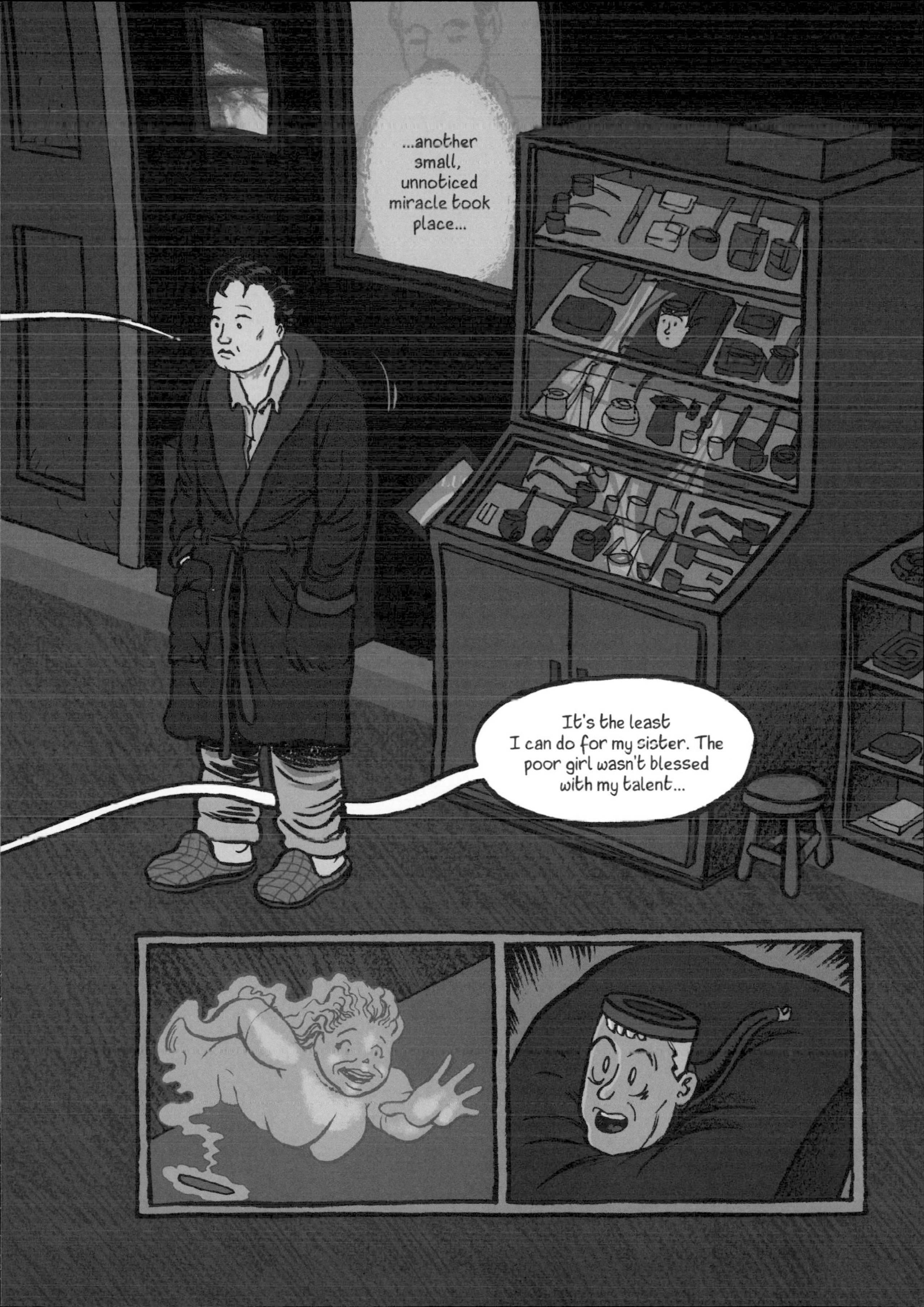
...another small, unnoticed miracle took place...
It's the least I can do for my sister. The poor girl wasn't blessed with my talent...

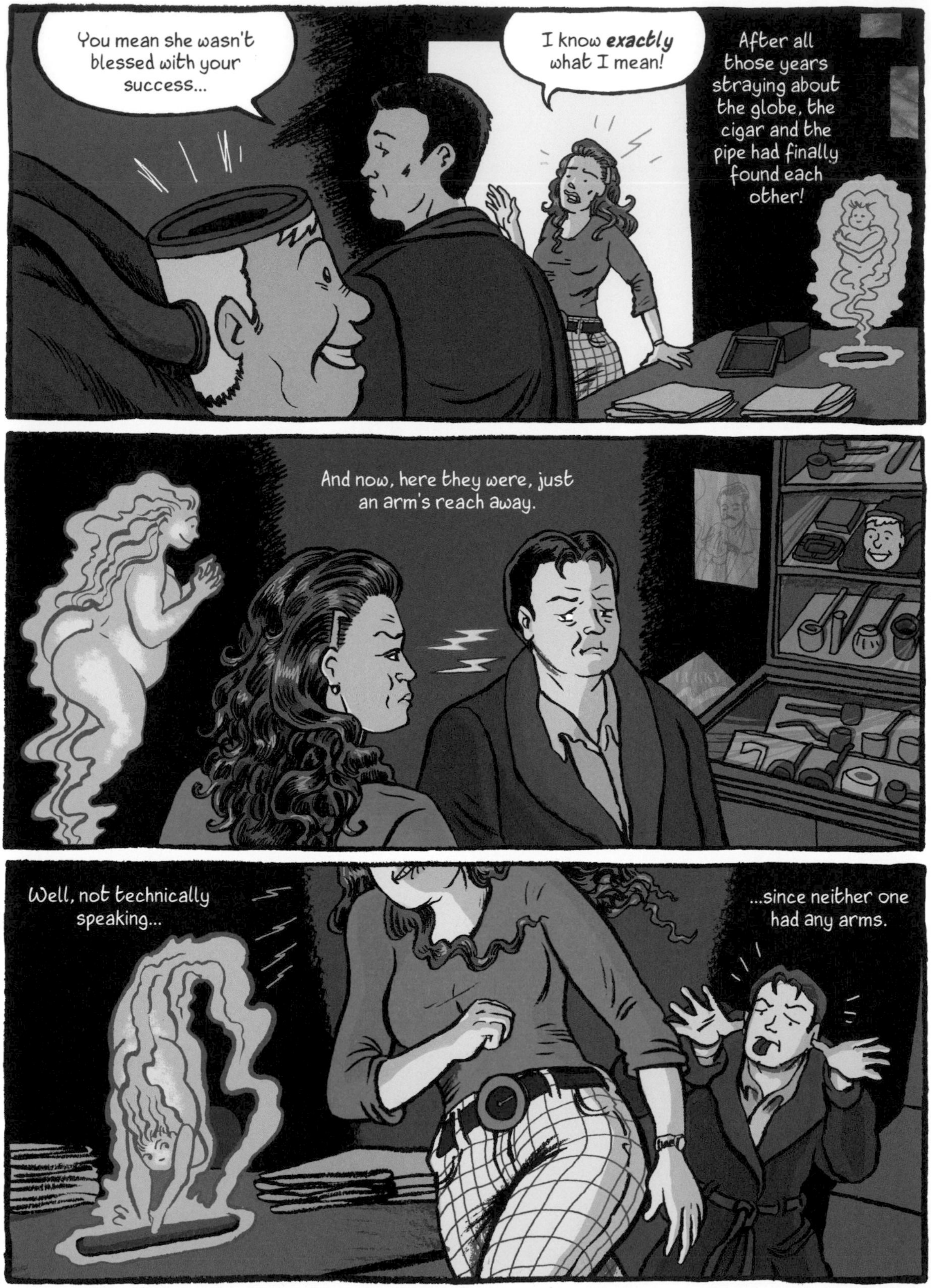
You mean she wasn't blessed with your success...
I know **exactly** what I mean!
After all those years straying about the globe, the cigar and the pipe had finally found each other!
And now, here they were, just an arm's reach away.
Well, not technically speaking...
...since neither one had any arms.

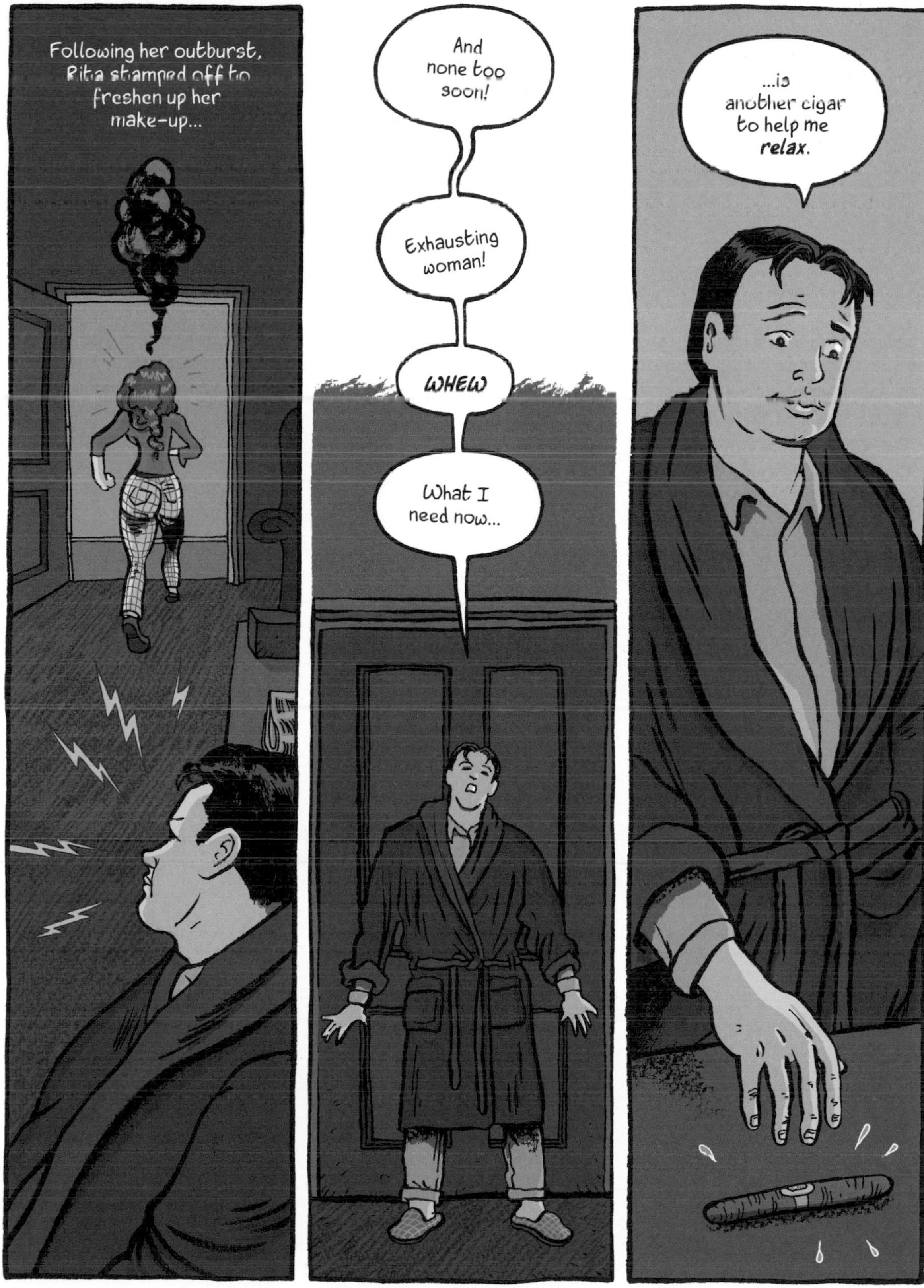
Following her outburst, Rita stamped off to freshen up her make-up...
And none too soon!
Exhausting woman!
WHEW
What I need now...
...is another cigar to help me relax.

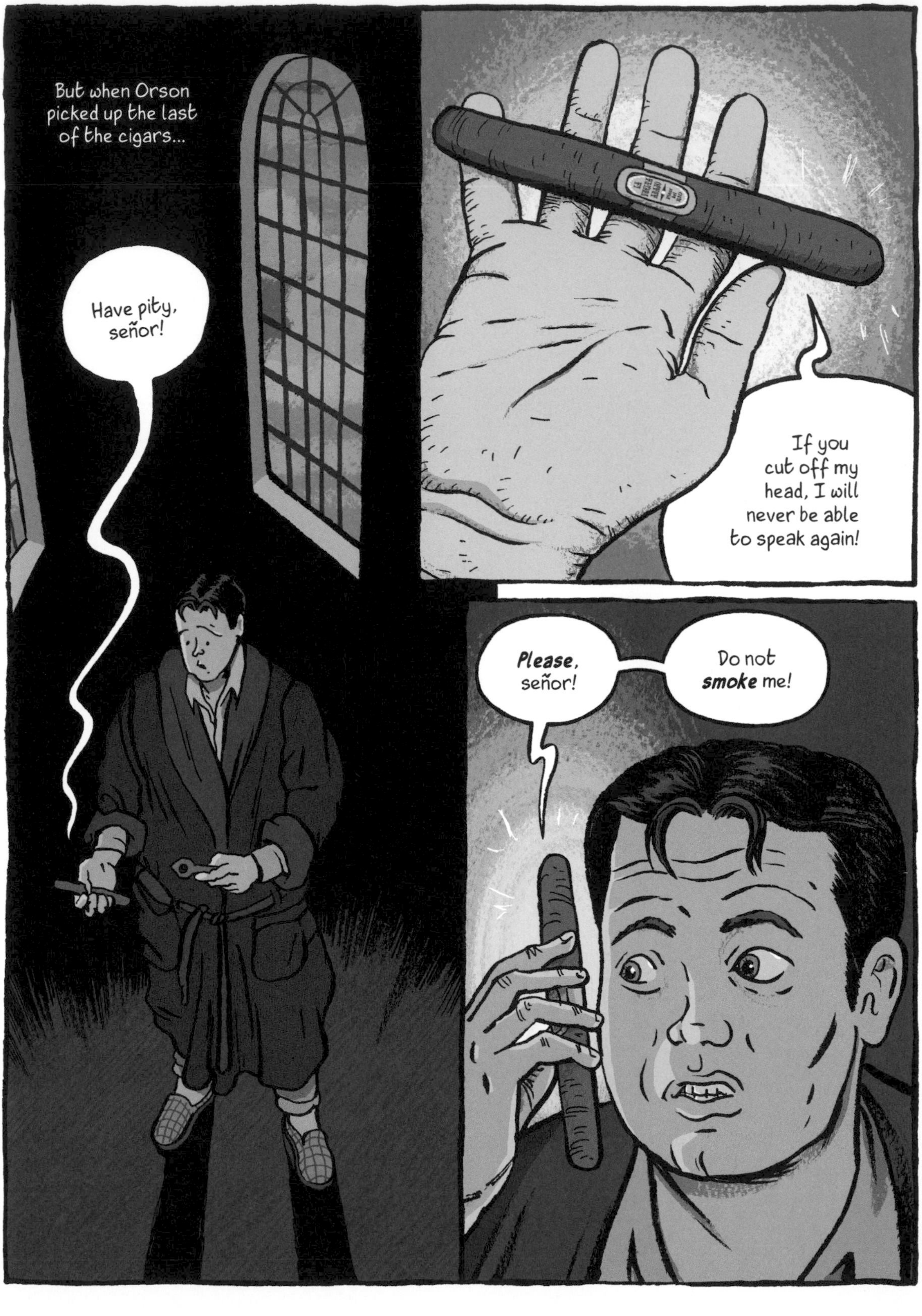
But when Orson picked up the last of the cigars...
Have pity, señor!
If you cut off my head, I will never be able to speak again!
Please, señor!
Do not **smoke** me!

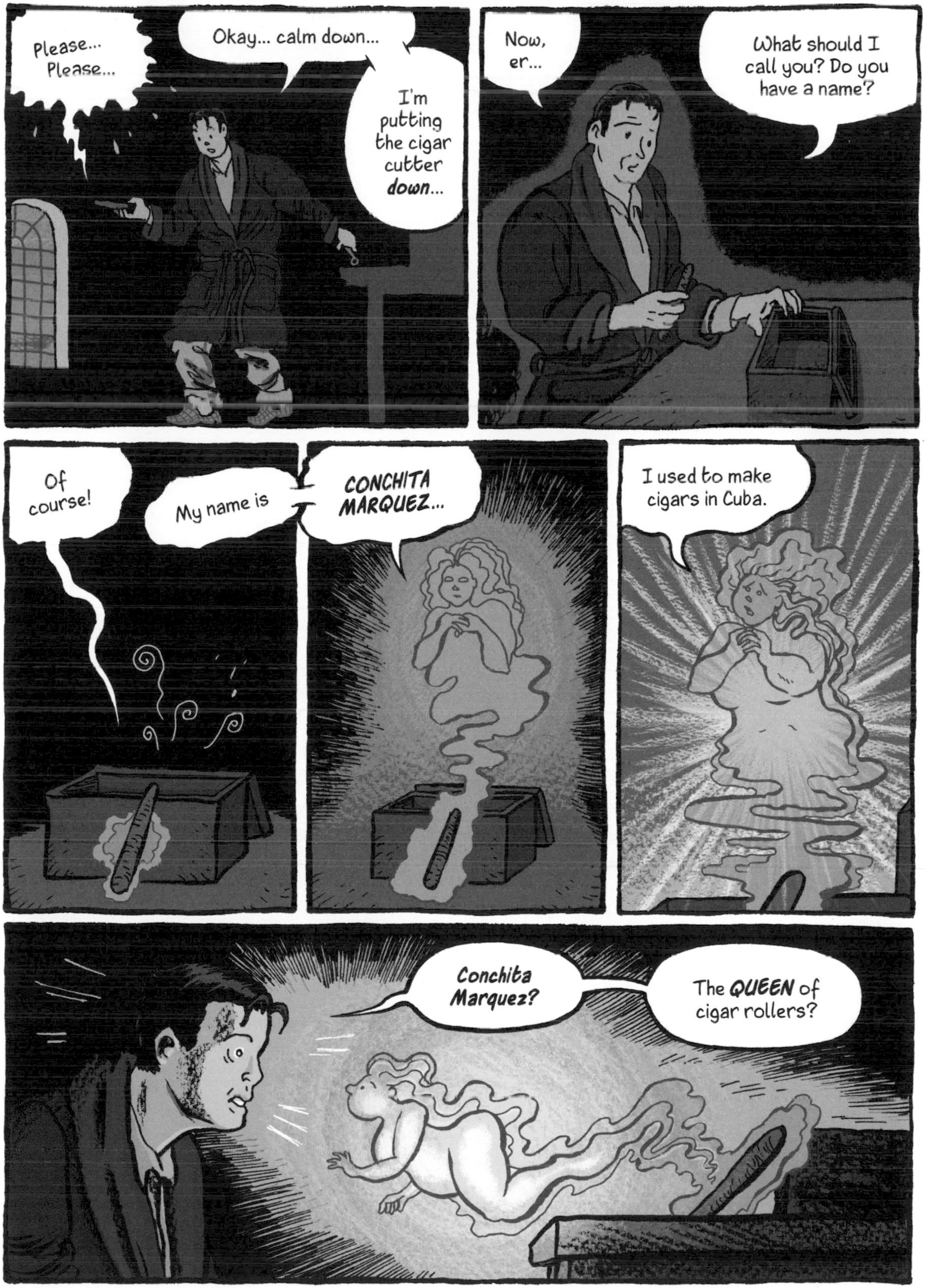
Please... Please...
Okay... calm down...
I'm putting the cigar cutter down...
Now, er...
What should I call you? Do you have a name?
Of course!
My name is
CONCHITA MARQUEZ...
I used to make cigars in Cuba.
Conchita Marquez?
The QUEEN of cigar rollers?

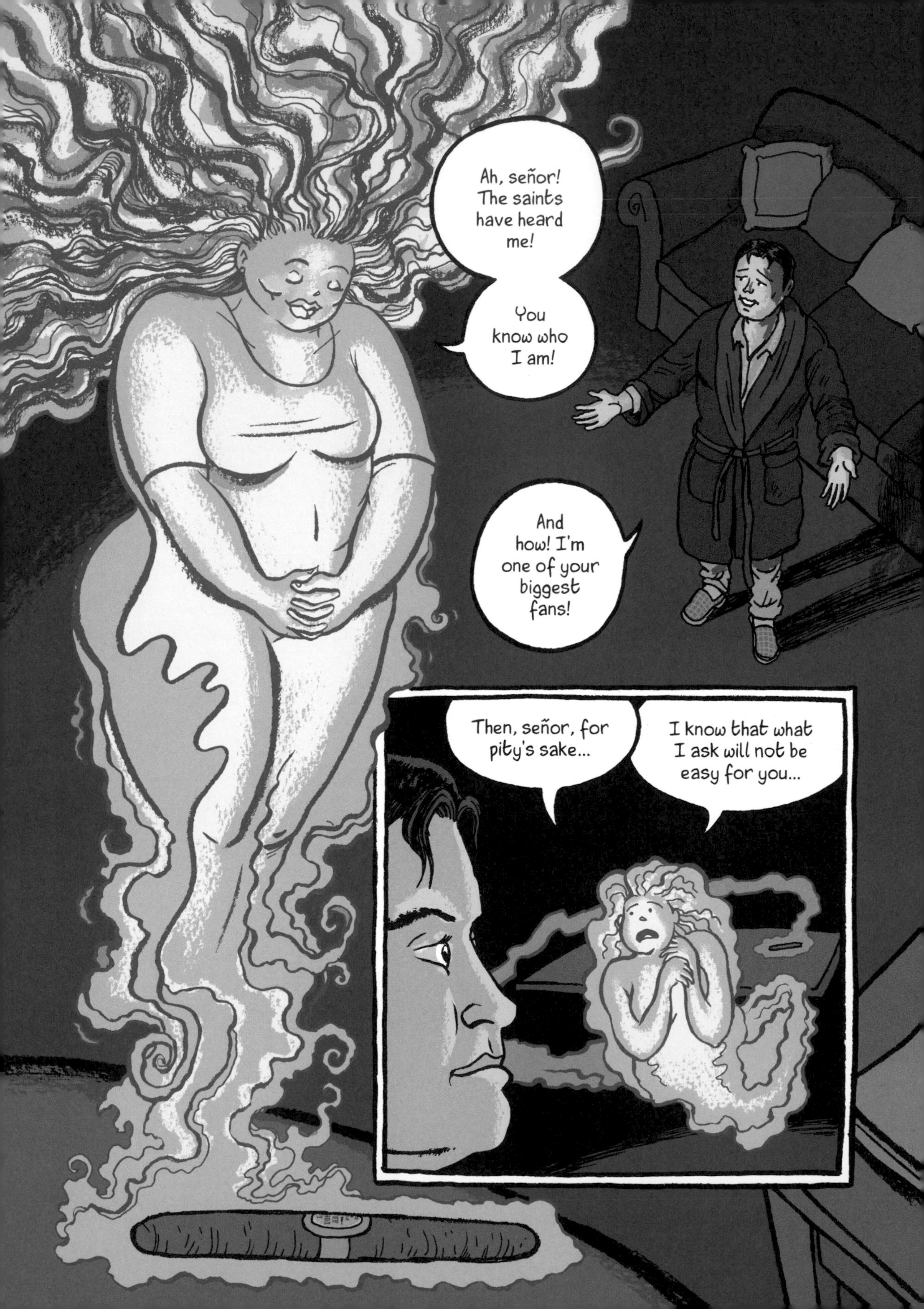
Ah, señor! The saints have heard me!
You know who I am!
And how! I'm one of your biggest fans!
Then, señor, for pity's sake...
I know that what I ask will not be easy for you...

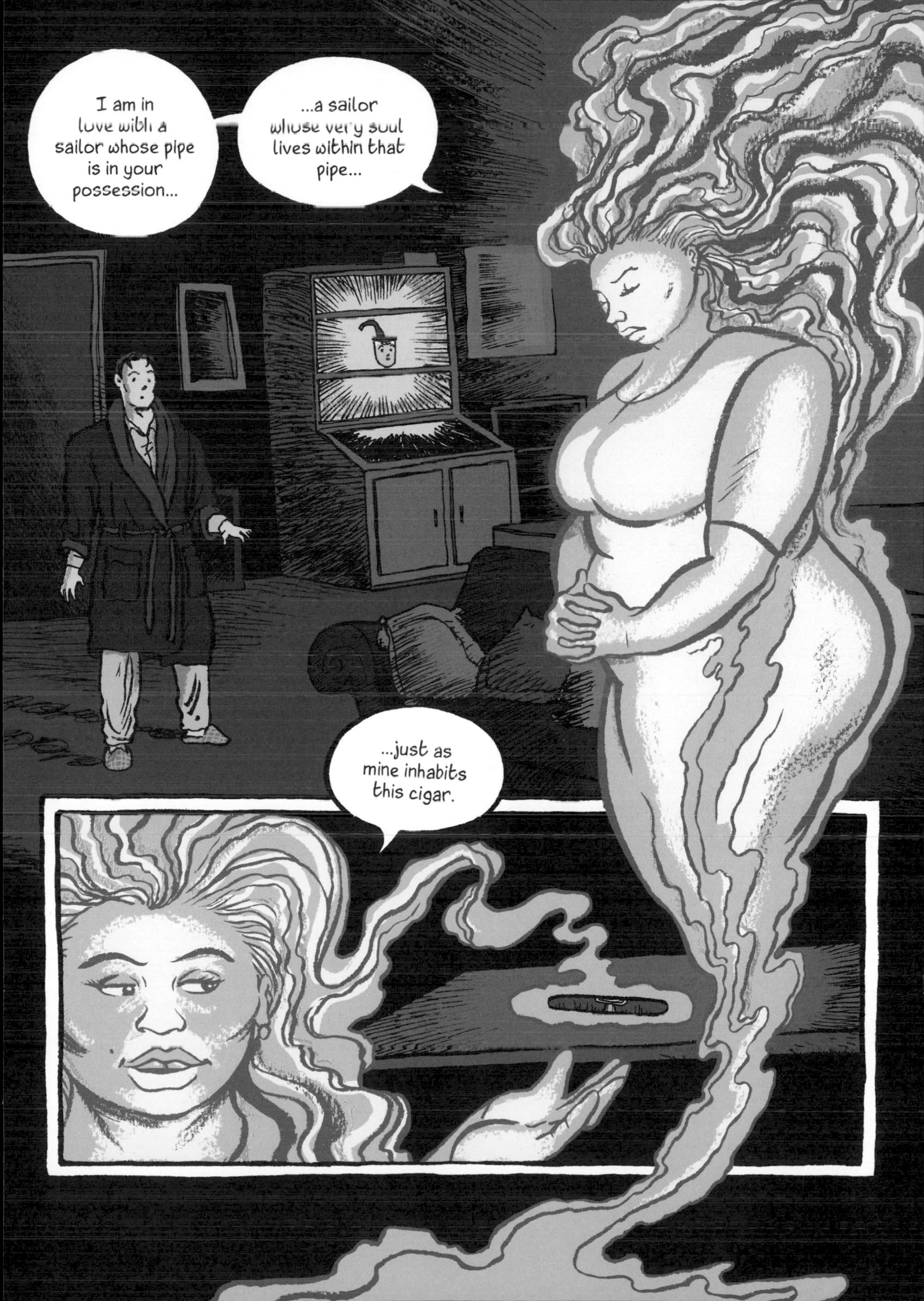
I am in love with a sailor whose pipe is in your possession...
...a sailor whose very soul lives within that pipe...
...just as mine inhabits this cigar.

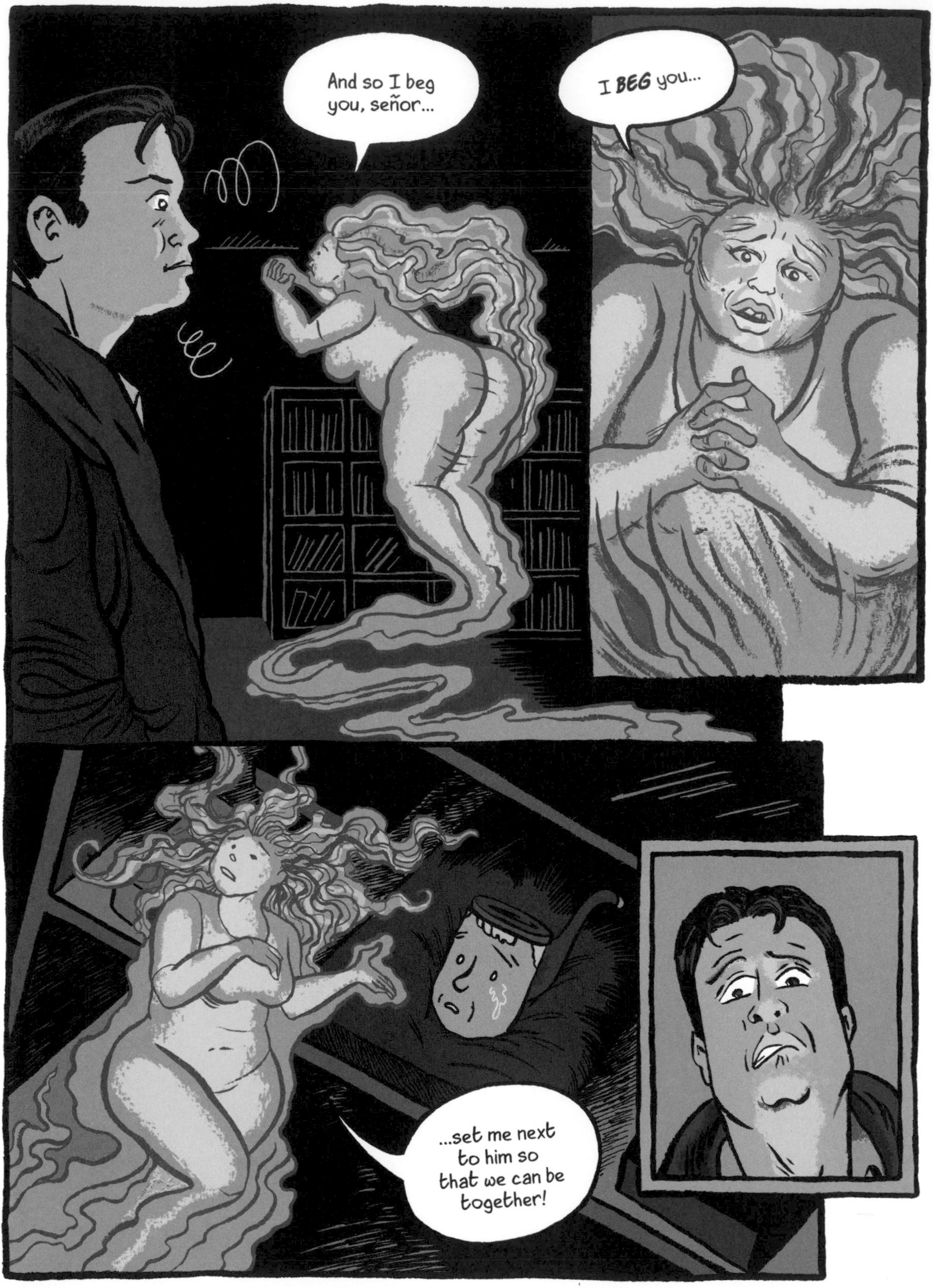
And so I beg you, señor...
I **BEG** you...
...set me next to him so that we can be together!

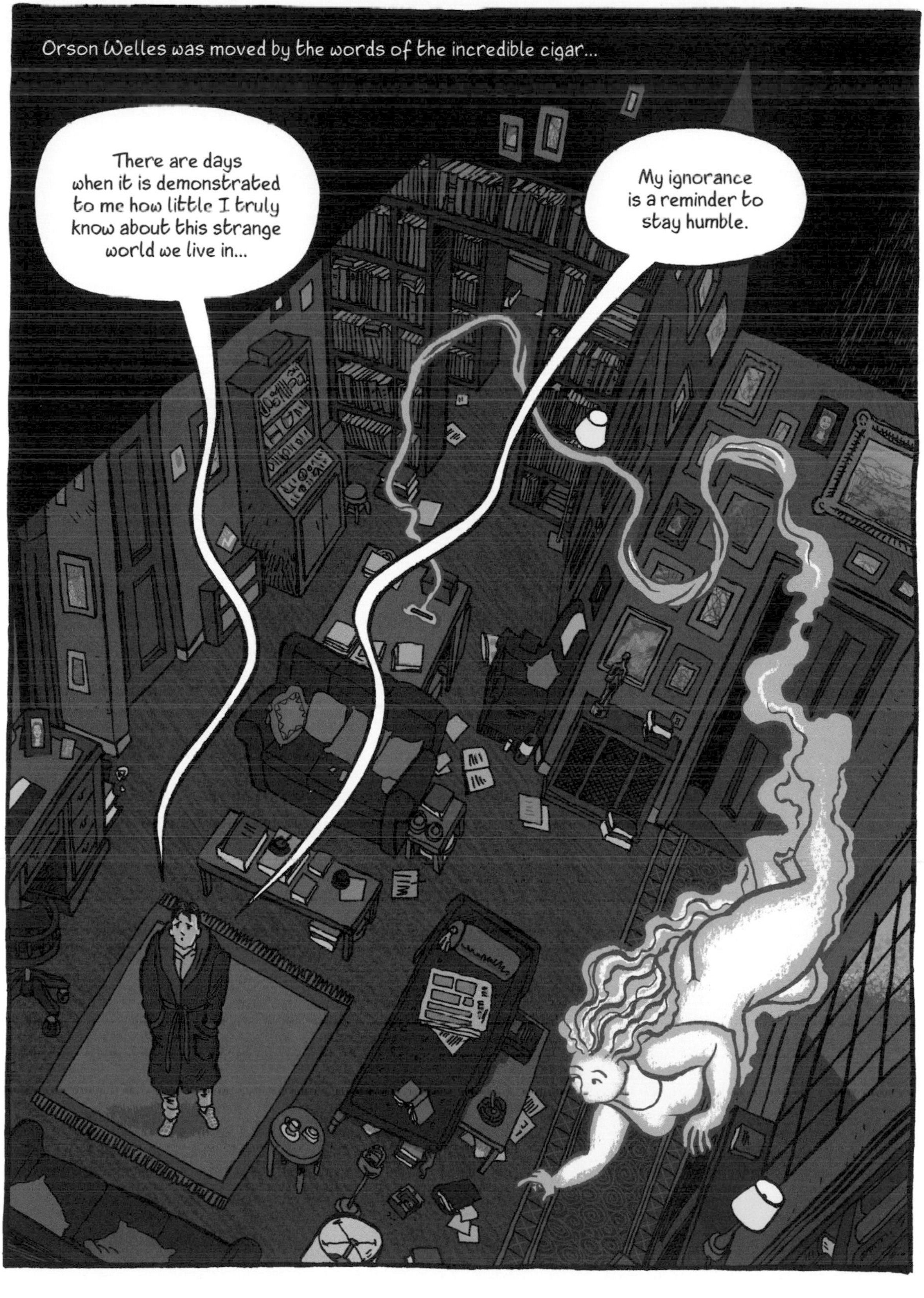
Orson Welles was moved by the words of the incredible cigar...
There are days when it is demonstrated to me how little I truly know about this strange world we live in...
My ignorance is a reminder to stay humble.

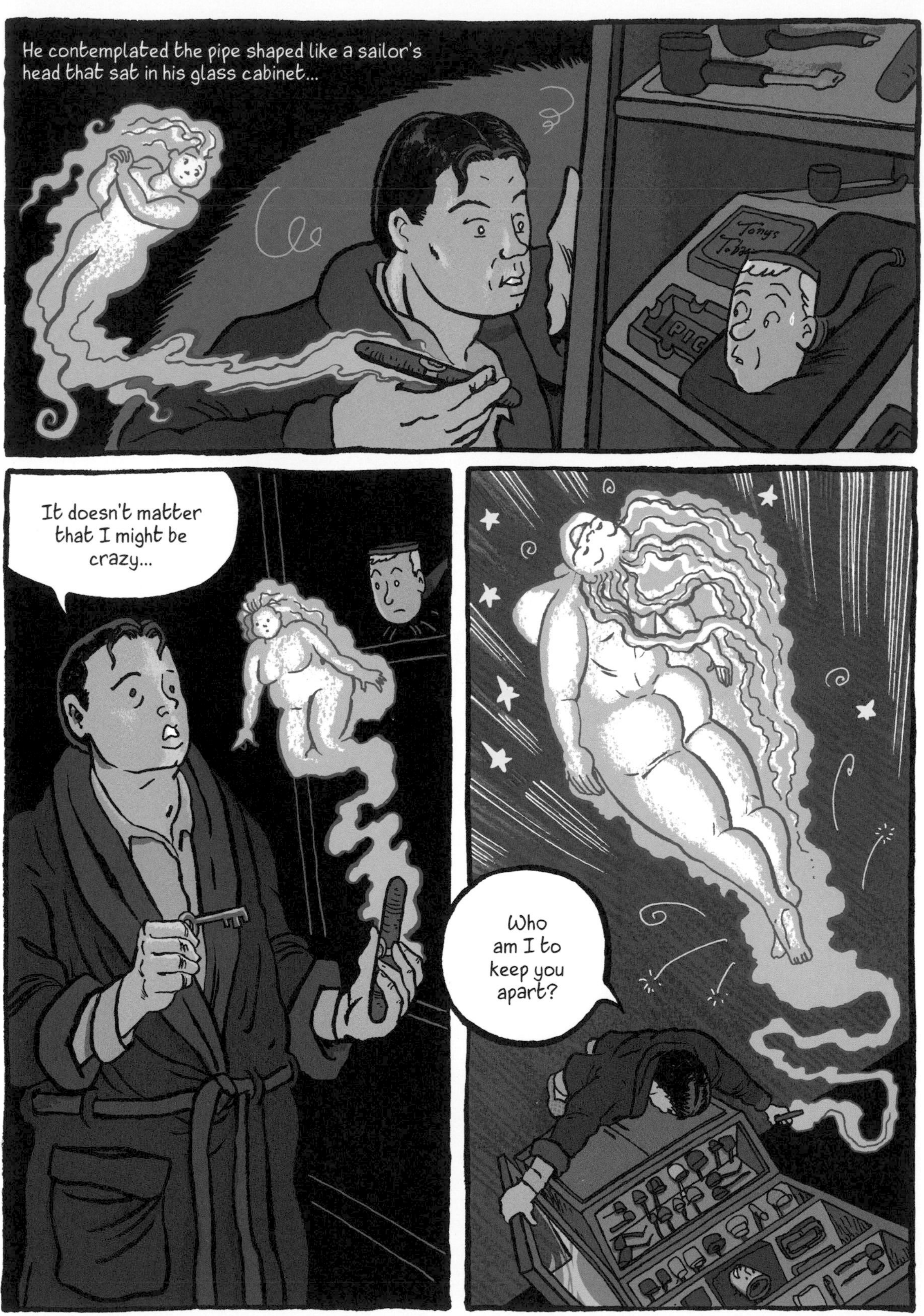
He contemplated the pipe shaped like a sailor's head that sat in his glass cabinet...
It doesn't matter that I might be crazy...
Who am I to keep you apart?

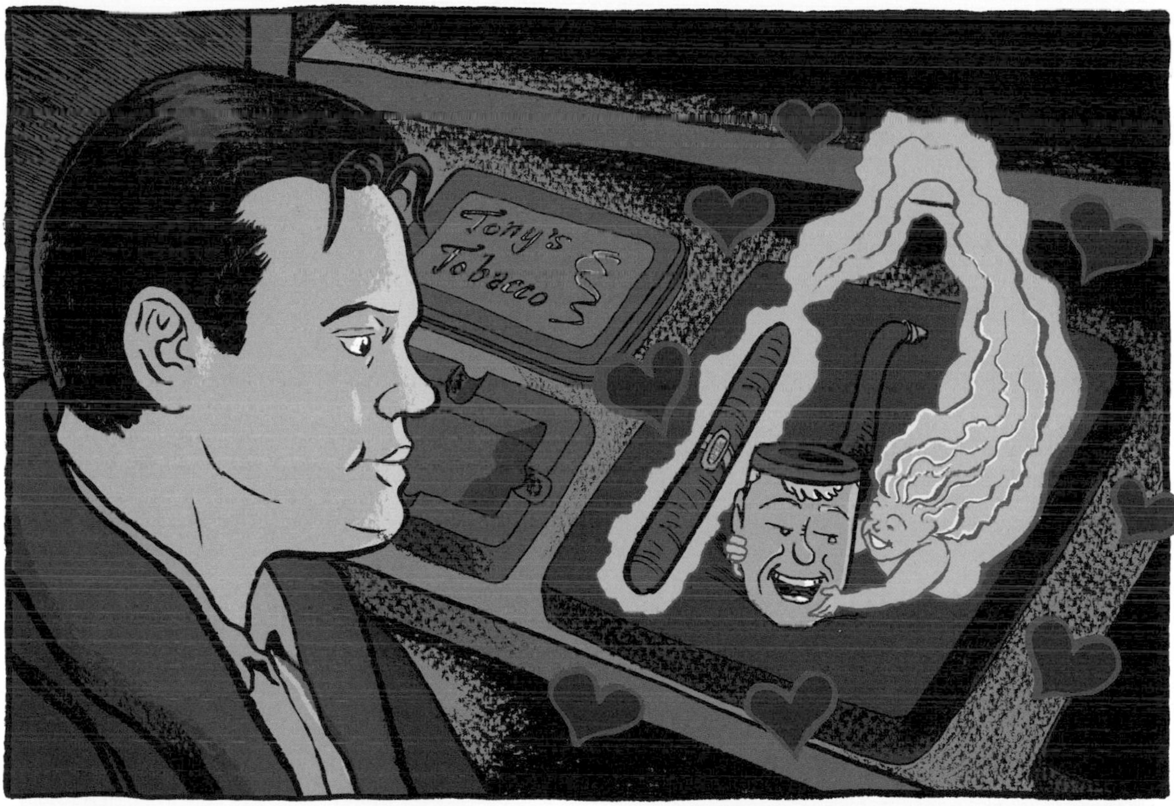
Tony's Tobacco

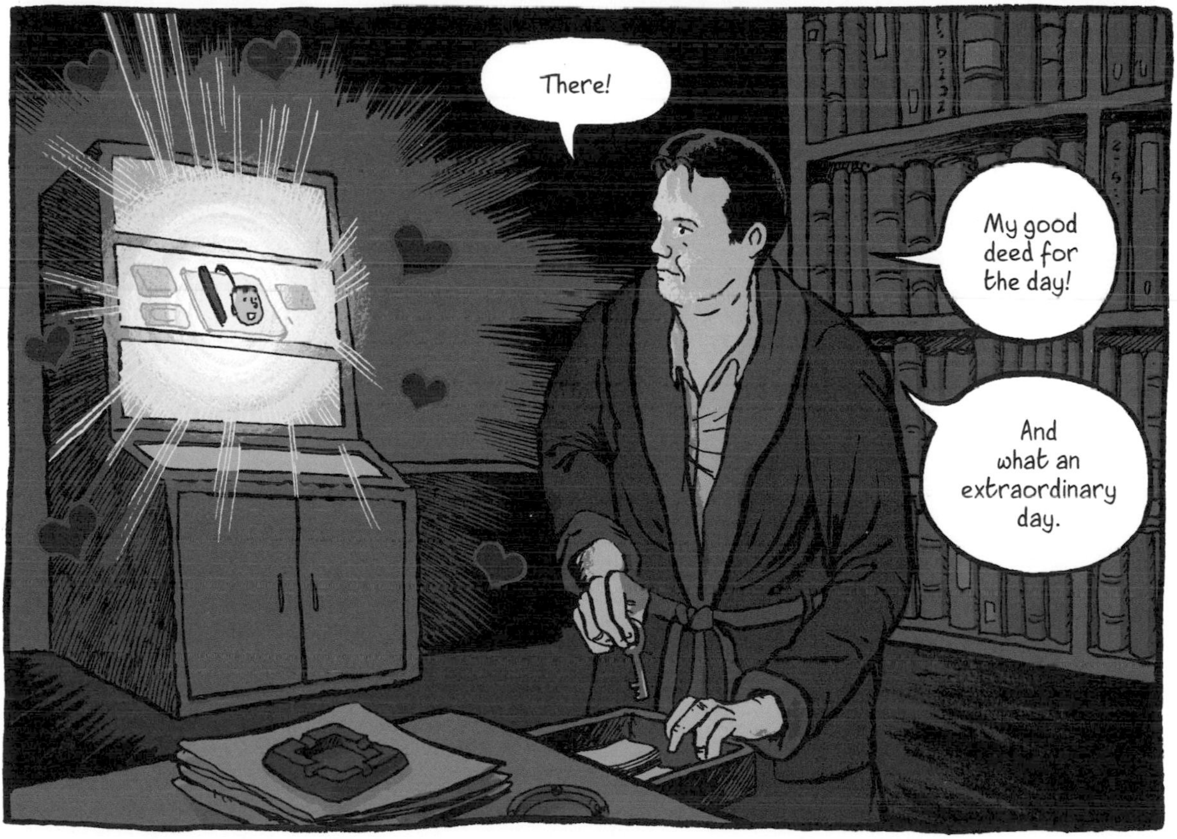
There!
My good deed for the day!
And what an extraordinary day.

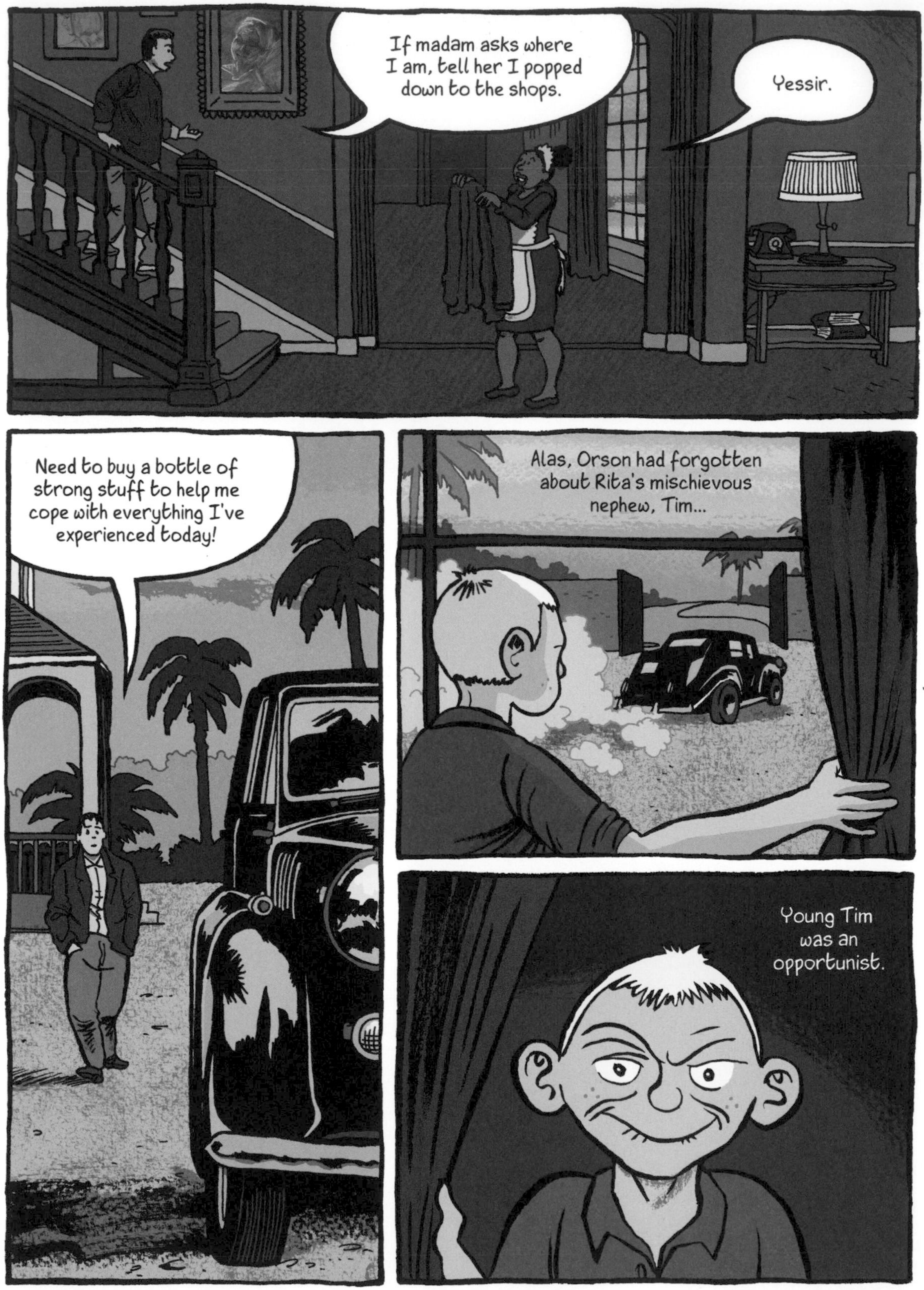
If madam asks where I am, tell her I popped down to the shops.
Yessir.
Need to buy a bottle of strong stuff to help me cope with everything I've experienced today!
Alas, Orson had forgotten about Rita's mischievous nephew, Tim...
Young Tim was an opportunist.

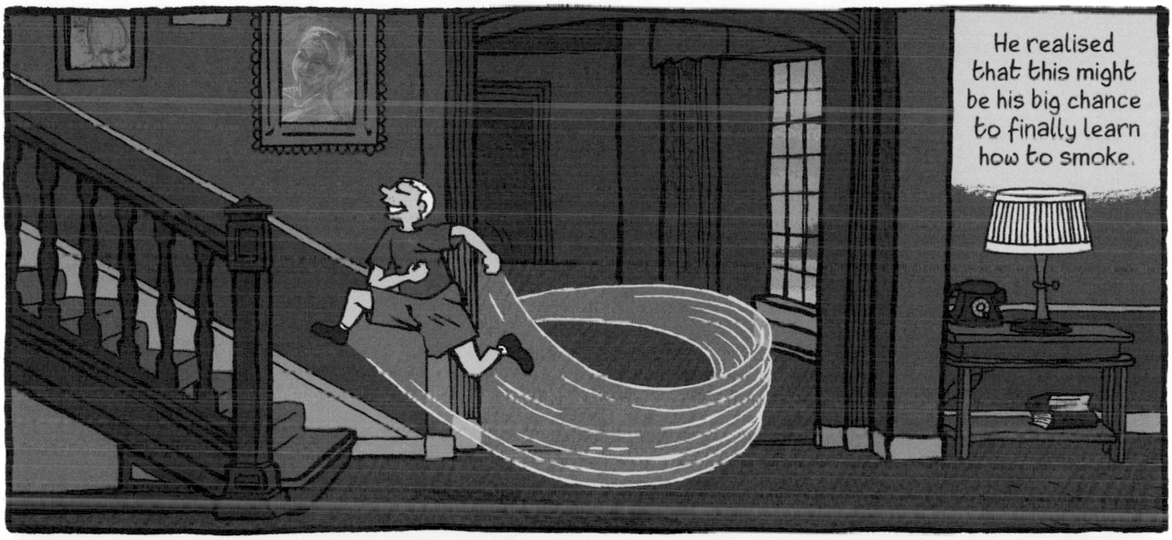
He realised that this might be his big chance to finally learn how to smoke.
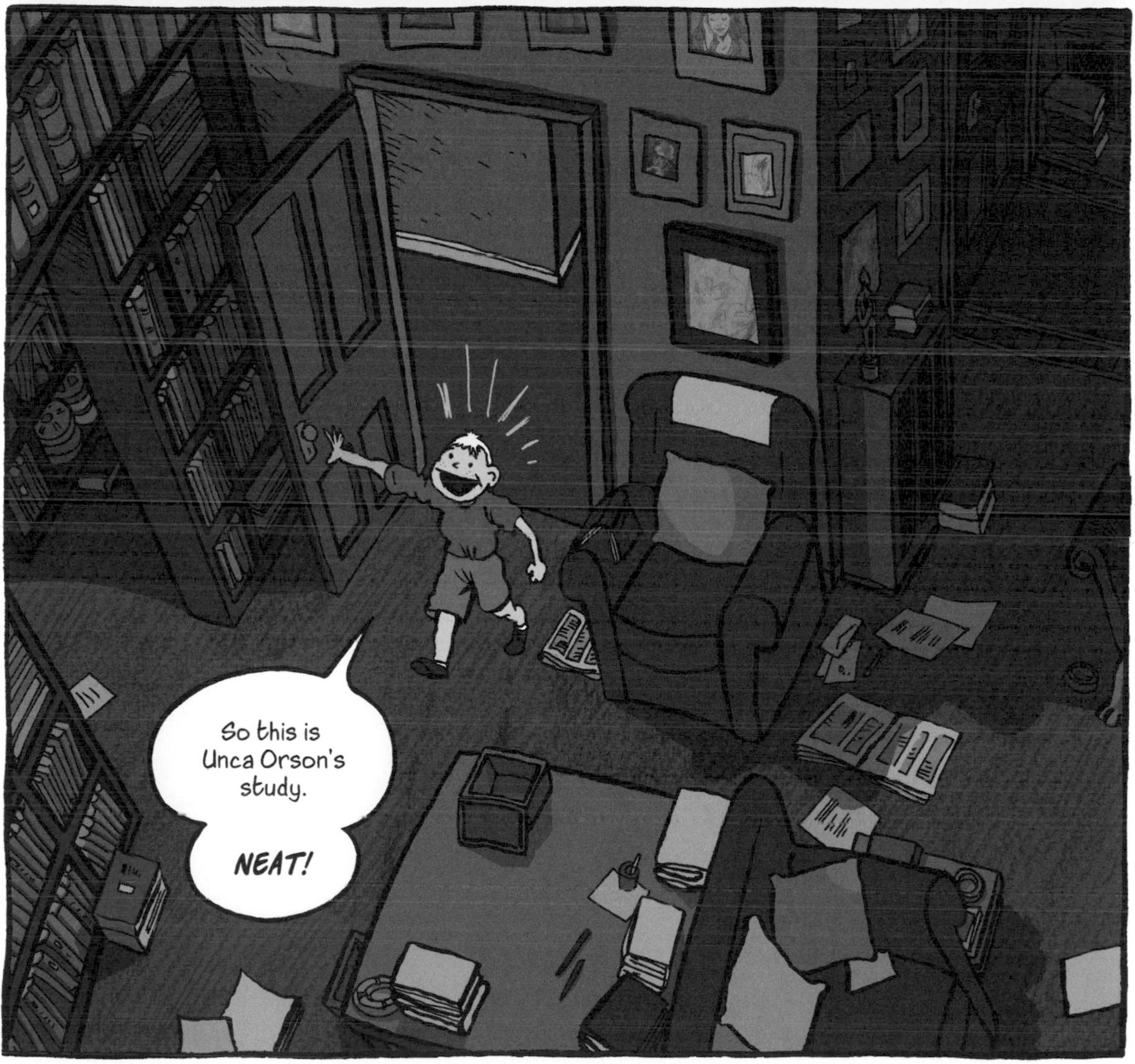
So this is Unca Orson's study.
NEAT!

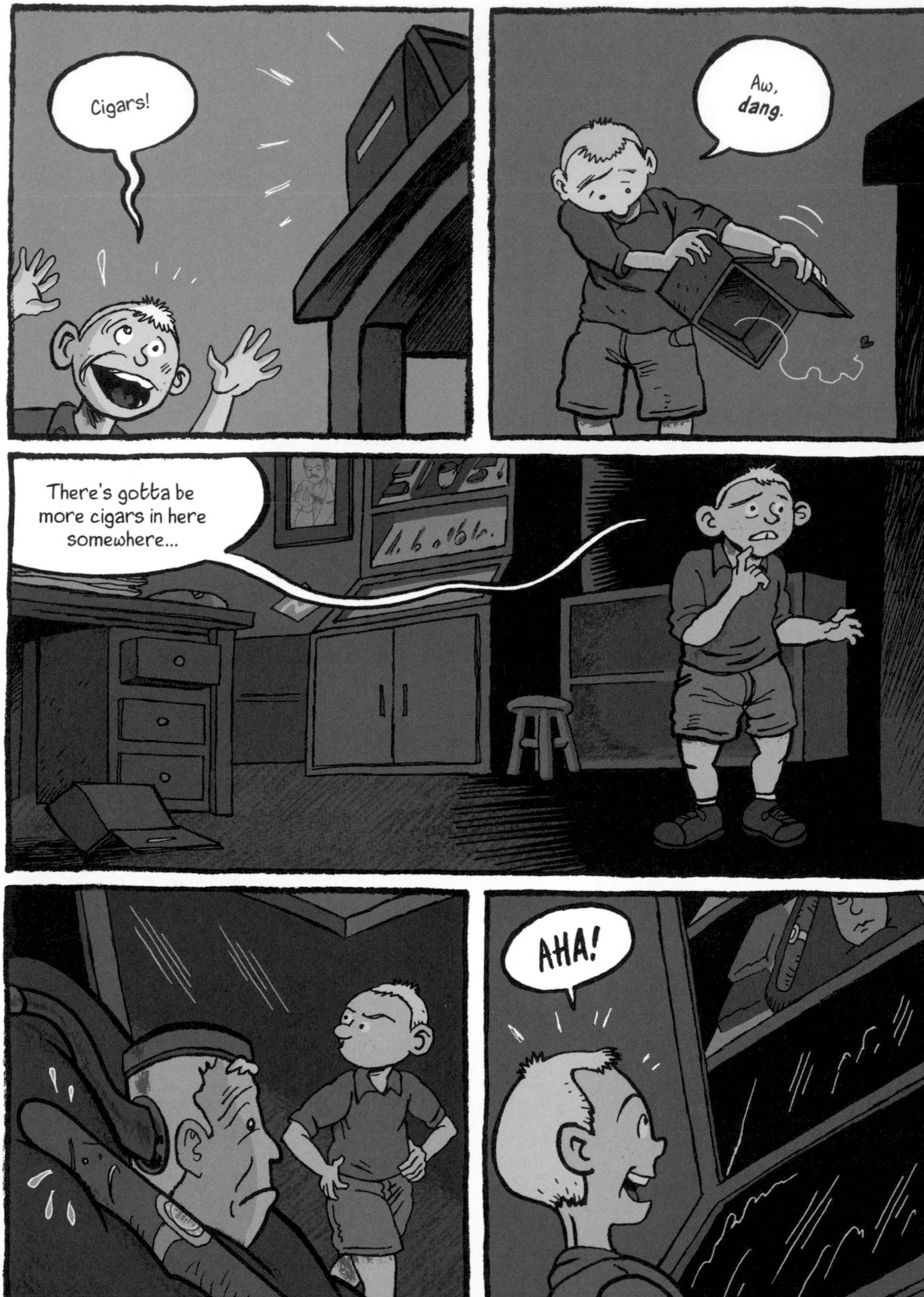
Cigars!
Aw, dang.
There's gotta be more cigars in here somewhere...
AHA!

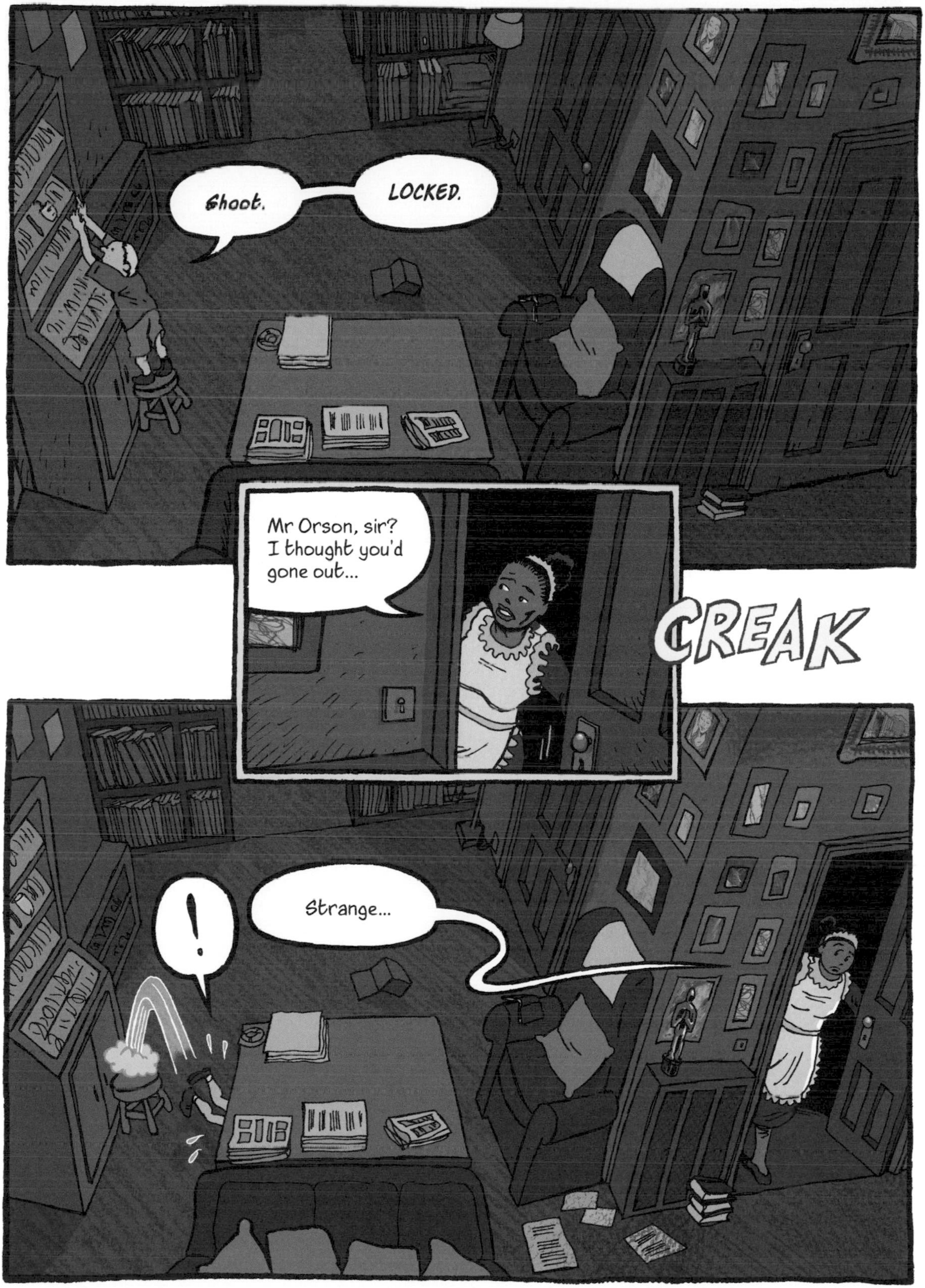
Shoot.
LOCKED.
Mr Orson, sir? I thought you'd gone out...
CREAK
!
Strange...

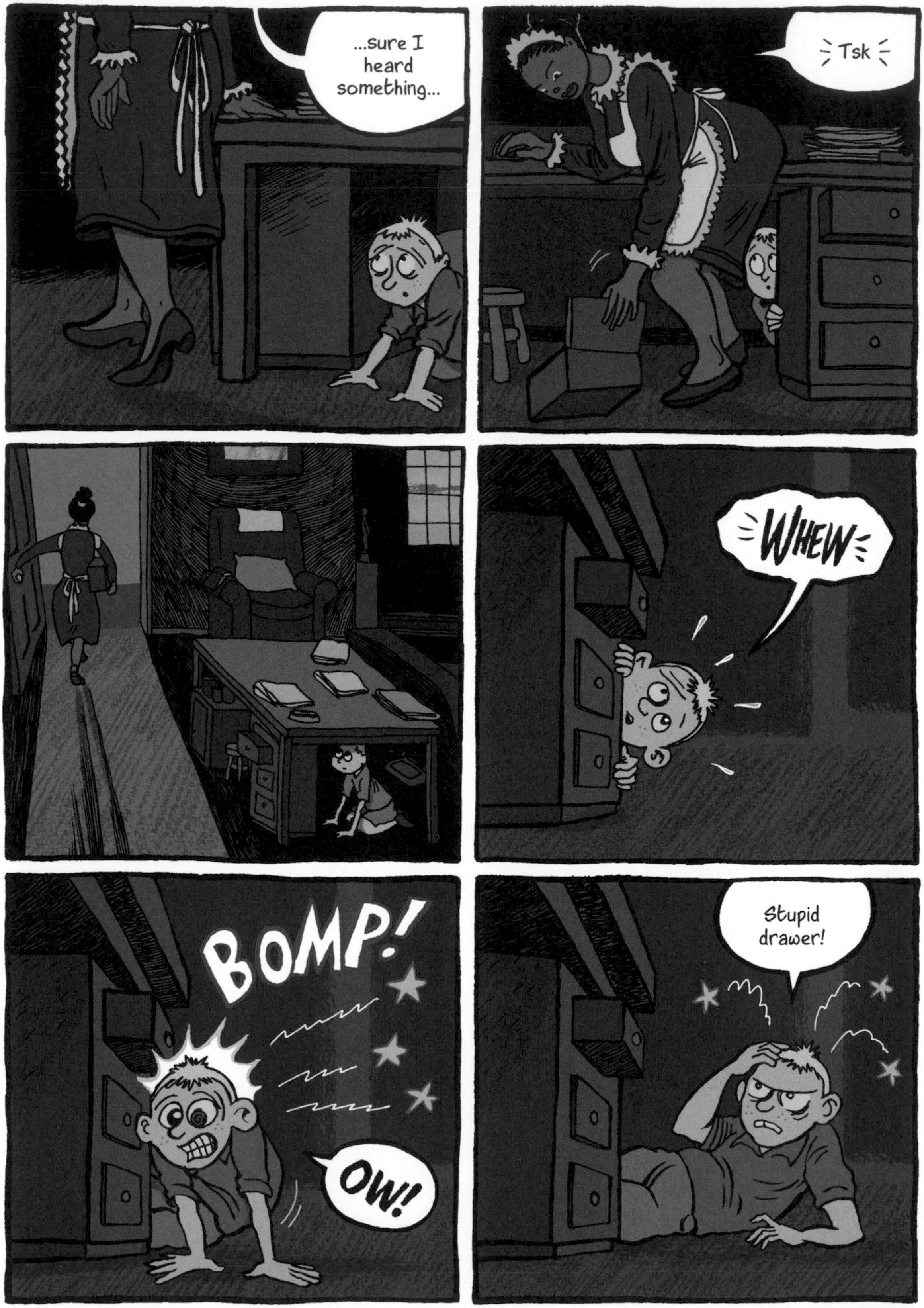
...sure I heard something...
Tsk
WHEW
BOMP!
OW!
Stupid drawer!

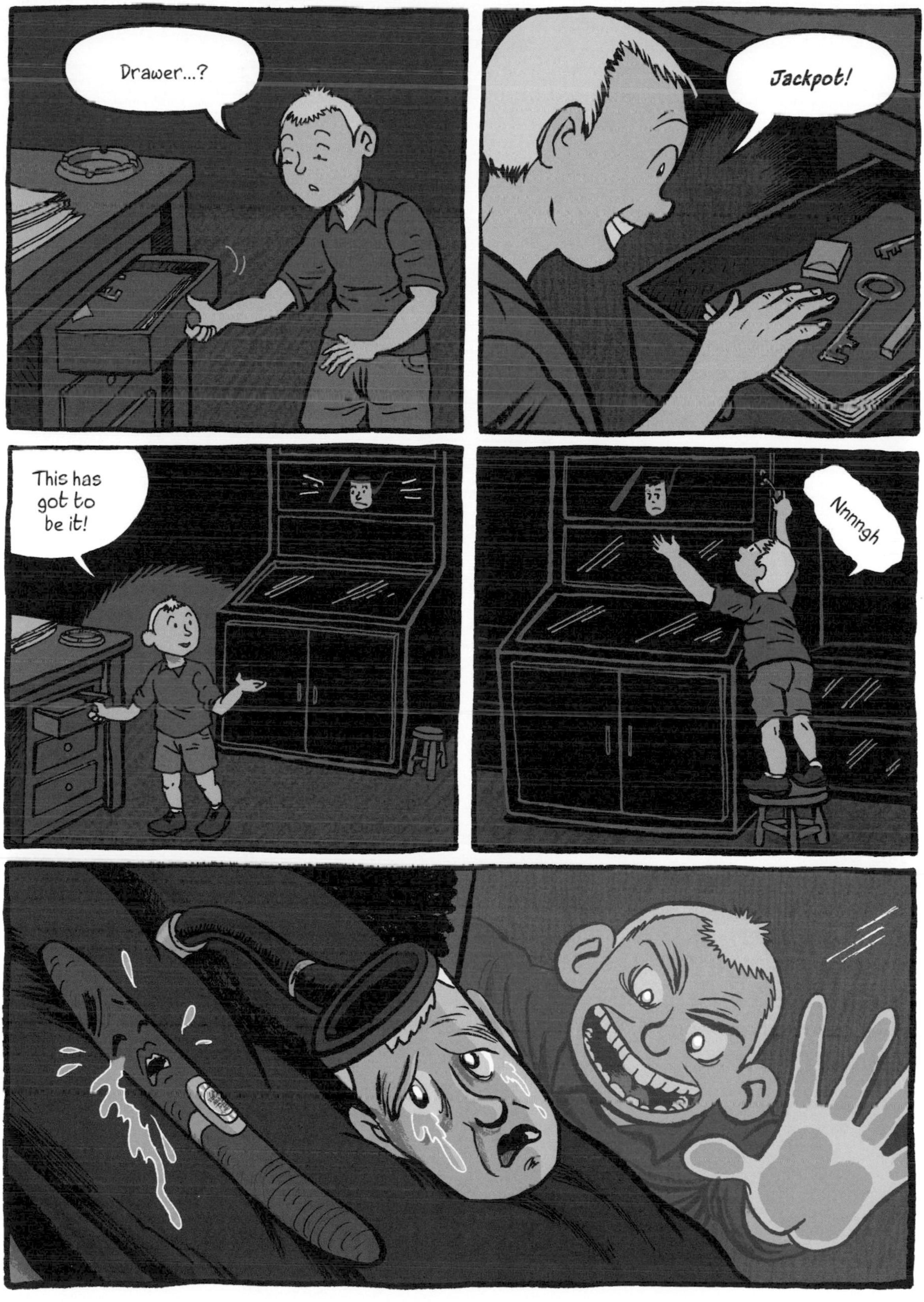
Drawer...?
Jackpot!
This has got to be it!
Nnnngh

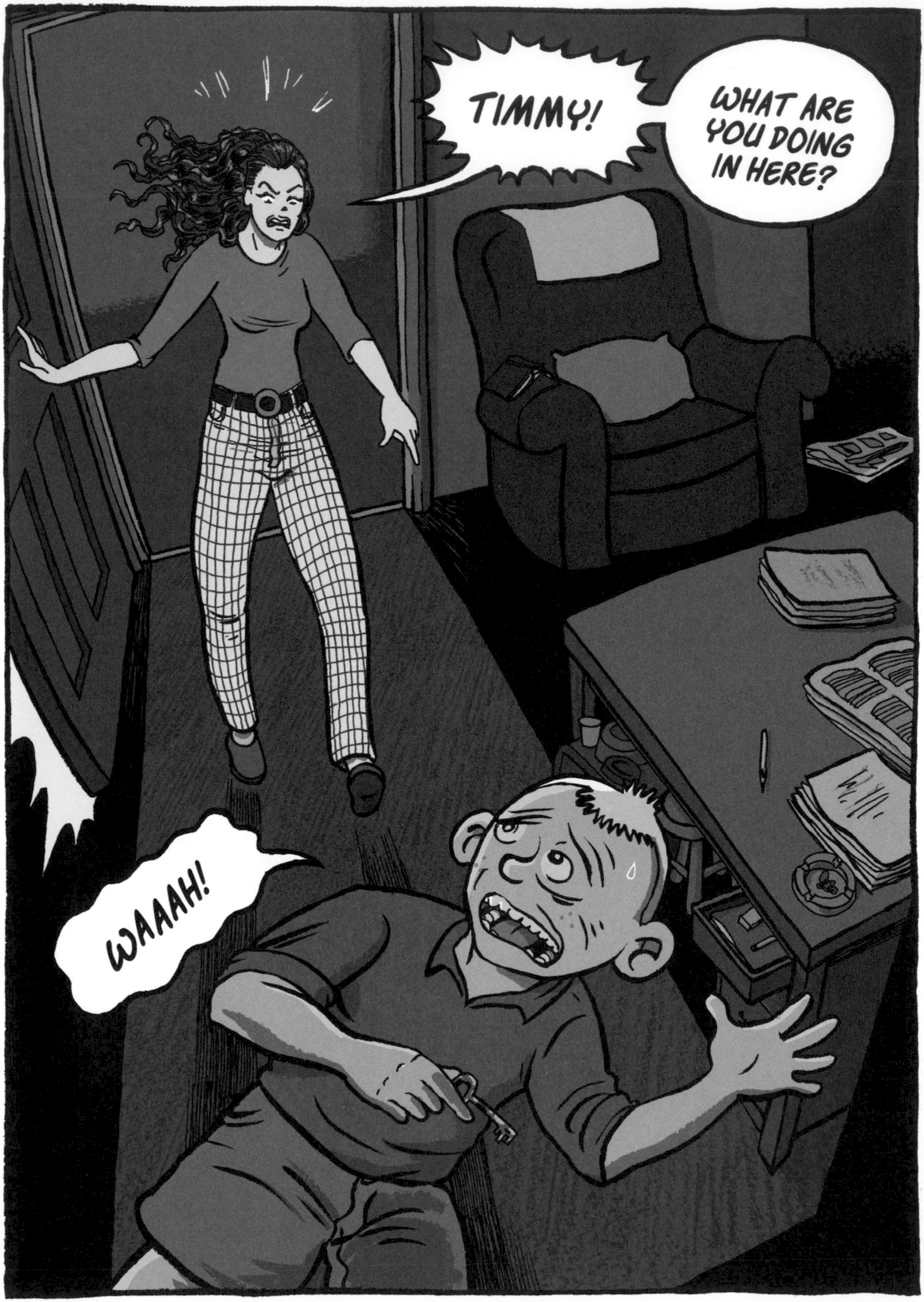
TIMMY!
WHAT ARE YOU DOING IN HERE?
WAAAH!

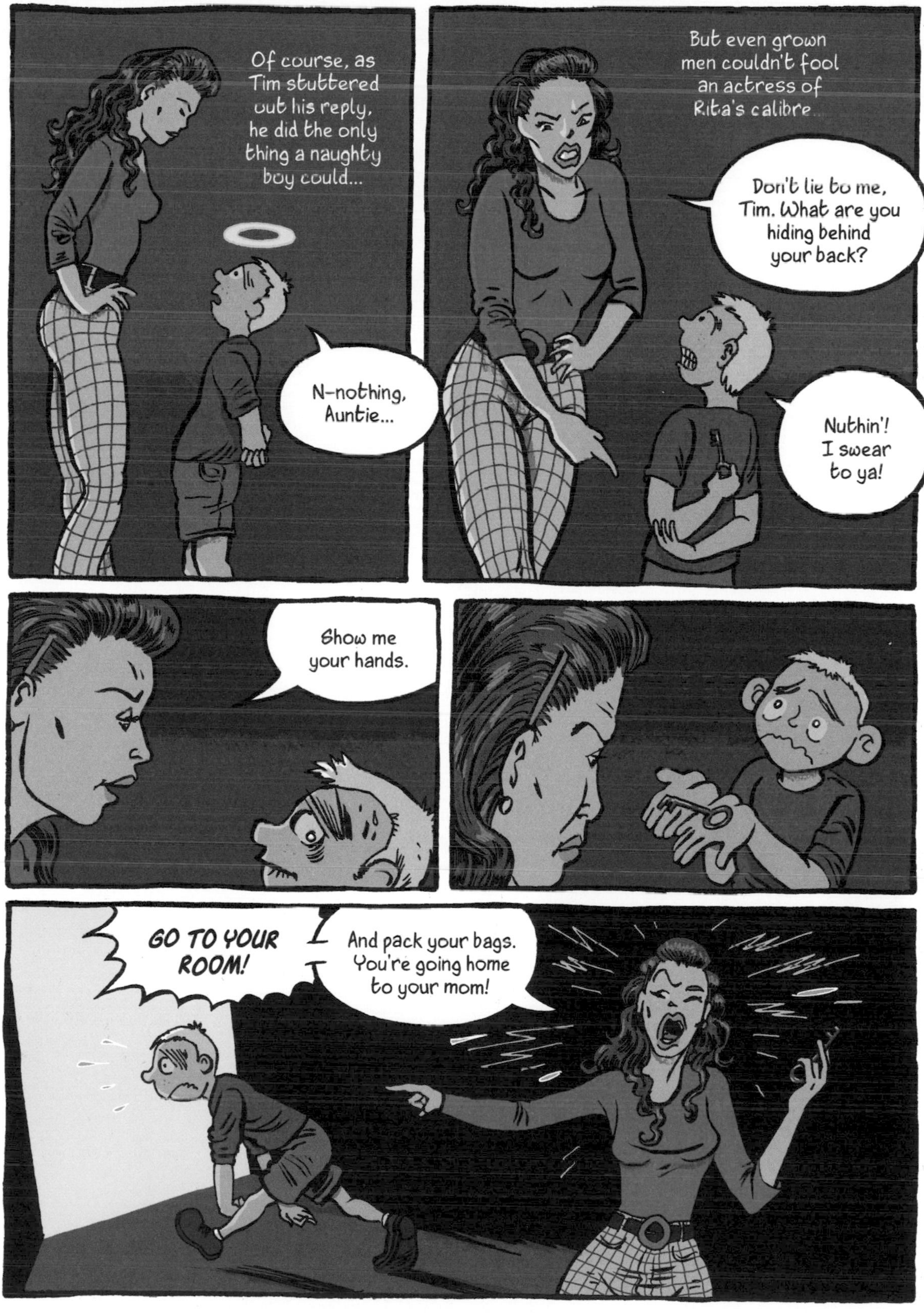
Of course, as Tim stuttered out his reply, he did the only thing a naughty boy could...
N-nothing, Auntie...
But even grown men couldn't fool an actress of Rita's calibre...
Don't lie to me, Tim. What are you hiding behind your back?
Nuthin'! I swear to ya!
Show me your hands.
GO TO YOUR ROOM!
And pack your bags. You're going home to your mom!

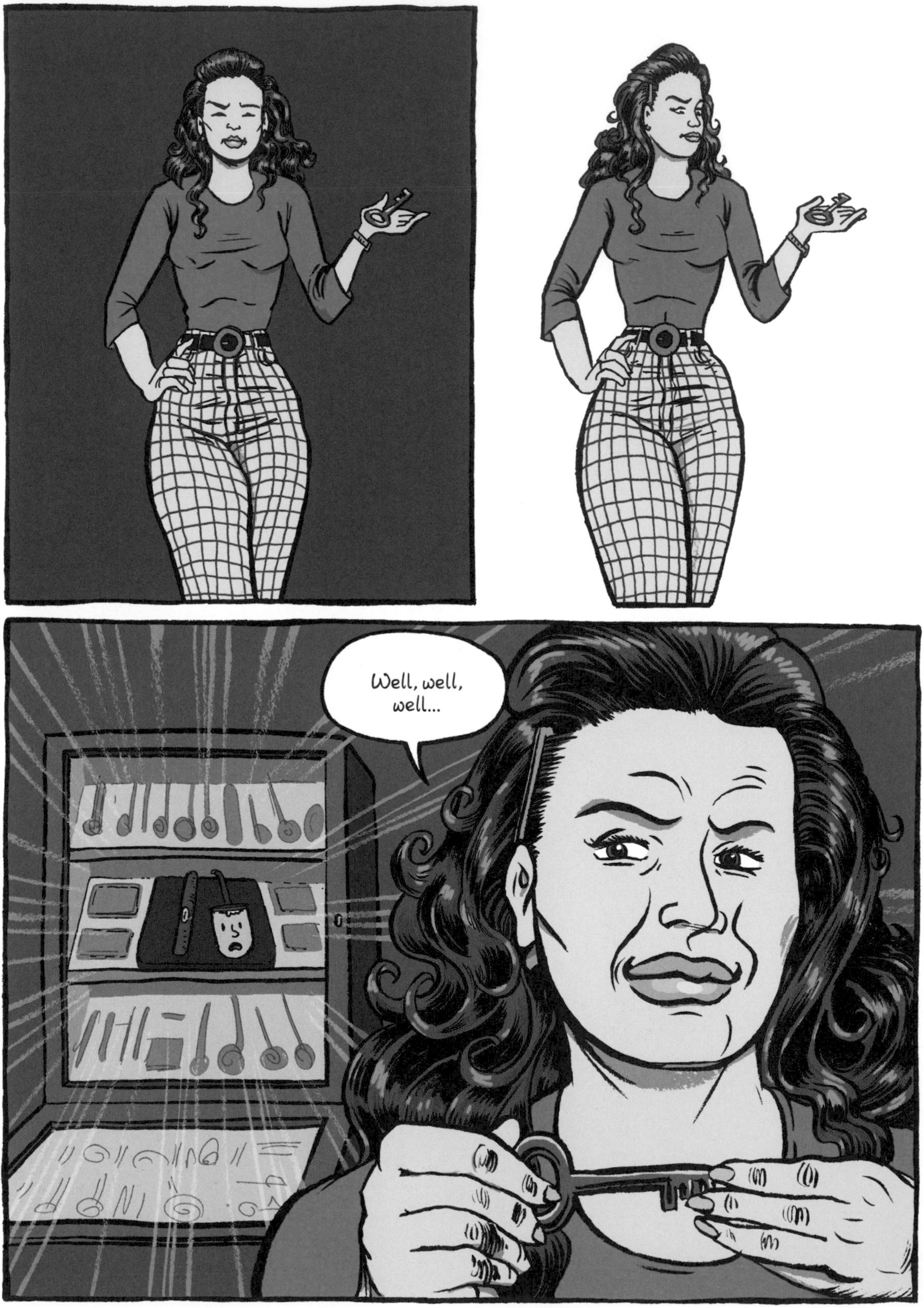
Well, well, well...

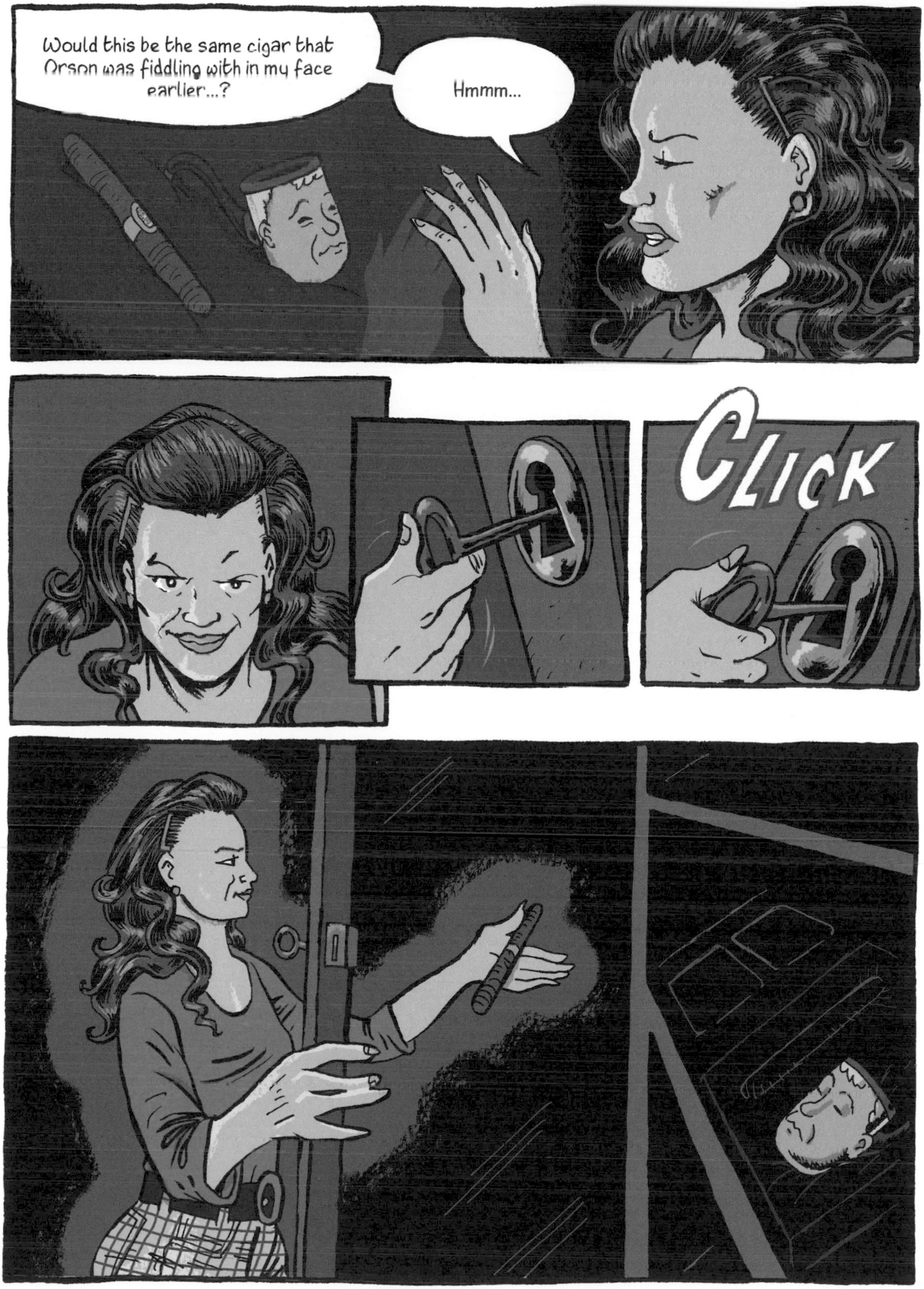
Would this be the same cigar that Orson was fiddling with in my face earlier...?
Hmmm...
CLICK

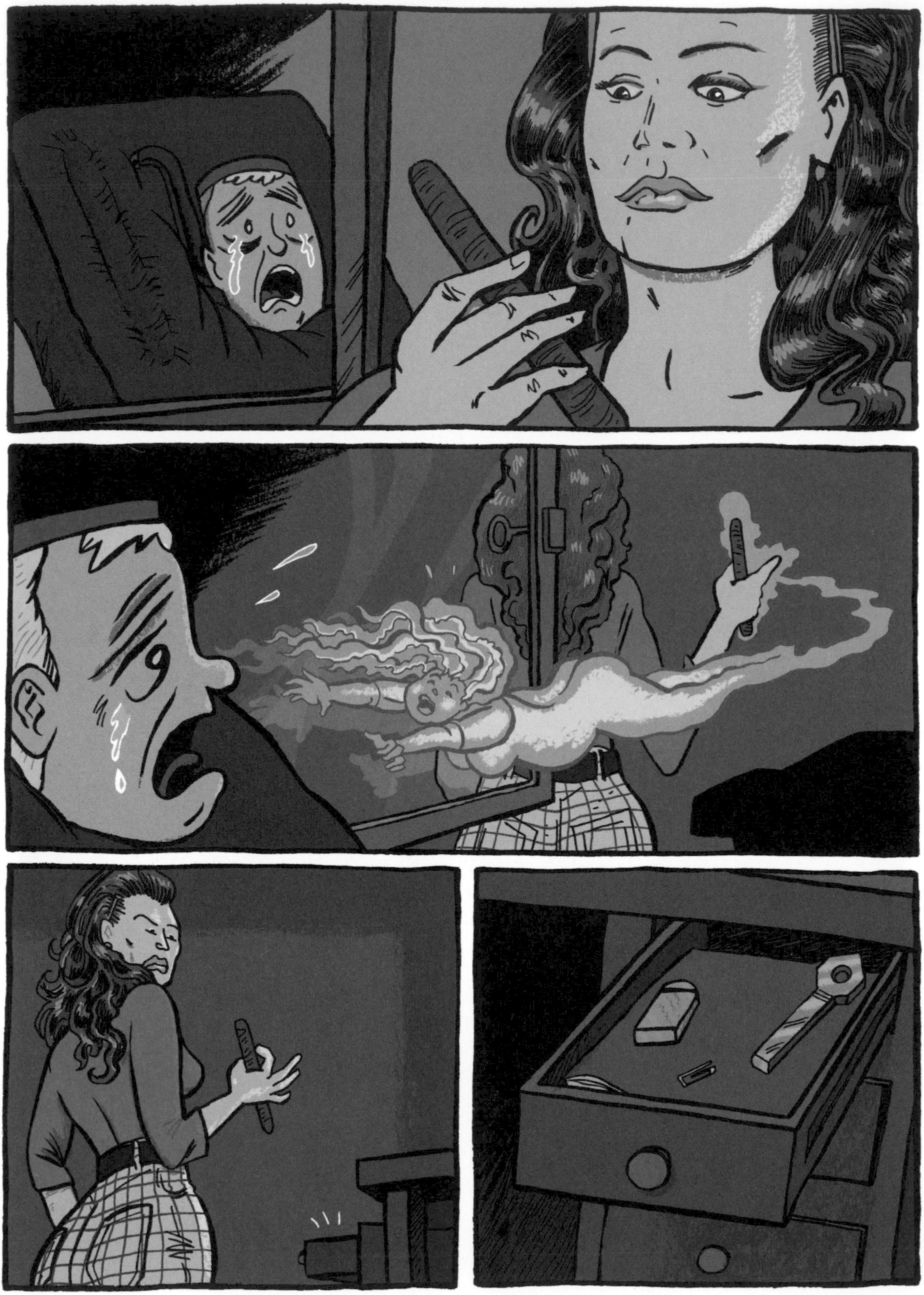

Impervious to its desperate squeals as she cut off its head...

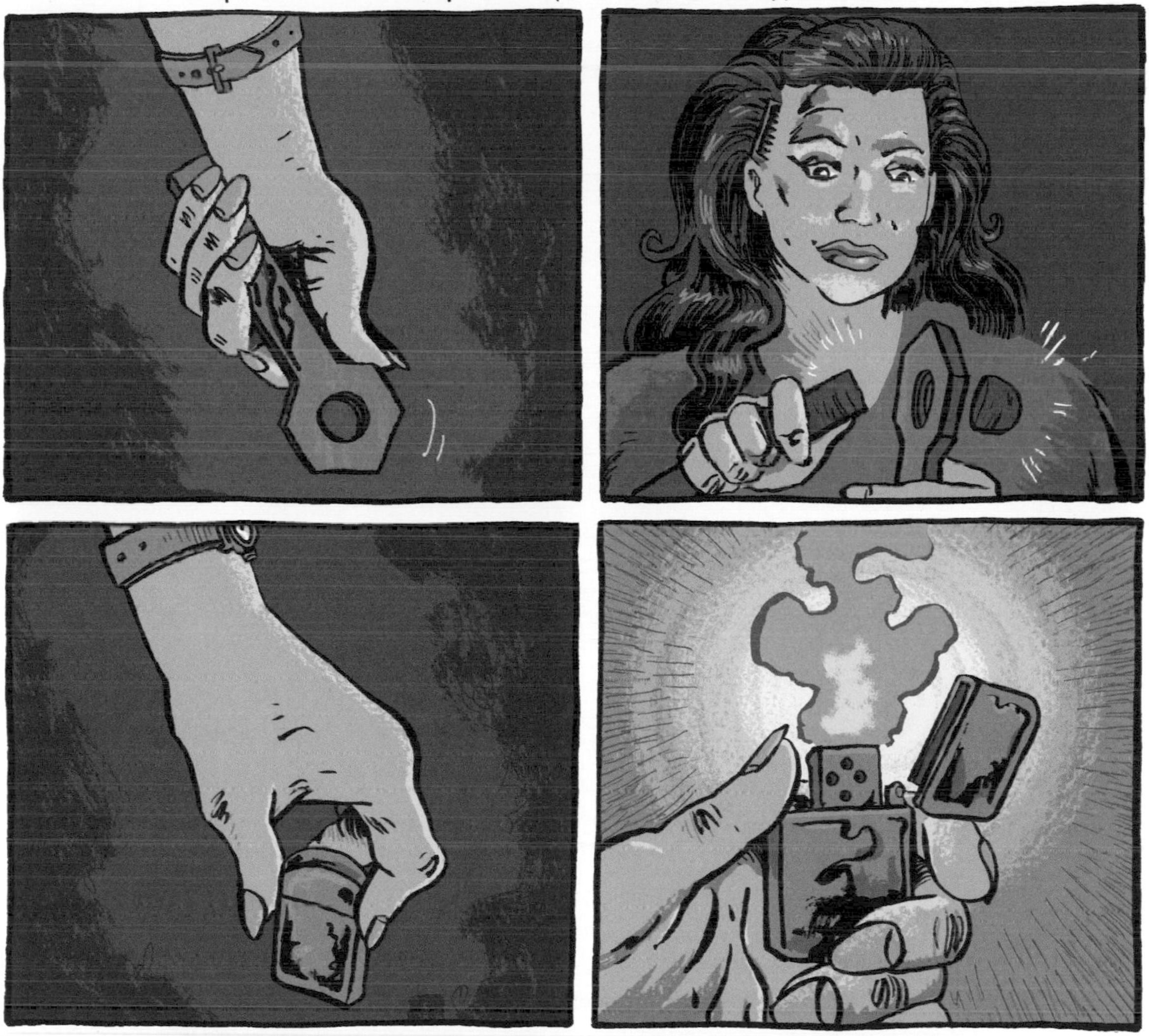

...Rita Hayworth ran the lighter's flame up and down the cigar's body to heat it...

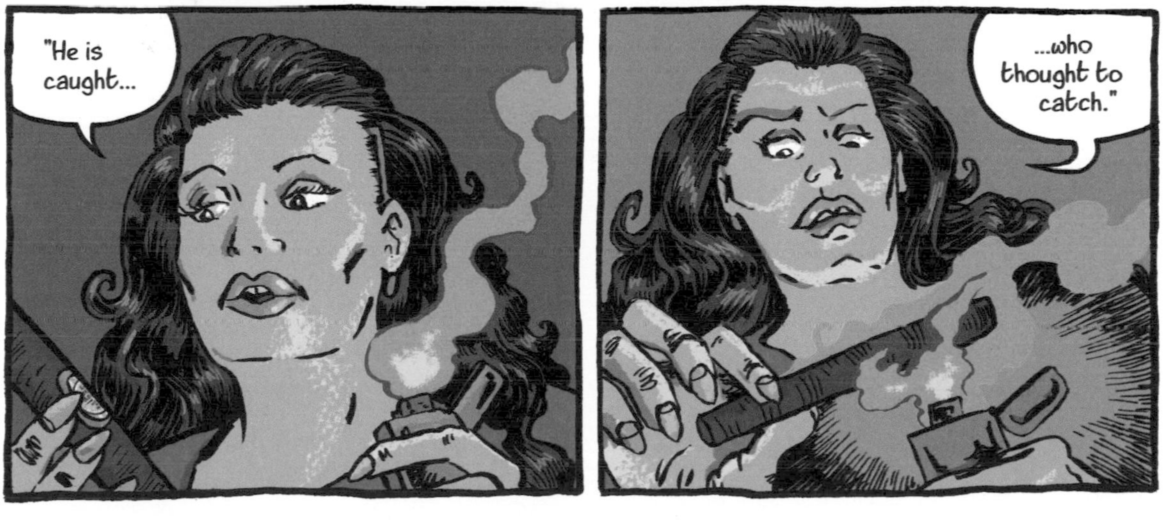
"He is caught...
...who thought to catch."

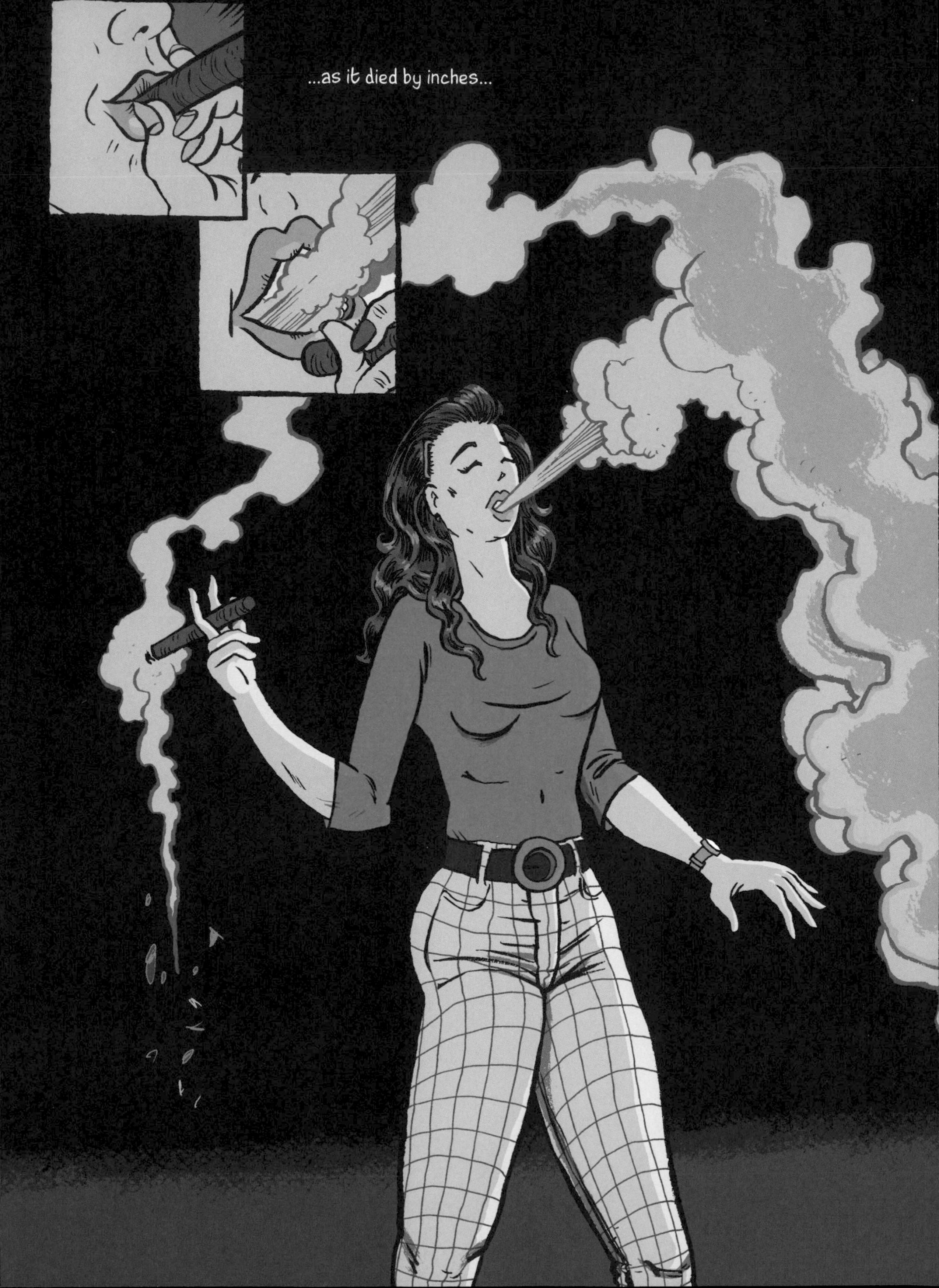
...as it died by inches...

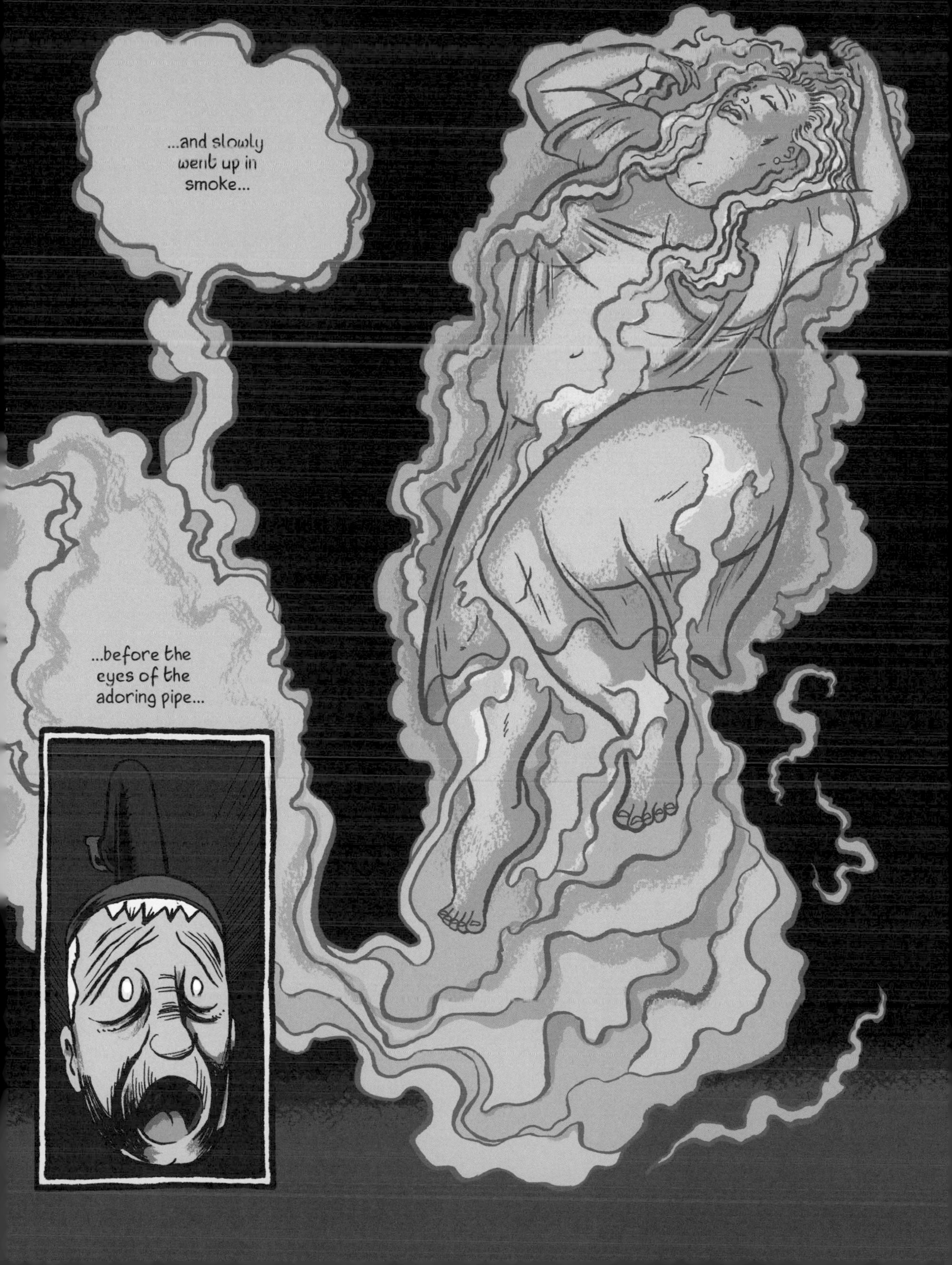
...and slowly went up in smoke...
...before the eyes of the adoring pipe...

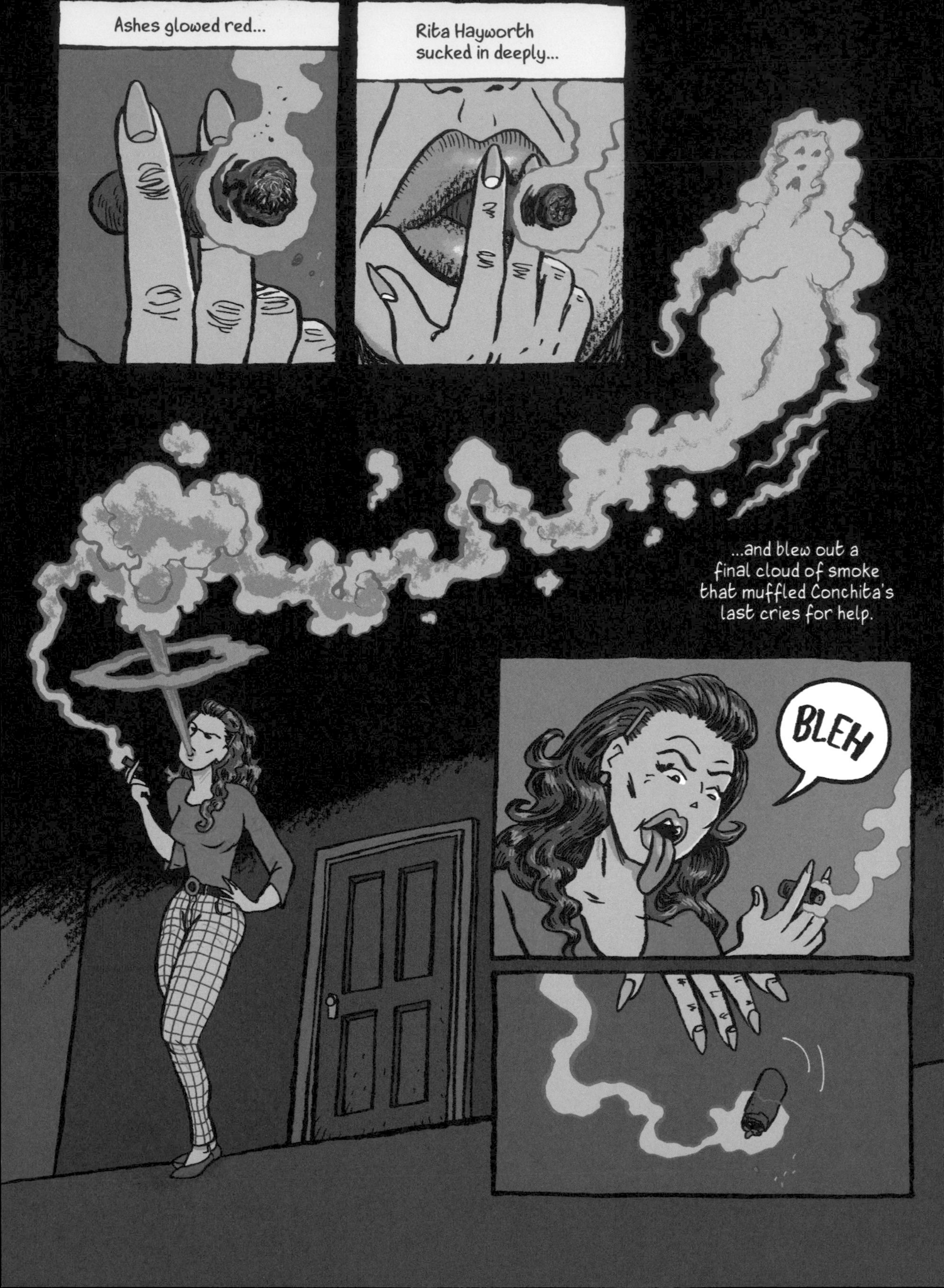
Ashes glowed red...
Rita Hayworth sucked in deeply...
...and blew out a final cloud of smoke that muffled Conchita's last cries for help.
BLEH

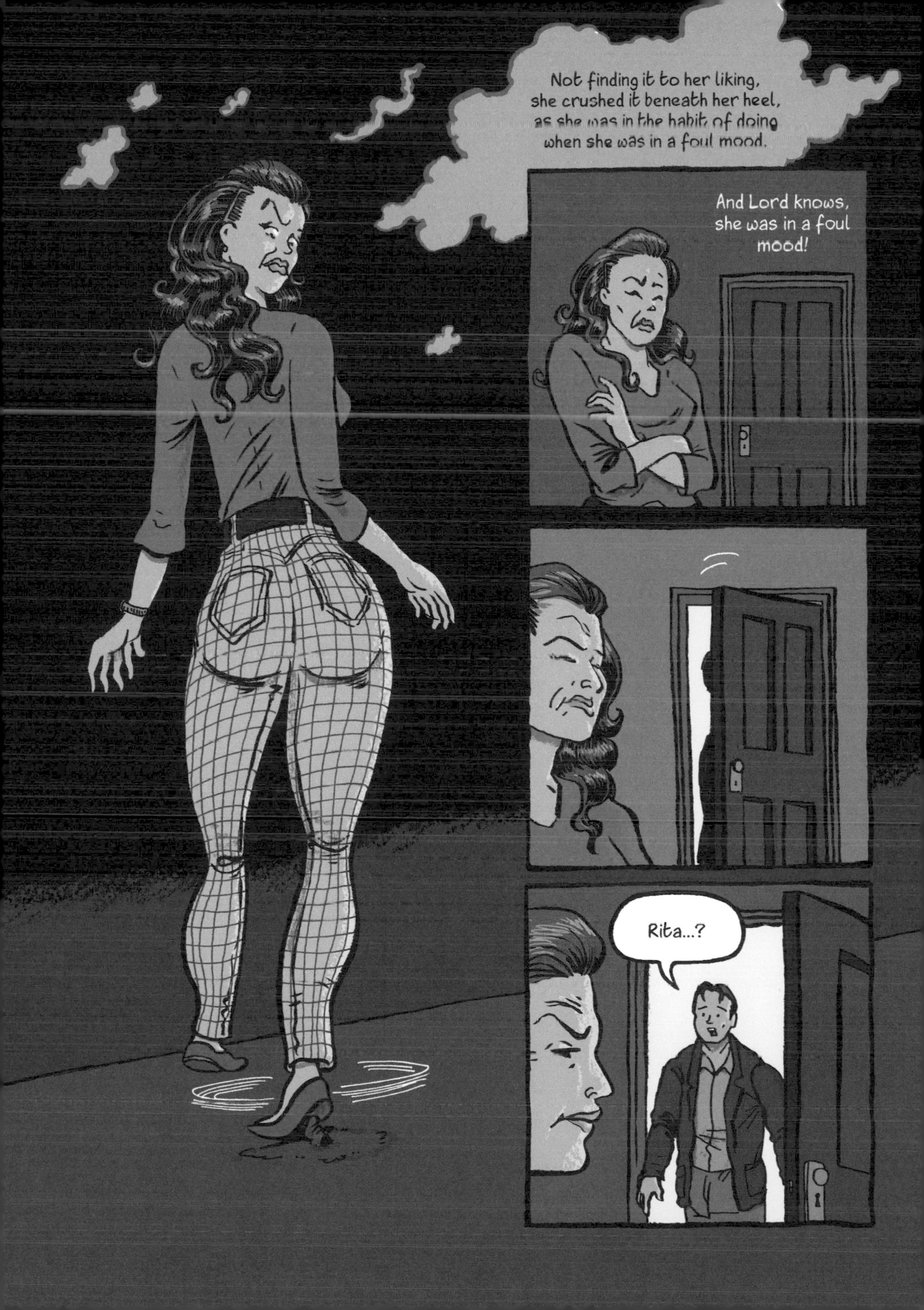
Not finding it to her liking,
she crushed it beneath her heel,
as she was in the habit of doing
when she was in a foul mood.
And Lord knows,
she was in a foul
mood!
Rita...?

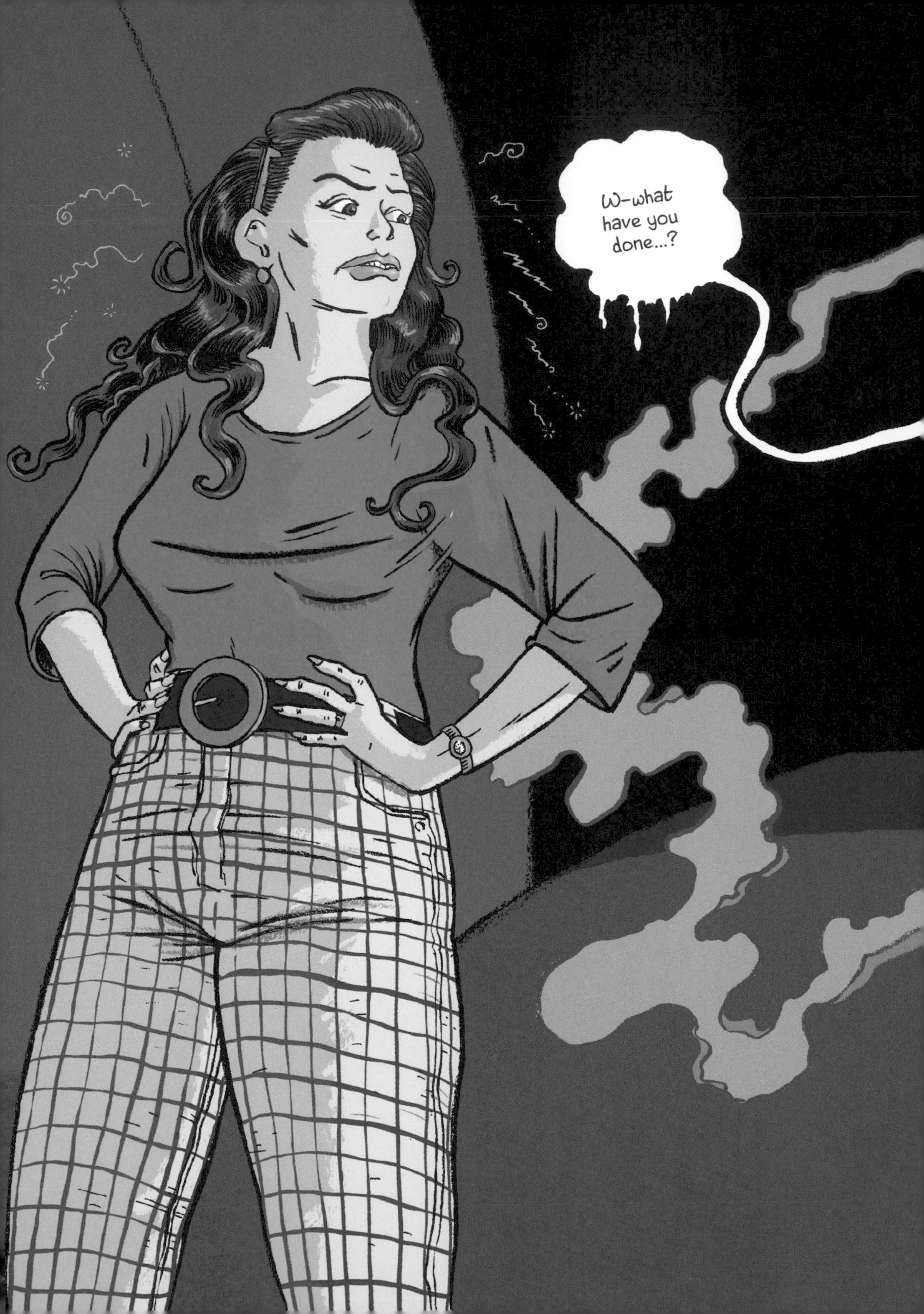
W-what have you done...?

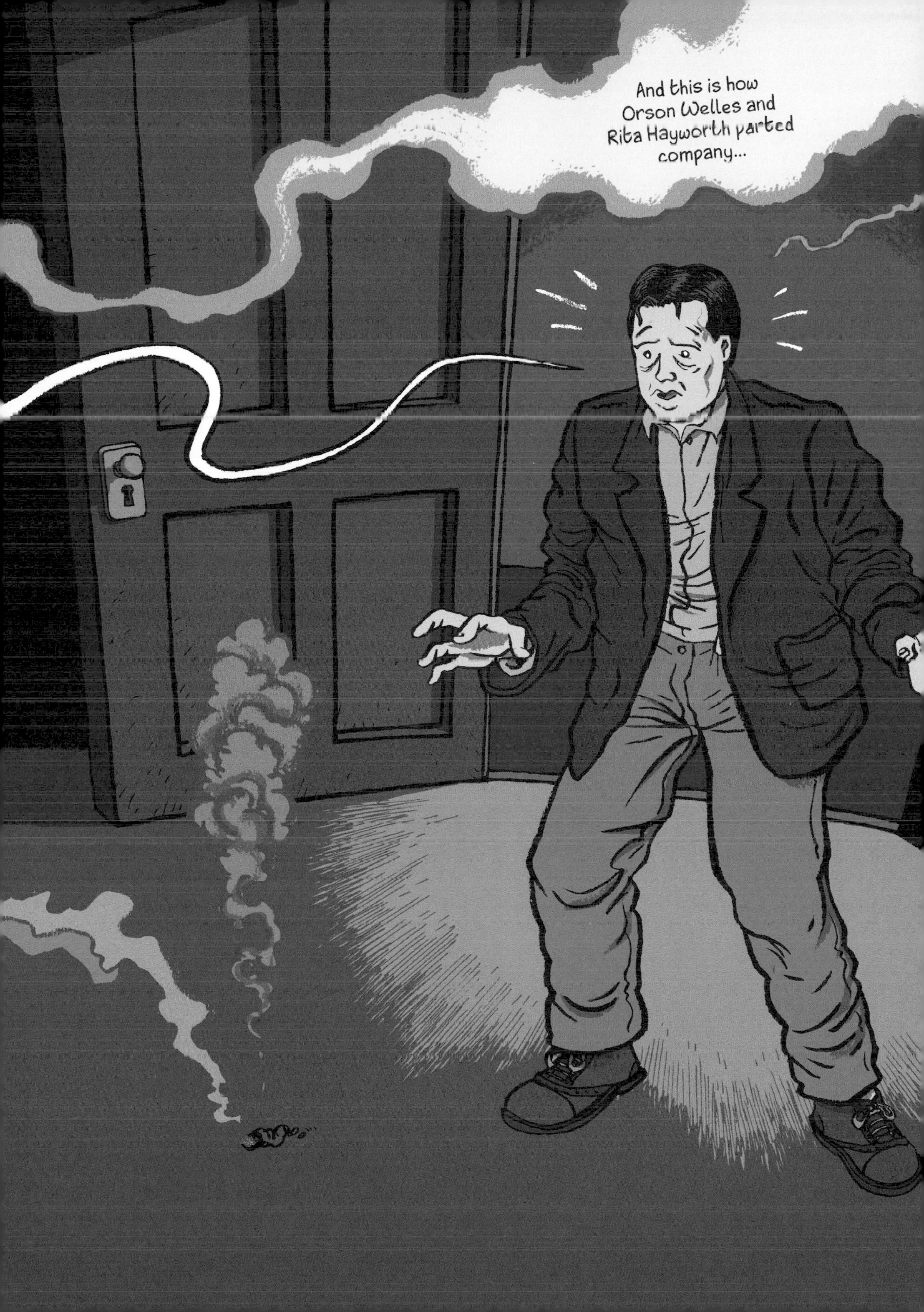
And this is how Orson Welles and Rita Hayworth parted company...

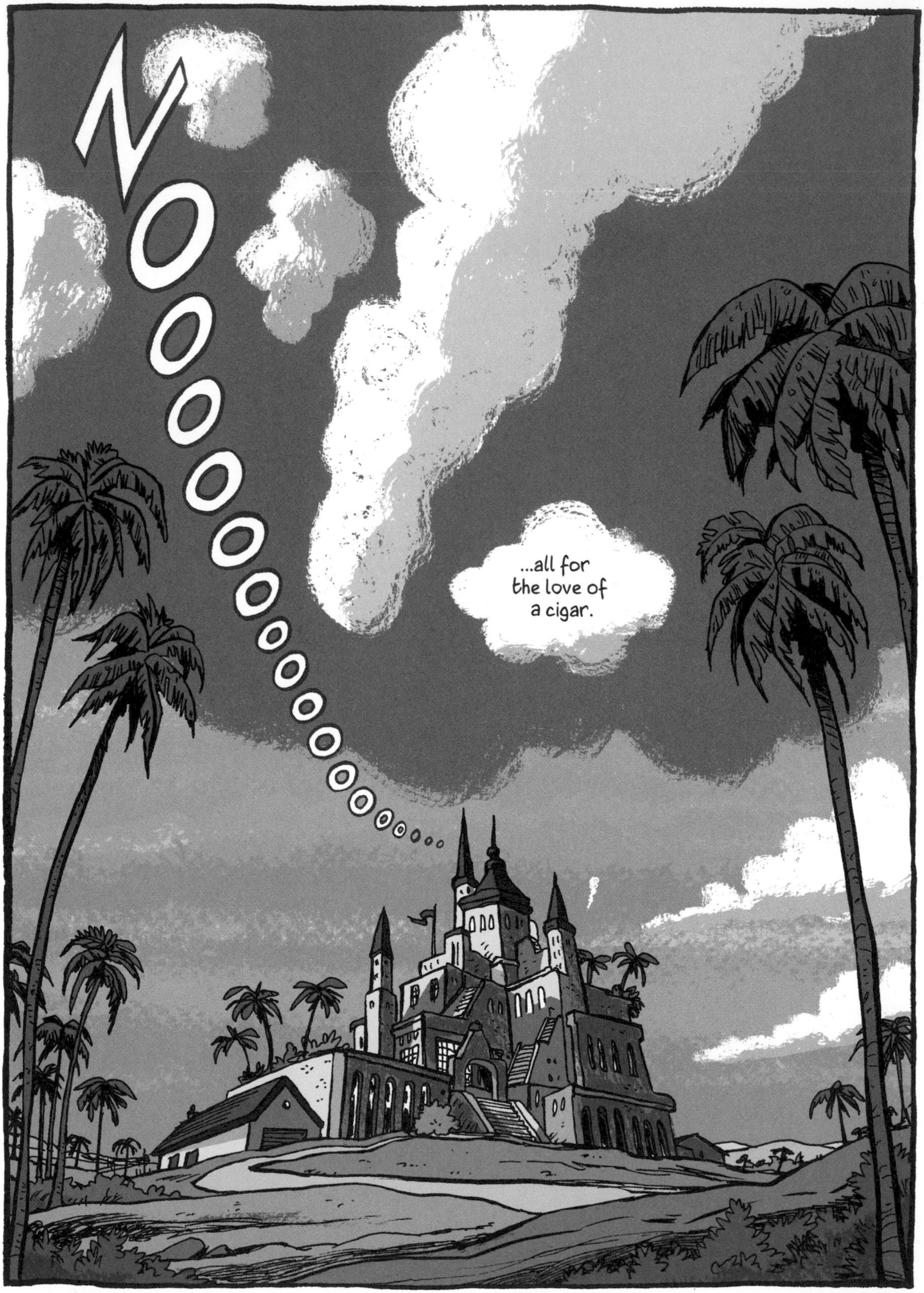
NOOOOOOOOOOOOOOOOOO...
...all for the love of a cigar.

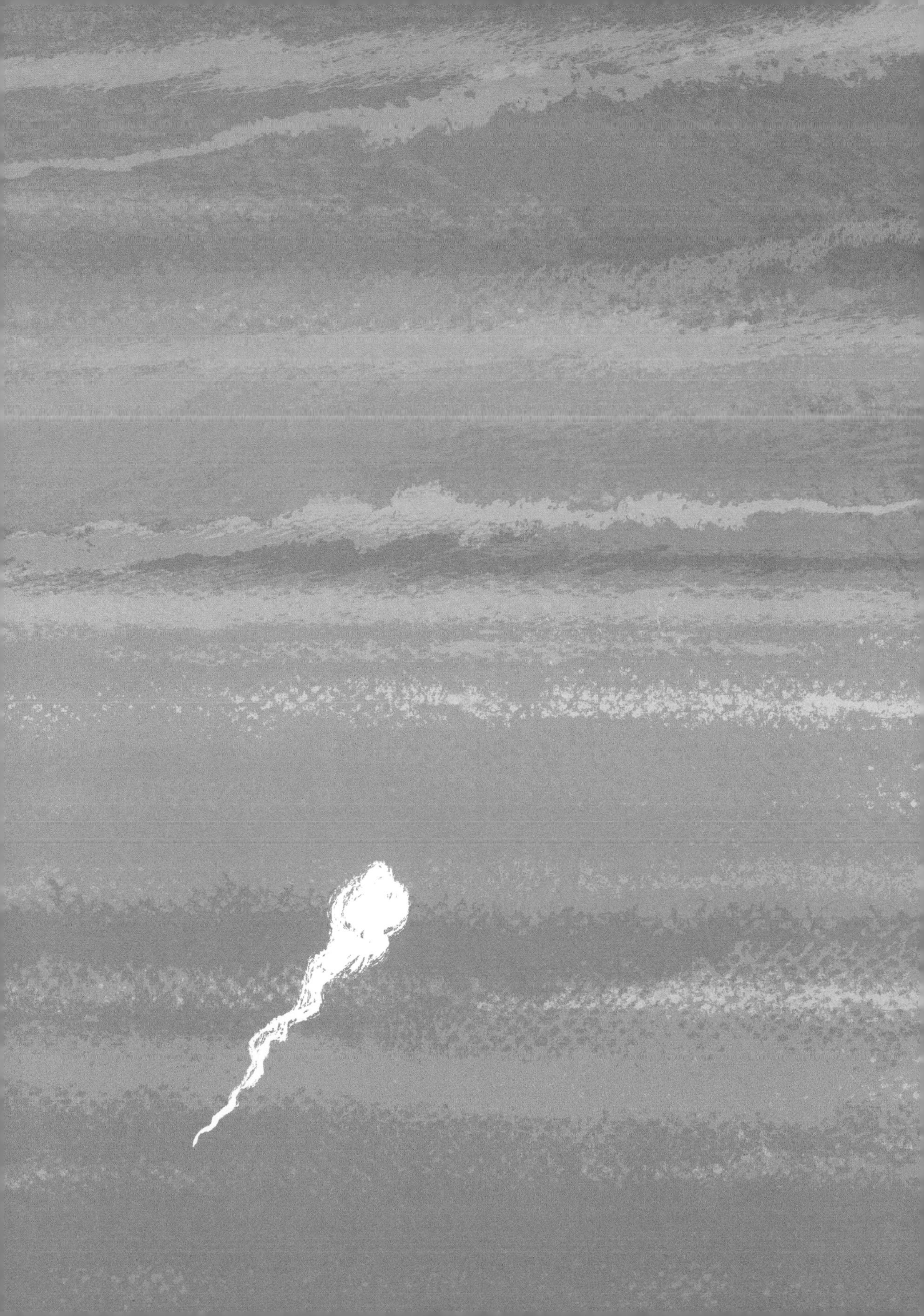

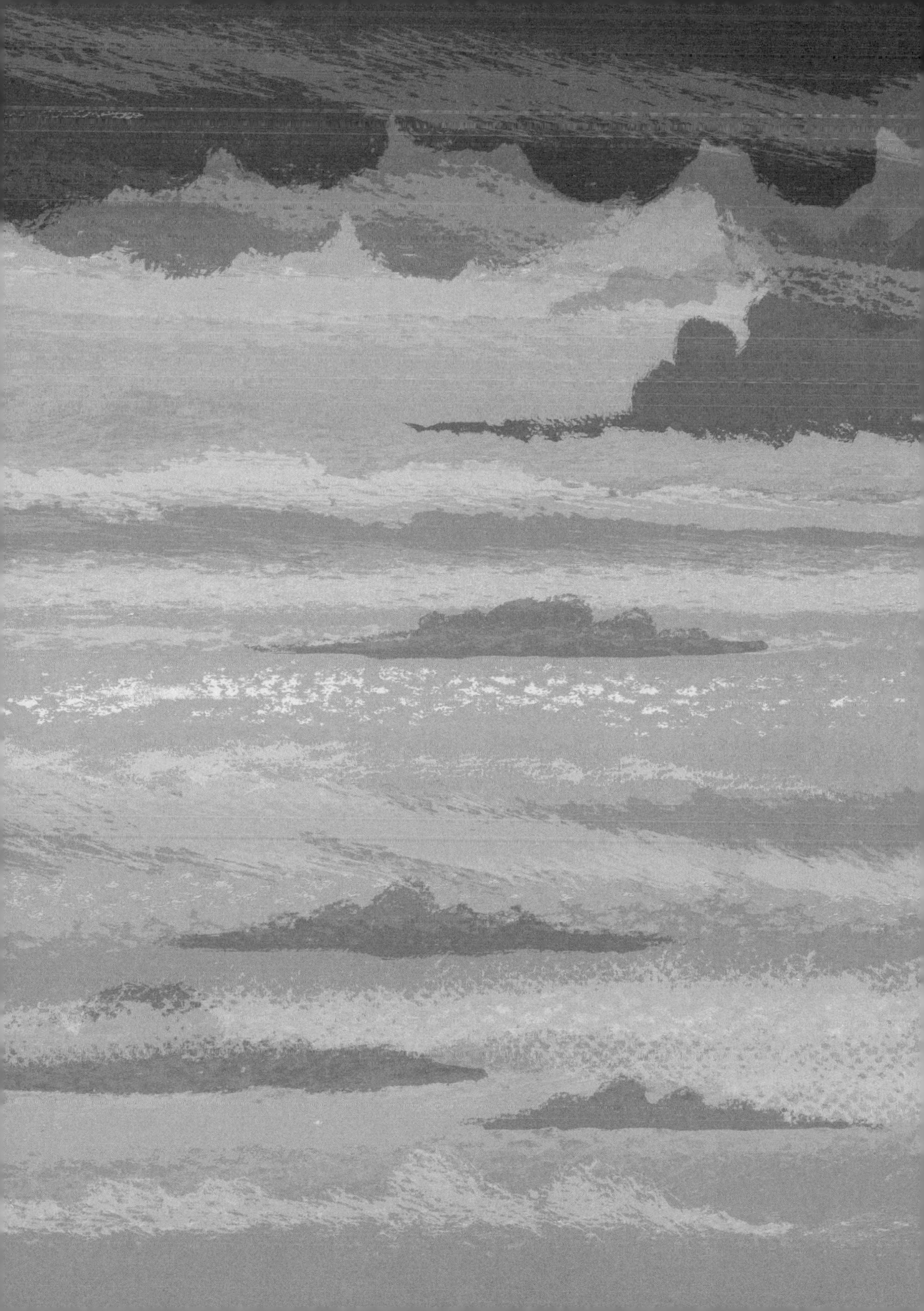

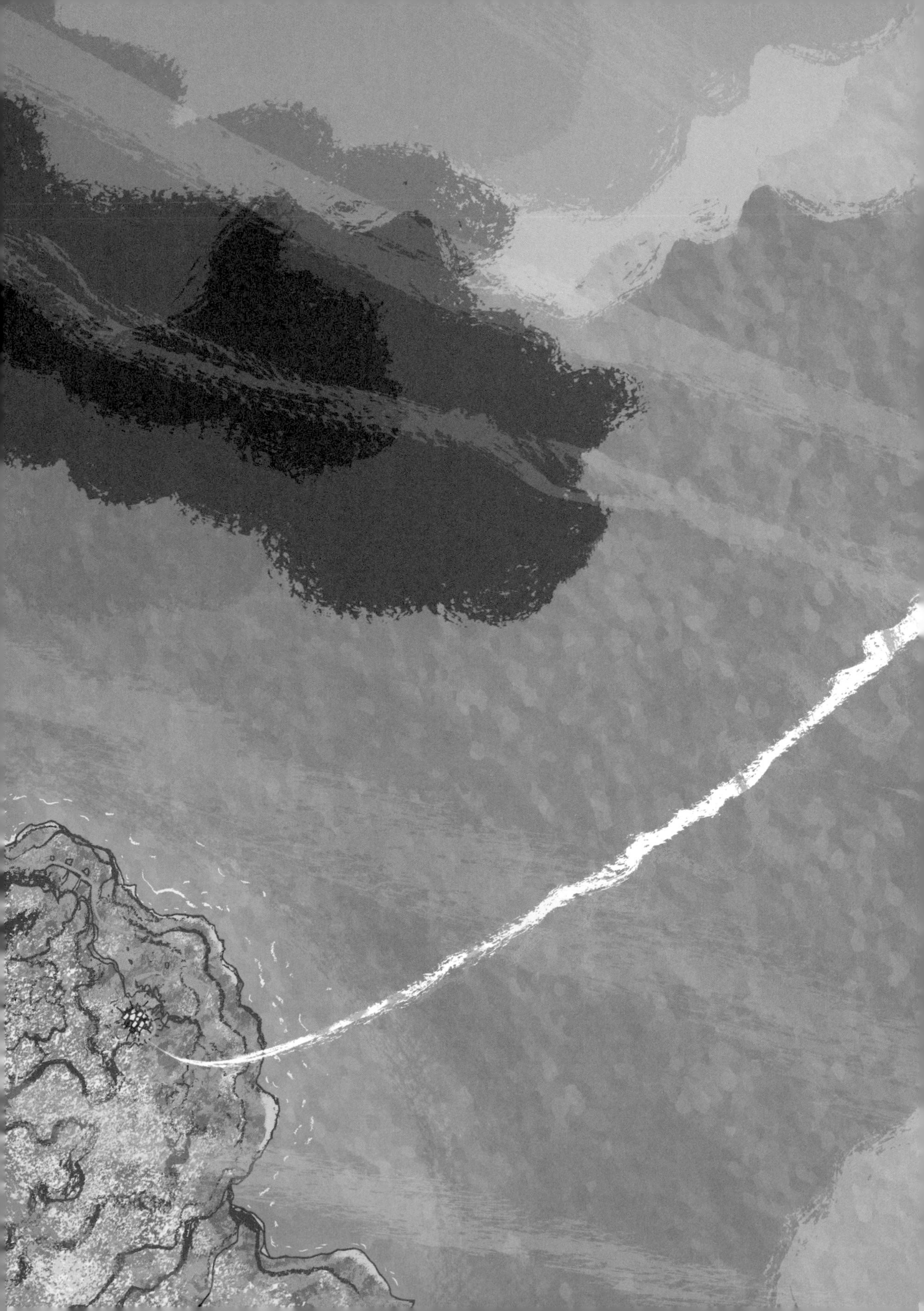

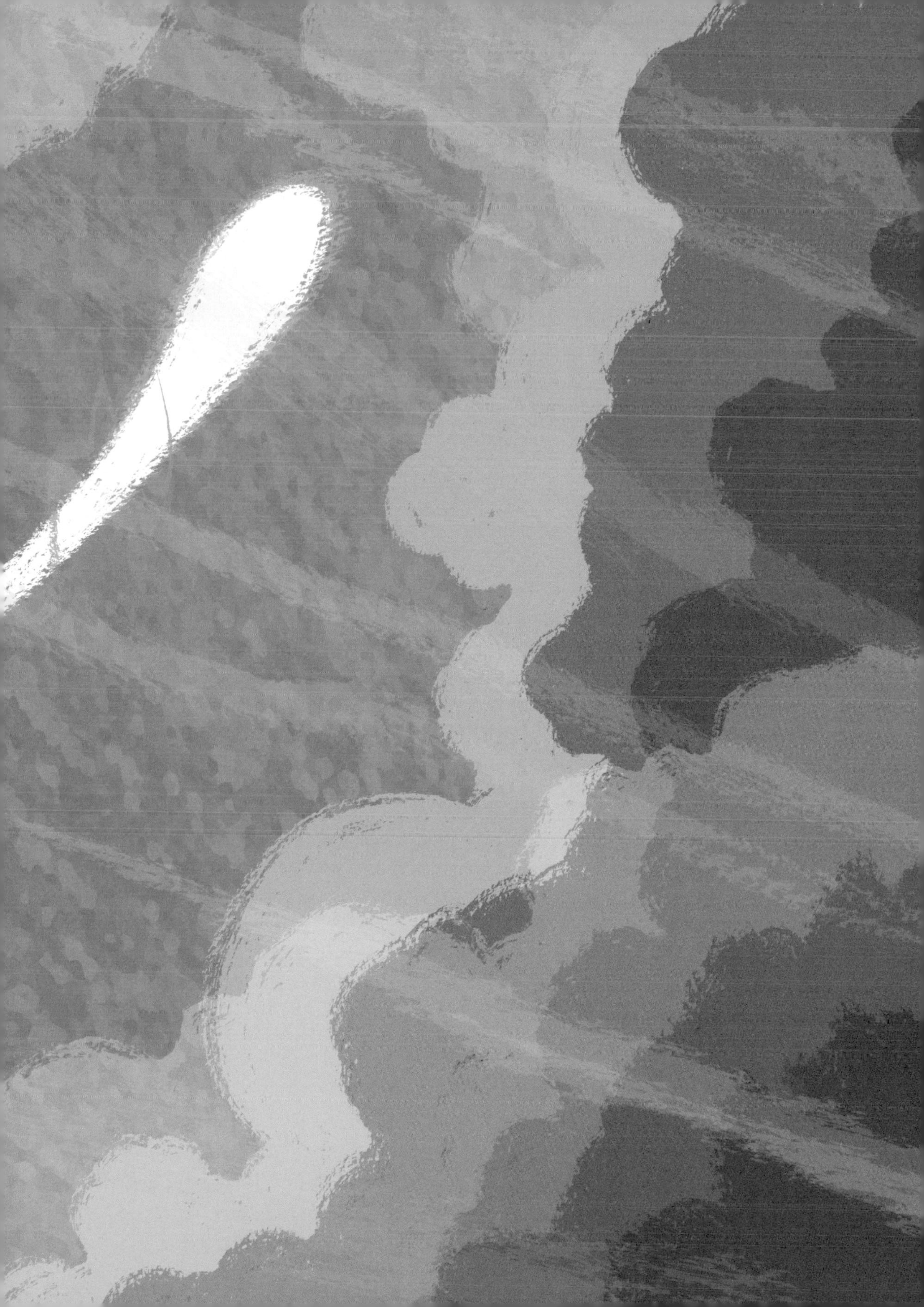

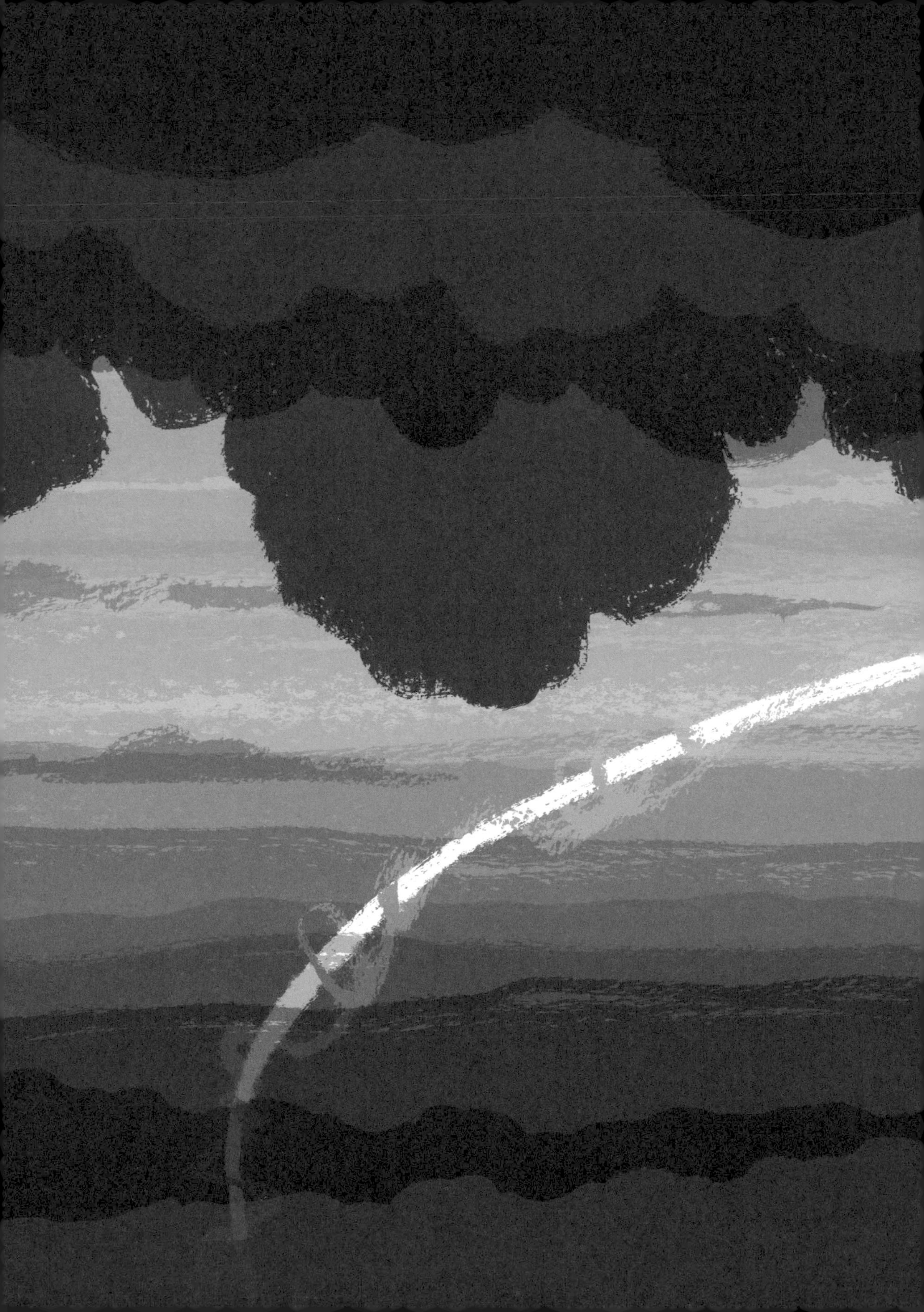

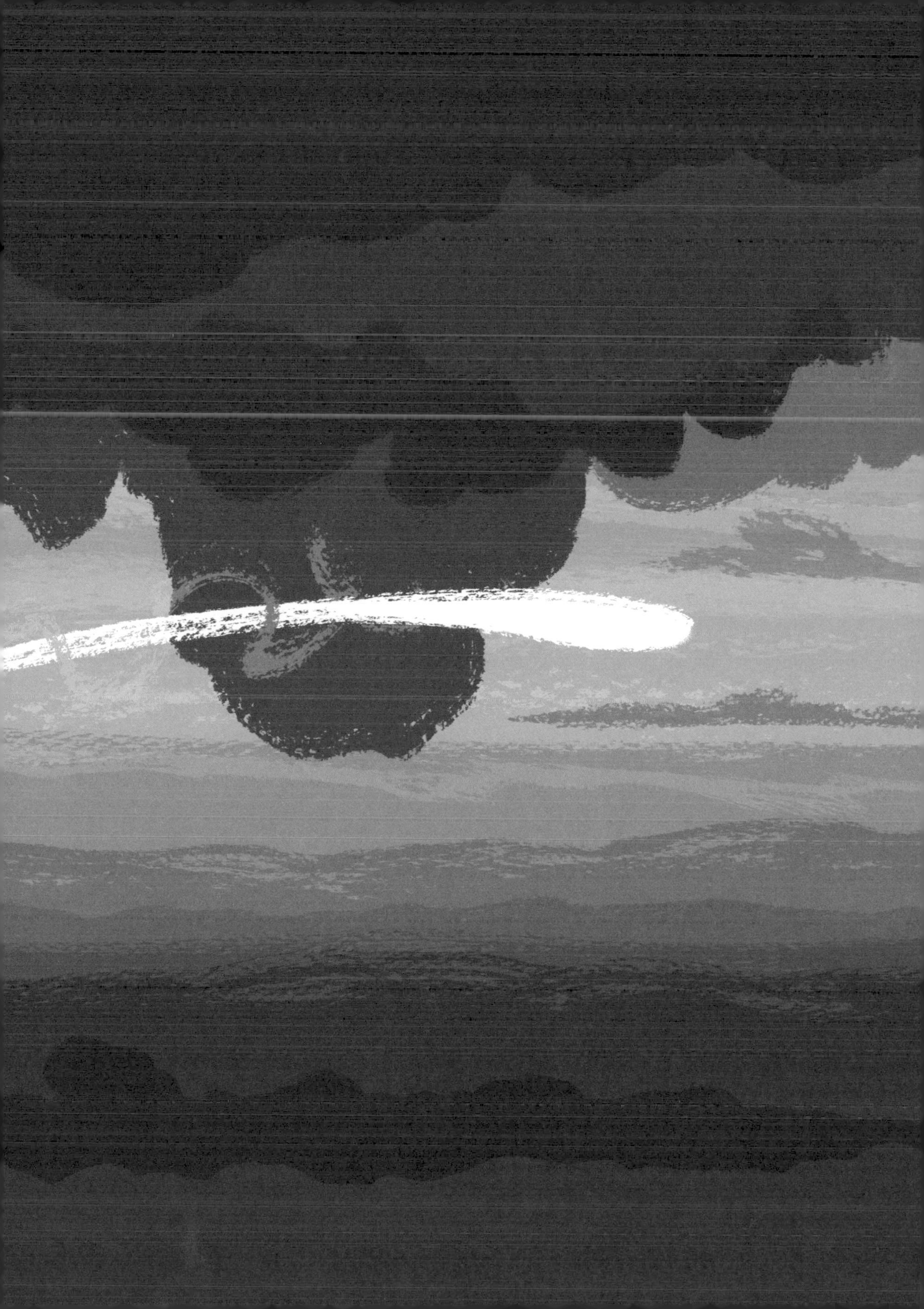

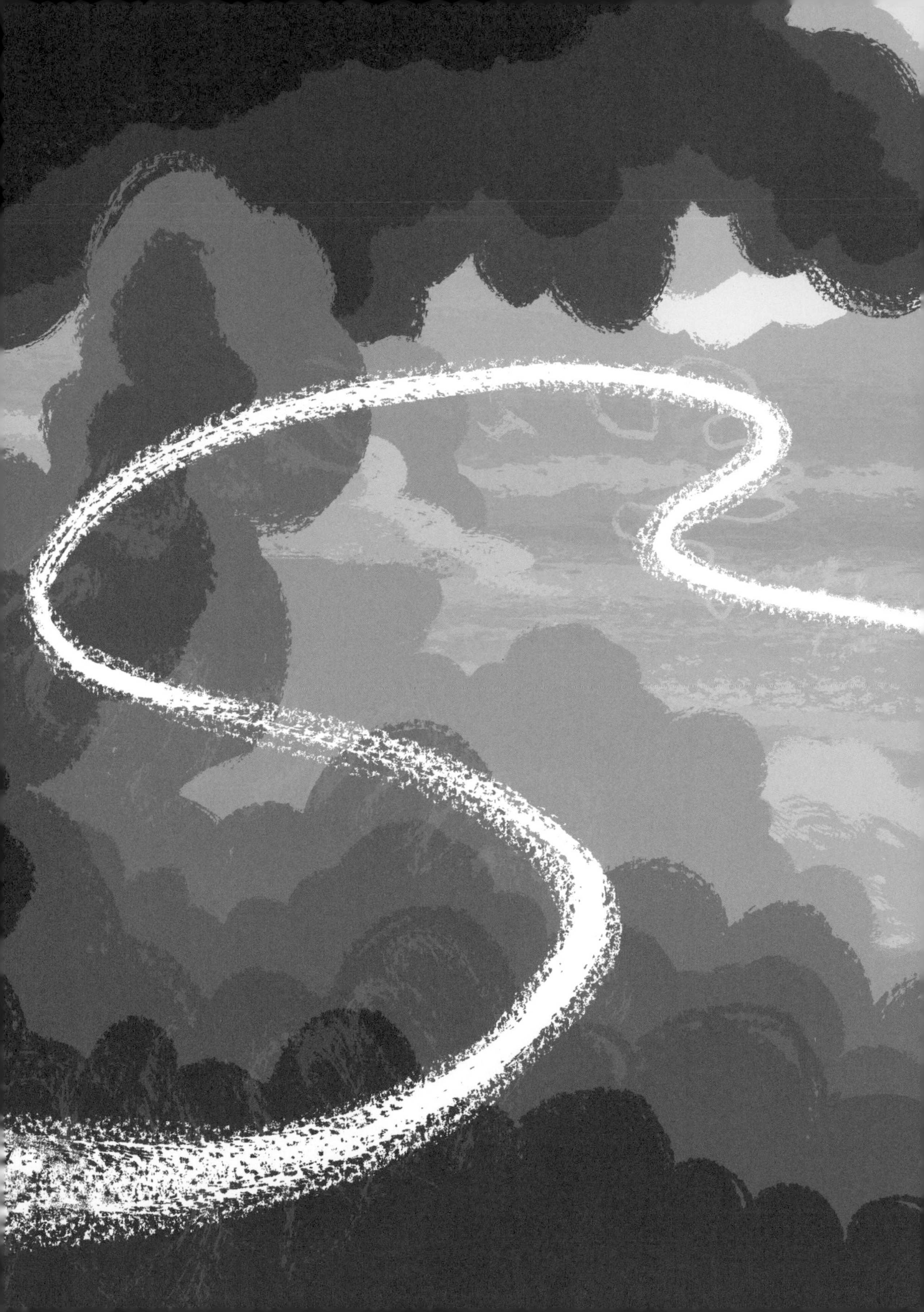

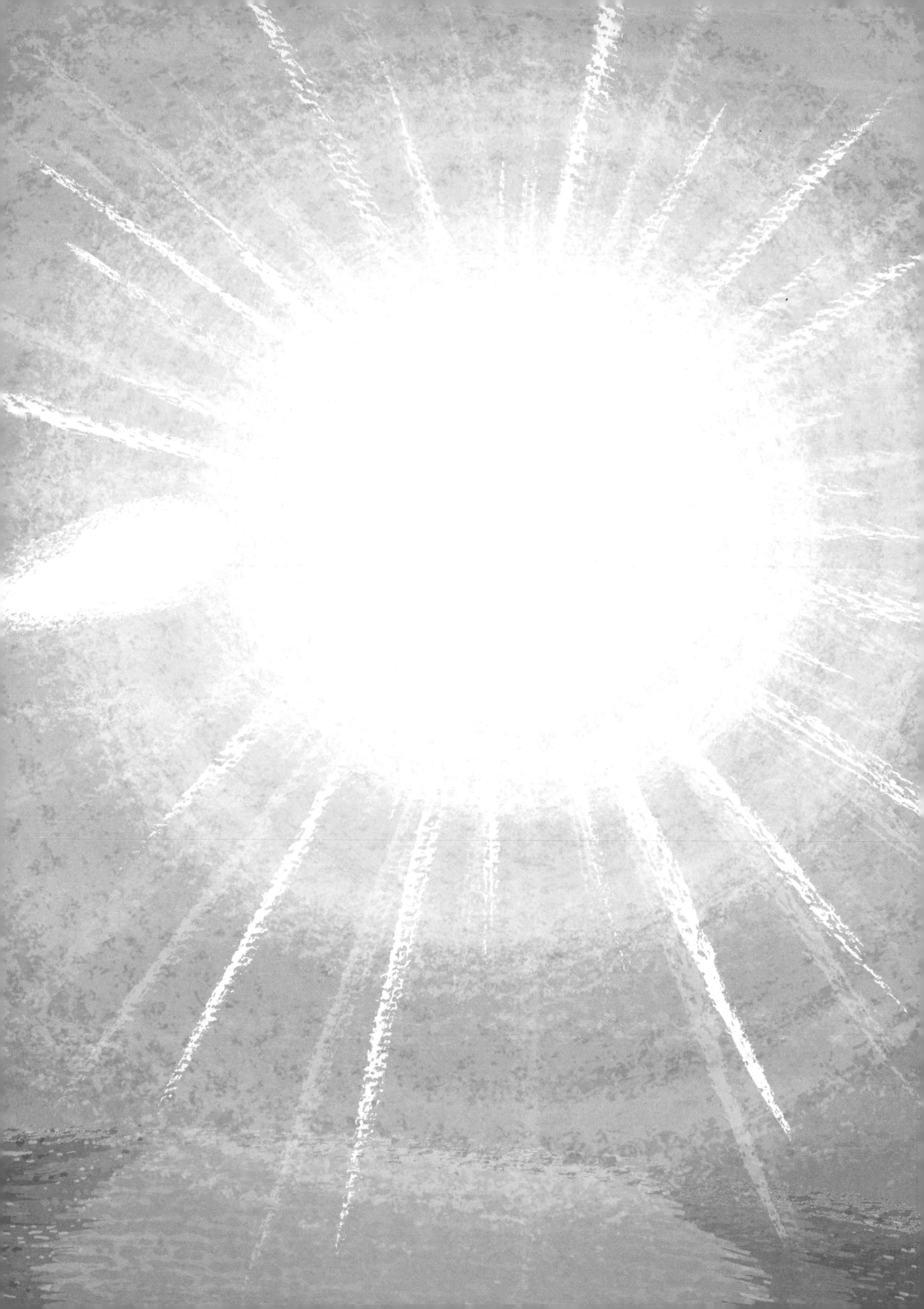

Author, translator, editor and documentary filmmaker, **David Camus** was born in Grasse, France in 1970. His literary career began in 2005 with his award-winning historical series, *The Book of the Cross* (Editions Robert Laffont), which has since seen publication in seven languages. His many translations include his award-winning work on the "Dreamcycle" by H.P. Lovecraft – his work in this area has been hailed as "definitive". He is currently retranslating all of Lovecraft's work into French and teaches Science Fiction, Fantasy and Horror Literature at the University of Paris III La Sorbonne Nouvelle. He lives in Paris, France, with his wife and two daughters.

Nick Abadzis was born in Sweden to Greek and British parents and was brought up in England and Switzerland. He has been writing and drawing comics and graphic novels for both children and adults for over twenty-five years. His work has appeared in numerous books, newspapers, magazines and other periodicals around the world and he has been honoured with various international storytelling awards, including an Eisner for his 2007 graphic novel, *LAIKA*. He also works as a publishing consultant, visual facilitator for corporate business and speaker on visual communication in culture. He lives in Brooklyn, New York, with his wife and daughter.

Thanks

Anna Jarota, my wonderful agent, who believed in this story and did "a hell of a job", PJ Mark, who knew that Nick would love it and sent it to him, to Emma Hayley and the SMH team, who made this dream come true, and – last but not least – to Jeffrey Probst, my friend, who knew how to find the words.

Very Special Thanks

...to Nick Abadzis, who breathed life into my words – and more than that: Nick, I think this is the beginning of a beautiful friendship.

- DC

Thank you

The family Abadzis (American and European branches), Jessica Abel, Rachael Ball, Greg Bennett, The Bentleys, Nick Bertozzi, Alan Cowsill, Glenn Dakin, Garth Ennis, Joan Hilty, Antony Huchette, Nikki Kastner, Jason Little, Matt Madden, PJ Mark, Luciana Mazzocco, Ed McGarry, Tom Motley, Kevin Mutch, Scott Teplin, Charlie Orr, Lark Pien, Steve Sargent, Caspar Sewell, Kristine Smith, John West and Sally Willis. -

Group Thanks

Emma Hayley, Lizzie Kaye, Dan Lockwood and everyone at SMH past and present, all members (you know who you are) of Zack Soto's SG13 'Bored' (or whatever it's called this week), everyone at Bergen Street Comics and everyone in or around the studios in Gowanus underneath the Culver Viaduct, Brooklyn, NY.

Special Thanks to my art assistant Andrew Foot for tireless clean-up and flat colour work, pointing out minor continuity errors, being more reliable than he knows and for supplying truly terrible jokes.

Extra Special Thanks to David Camus for true and joyous storytelling collaboration – two heads, one heart.

- NA